D0630167

THE MODERN PARISH COMMUNITY

THE MODERN PARISH COMMUNITY

Alex Blöchlinger

GEOFFREY CHAPMAN—LONDON 1965

This book was originally published in German under the title *Die Heutige Pfarrei als Gemeinschaft* by Benziger Verlag in 1962

English translation by Geoffrey Stevens
Adaptation and abridgement by Hilda Graef

Imprimatur: H. Gibney, Vicarius Generalis
Nihil obstat: R. D. Dermitius Fogarty, D.D., L.C.L. Censor deputatus
Datum Southwarci die 28a Augusti, 1964

MADE AND PRINTED IN GREAT BRITAIN BY
BILLING & SONS LIMITED, GUILDFORD AND LONDON, FOR THE PUBLISHERS,
GEOFFREY CHAPMAN LTD., 18 HIGH STREET, WIMBLEDON, LONDON, S.W.19

CONTENTS

FOREWORD

It is fortunate that those interested in the apostolate today should show an ever increasing interest in the parish and its problems.

This interest is not restricted to Europe but can be seen throughout the Catholic and Christian world. It may to some extent be regarded as an answer to de-christianization. Large sections of the population have abandoned all interest in religion and the masses know little or nothing about the Church.

Thus the parish today is once more seen as a factor of decisive importance in pastoral work, and must be given its rightful place in it. It is a matter of urgency that the apostolate render its own action more fruitful by making use of all the means of assistance that the parish has to offer.

The Church's pastoral office is essentially connected with the parish, though this does not mean that the higher echelons can be neglected. The parish today has new problems set in new dimensions: its usefulness is by no means at an end, but it must re-think the apostolate as a whole if it is not to risk showing signs of ossification.

The parish is not, as has for so long mistakenly been held, a part of the Church; rather, in it the whole Church of Christ works in a limited space. Through the parish the living Christ realizes a marvellous plan among men, of which St Paul tells us in his Epistle to the Ephesians. In his love, God 'has chosen us out . . . marking us out beforehand (so his will decreed) to be his adopted children through Jesus Christ' (Eph. 1: 4–5). This plan was worked out in the mysteries of the incarnation and the redemption; it is being continued in the Church, and fulfilled in the parish.

In this building up of the Body of Christ man must play his part. The parish is also the work of the parishioners. In this connexion we should remember Dostoyevsky's dictum that everyone is responsible to everyone else for everything.

The role of the faithful in the growth and development of the parish has its sociological, psychological and juridical aspects. All these elements must be activated in the building up of a parish. Nothing may be left unused or idle. All are called upon to work and to work together, for the parish can only grow if it is built from below as well as from above.

All these problems are dealt with by the Rev. Dr Alex Blöchlinger, the author of this book. He deals with them as an expert, thoroughly, clearly and graphically, and seeks to arrive at a synthesis.

This book should make a considerable contribution towards arousing the parish spirit among clergy and laity alike.

Fribourg
May 1962

F. X. von Hornstein
Rector of the University

INTRODUCTION

Introduction

I—The Parish in Pastoral Theology

The parish is without any doubt one of the most important means in the Church's cure of souls. It is a tool that has been in use throughout the centuries of the Church's tradition, in the most varied times and civilizations, and is still in use today.

In view of this really unique importance it may surprise one that up till now there has been no fundamental, synthetic, *pastoral-theological* study of the parish. True, there is no lack of literature on the parish: on the contrary. But this consists largely of practical instructions, treats only individual aspects or takes the form of collective volumes. What is missing is particularly a pastoral-theological study of the parish that deals not only with its official organization but sees in it a *community* and as such treats it as a form of the pastoral work of the Church; a study which regards the parish community not only as an object for pastoral activity but also one of its channels.

This gap in pastoral theology—which is not just a *technique* or any kind of science but a genuine theology—this gap is explained by the internal problems and the evolution of pastoral theology itself. For a pastoral-theological treatment of the parish is only possible after a one-sided view of pastoral theology has been set aside and the very notion of it has been freed from its traditional narrowness. For this reason we start with an analysis of the problems of pastoral theology before proceeding to the actual theme of this work.[1]

1. *The Internal Evolution of Pastoral Theology*

Pastoral theology is a product of the *Enlightenment*. The very term leads to misunderstanding, and even today bears the

[1] Cf. Arnold, *Grundätzliches*, 105 ff.; Füglister, 11–41; Bopp. For the Protestant side, cf. Böhm, 209–71, Pt. II, 'Amt und Gemeinde in der praktischen Theologie'.

traces of this, which are difficult to eliminate, suggesting that it is solely concerned with practical conclusions and advice for the shepherd of souls. But the name has come to stay.[1] On account of this misunderstanding and its historical background, pastoral theology is often taken rather less seriously by 'other' theologians.

The actual Enlightenment period is in this matter of relatively small importance, for at that period it could not yet really be called a theology.[2]

Pastoral theology was first seen in its theological aspect when Christian thinkers strove to defeat the Enlightenment. The Tübingen school played the leading part here, and is still loyal to this tradition. The battle with the Enlightenment was fought principally on the field of the concept of the Church and the revival of a theology of the Church. The development of pastoral theology is very closely tied up with this battle. How hard the struggle was can be judged from the inconsistency in the fact that the deeper and wider concept of the Church does indeed find its place in the definition of pastoral theology, but until very recent times has in practice not been allowed to serve as its actual structural principle.

The first break in the deistic current was made by Johann Michael Sailer (1751–1832) with his renewal of the notion of the Church. 'But', writes Arnold, 'he failed to make it into a structural law of his pastoral theology.'[3] True, Sailer's concept of the Church goes far beyond the mechanical Church, but in his lectures he fell back on the threefold office of the pastor of souls, although this was not required by his definition.[4]

[1] According to Stolz it was Canisius who first used the term *theologia pastoralis* in 1556 (*LThK* VII, 1024), but Bopp attributes it to Peter Binsfeld (ob. 1598) in his *Encheiridion theologiae pastoralis* (1591) (Bopp, 29, cf. Noppel, *Pfarrei*, 32).

[2] Cf. Pitroff, *Anleitung zur praktischen Gottes Gelahrtheit. Nach dem Entwurf der Wiener Studienverbesserung*, 1744, 4 vols., Prague, 1783. Definition I, 11. Pitroff was the first holder of the chair of Pastoral 'Theology' set up at Prague University in 1777. Cf. also Reichenberger, *Pastoral-Anweisungen nach den Bedürfnissen unseres Zeitalters*, Vienna, 1805, definition I, 101; also Giftschütz, Gollwitz *et al.* and Füglister, 23–27.

[3] Arnold, *Grundsätzliches*, 107.

[4] 'Pastoral theology is . . . the science of bringing men, who are separated and far from God and disunited among themselves, to a rapprochement among themselves and with God, in the Spirit of Christ and of his Church; in the Spirit of Christ who came down to earth to draw men to himself

Whereas Fr Maurus Schenkl, O.S.B., who was the first to take Sailer's attempt any further,[1] himself advances one-sidedly in the direction of the clerical Church,[2] Anton Graf, the Tübingen pastoral theologian and a pupil of Möhler, achieved a balanced definition in which the Church appeared for the first time in its totality and full meaning,[3] although the clerical Church still retained a certain pride of place.[4]

In the thought of Josef Amberger (1816–89), whose work is unanimously accepted as the high-water mark of the development so far discussed,[5] the discrepancy between his profound concept of theology in general and pastoral theology in particular, on the one hand, and the actual structure of his pastoral theology on the other, is most clearly seen. He conceives theology as an all-embracing ecclesiology and allows this view to enter also into what he calls practical theology.[6] The active subject is for him the Church as a whole and not solely or principally the clergy.[7] In his practical development of pastoral theology, however, he slips back into the narrower field of clerical office and the ordained priesthood,[8] so that Arnold resignedly comments: 'Even with Amberger the preponderance given to the hierarchical apostolate is so great that it is no accident that active function of the (lay) "community" receives only marginal notice at the end.'[9]

---

and to unite them through himself with God; in the Spirit of his Church, which is none other than the union of *all members among themselves and with their Head*.' Sailer, *Vorlesungen*, I, 8.

[1] Füglister, 28.

[2] He defines pastoral theology as: 'bene ordinata institutio ad munus pastorale rite exercendum, seu est aptum riteque coordinatum systema, quo officia muniaque pastoris animarum et eorum modo optimo saluberrimoque exsequendorum methodus ordinatim distributeque explicantur.' Schenkl, 8.

[3] Arnold, *Grundsätzliches*, 107; Füglister, 30.

[4] He conceives pastoral theology as 'the science of ecclesiastical, divine–human activities by means of authorized ecclesiastical persons, principally those in Holy Orders, and designed to build up the Church'. Graf, 149.

[5] Cf. Krieg, *Seelenführung*, Foreword, V; Bopp, 19; Arnold, *Grundsätzliches*, 107; Füglister, 30 ff.

[6] 'Pastoral theology is the science of the divine–human activity of the Church directed towards the building and spread of God's kingdom on earth.' Amberger, I, 6; cf. also 10.

[7] Cf. op. cit., I, 13, 16, 17, 19, 21, and Füglister, 31.

[8] Op. cit., I, 22.

[9] Arnold, *Grundsätzliches*, 108. We find a similar development in Protestant pastoral theology. Cf. Böhm's effective summary, 209–71.

Amberger's profound concept was not taken up. It disappeared because theologians clung obstinately to the narrow hierarchical notion of the Church.[1] True, Cornelius Krieg (1838–1911) assigns much space to the community care of souls, but he does not include this in the sphere of Church activity.[2] Schubert, reprinted for the third time in 1934–35, actually presents a low-water mark.[3]

Linus Bopp was the first once more to make a critical study of the development of pastoral theology.[4] For him the laity can also be the subject of the cure of souls, that is of the activity of the Church,[5] whereas Noppel confines this to the ordained clergy.[6] Vagaggini gives yet another definition which is a long way behind Amberger.[7]

Finally in the spirit of the best Tübingen tradition, Franz-Xaver Arnold, one of the greatest pastoral theologians of our time, has in a number of profound historical studies freed pastoral theology from its narrowness and from the remaining burden inherited from rationalism and Enlightenment. For him pastoral theology is not a technique but a true theology with its own subject matter,[8] namely 'the Church's activities comprising the Word, the sacraments and the care of souls in the widest sense'.[9] Thereby he deliberately and emphatically frees the concept of the Church from the narrowness of its 'official' aspect to include the company of all the baptized.[10]

[1] Cf. Pruner (1827–1909), *Pastoraltheologie* I, 1; Renninger, *Pastoraltheologie*, 1893, 1; Ignaz Schüch, O.S.B., (1823–93), *Pastoraltheologie*, 4.

[2] Krieg, *Seelenführung*, I.

[3] Schubert, *Pastoraltheologie*, 3 vols., 1934–35.

[4] Bopp, *Zwischen Pastoraltheologie und Seelsorgewissenschaft.*

[5] Op. cit., 25–40; 72.

[6] Noppel, *Aedificatio*, I; cf. Böhm, 223.

[7] Vagaggini, 403.

[8] In contrast to Fr Deman, for whom pastoral theology is not a branch of knowledge on its own, but is a theology 'in so far as it helps the pastor of souls'. Deman, 'Grundsätze einer Seelsorgewissenschaft' in *Anima*, I (1946–47), 15.

[9] Arnold, *Pastoraltheologie*, 194; cf. also 196.

[10] 'Where the Church and its future are mentioned, what is meant is *the Church in the fullest sense of its dogmatic and personal status*; the Church as the company of all baptized persons of whom the original and best Catholic tradition says that they all, through faith and charity, through penance and prayer, work together in the forgiveness of sins and the mediation of salvation. This universal view is opposed to the obstinate misconception that pastoral theology is exhausted when it has guided the officials of the Church in the practice of the care of souls. In reality and as a matter of

Very closely linked with this struggle for the overall concept there is, for Arnold, another demand: 'to anchor pastoral doctrine, which has largely been pursued according to no fixed principles, firmly *in the dogmatic teaching about Christ*, the God-man'.[1] The mediation of the Church must follow the lines of the absolute mediation of Christ, since the Church is his living *instrumentum coniunctum*. Since the Church has this role of mediation between God and man, pastoral theology is ordered to both factors: 'God and his revelation as well as man in his concrete situation. Thus the immense scope of the subject and its sources will be realized.'[2]

As we have said, this outcome in pastoral theology is closely linked with an analogous development in *ecclesiology*. In the nineteenth century Möhler, Pilgram, Franzelin and Scheeben had already made valuable contributions towards a better understanding of the nature of the Church. Today names like Feckes, Congar, de Lubac and Semmelroth are very closely linked with the building up of an ecclesiology which makes the best Catholic traditions fruitful in our own day and which has found expression in the important encyclicals of recent popes.[3]

---

principle, all baptized persons are subjects of the activity of the Church and responsible bearers of its work. All are called on, though not all in the same way, to the service of the Word and the faith, to participate in the celebration of sacraments and liturgy. To bring back to the general consciousness the full concept of the Church in her care of souls, a concept long overshadowed among Catholics by the defensive attitude in face of the reformers' denial of the mechanical priesthood, was and remains one of the most urgent tasks of modern pastoral theology.' Arnold, op. cit., 196.

Cf. Arnold, 'Kirche and Laientum', address at the solemn handing over of the Rectorship at the start of the Summer Term on 7 May 1954, in: *Reden bei der feierlichen Übergabe* . . . 23–45; and Arnold, *Grundsätzliches*, 80 ff.; Böhm, 221 ff, 240 ff.

[1] Arnold, op. cit., 197; cf. by the same writer, *Der geschichtliche Weg theozentrischer Pastoralwissenschaft; Das gottmenschliche Prinzip der Seelsorge in pastoralgeschichtlicher Entwicklung;* and *Das Prinzip des Gottmenschlichen und seine Bedeutung für die Seelsorge.*

[2] Arnold, op. cit., 198. Schoellgen, Schurr, Häring, Hitz and De Coninck, to name only a few, bend their efforts in the same direction.

[3] Semmelroth remarks, as Arnold does, that we are still largely inhibited by a counter-reformation viewpoint which often places too much emphasis on the office, so that it is divorced from the community it is there to serve, and that the concept of the Church thereby remains narrowed down to its official aspect. In contrast to this he emphasizes the mutual nature of the relationship between the official Church and the lay community, and their oneness, and concludes: 'As a result of the meaning we have given to the duality of office and community in the Church, the two directions of the

The broadening of pastoral theology to include the laity as well as the clergy has been assisted by pastoral or *religious sociology*. Although pastoral sociology is a young science, still in its early stages and far from having found its final form, it is well on the way to being one of the most important ancillary sciences to pastoral theology. Some scholars would even give it the status of a theological discipline elevated by a social theology.[1]

Fr Chenu sees the breakthrough of the community idea as one of the principal reasons for the revolution in modern theology, particularly pastoral theology with its influence on the whole field.[2]

2. *The Present Position of Pastoral Theology*

Through the work of its eminent exponents, pastoral theology has today broken through to a new and comprehensive concept which follows the best Catholic tradition and which has effectively overcome the Enlightenment and defeated rationalism and individualism. Properly so conceived, pastoral theology is fundamentally an ecclesiology[3] dealing with the Church's mediating action. It is both speculative theology—since this action can and must be considered also in its essence—

---

saving movement between God and man is visibly realized in the movement between the bearers of the pastoral office and the lay community.' This is equivalent to saying that the life of the Church depends equally on clergy and laity. The life of the Church is never borne by the pastoral office or the laity alone. One cannot say that the Church lives either more fully or in greater reality in one or the other. A life which consists essentially of contact between two parties can only be lived by the two parties together. In this, the life of the Church shows in fact a clear analogy with the life of the triune God of which it is the sacramental representation. Semmelroth, *Das geistliche Amt*, 205, cf. also 15 ff., 30, and Congar, *Paroisse*, 60 ff.

[1] Cf. Häring, *Macht*, 17; Chenu, *Position théologique de la Sociologie rel.;* Ermecke, *Die Sozialtheologie als christliche Gemeinschaftslehre und ihre Beziehung zu verwandten Wissenschaften;* Geck, *Christliche Sozialprinzipien. Zum Aufbau einer Sozialtheologie; Sozialtheologie als Aufgabe; Sozialtheologie.* See also Birou, 74 ff., 85.

[2] Chenu, *Die Erneuerung der Seelsorgewissenschaft*, 308–11. Only two practical examples are given: Abbé Michonneau, who wants to educate his community to become the bearer of the message of Christ (Michonneau, *Parish*); and the general missions of Fr Motte, called 'general' because they enlist the whole church in an area and not just the clergy in missionary work (Motte, *Mission Générale*).

[3] Cf. De Coninck, *Les orientations actuelles de la théologie pastorale*, especially 137.

and practical theology,[1] since pastoral theology is concerned not only with the understanding of the essence of the Church in its work, but then this knowledge is *directly ordered to the corresponding action* of the various members of the Church.[2] Again, practical theology can be more speculative when it leads to the formulation of general rules of conduct, or more practical when it leads to conclusions concerning individual concrete cases. A distinction must be made between practical theology and prudential knowledge, which has a great part to play in pastoral work but is not a part of scientific pastoral theology.[3]

Naturally, pastoral theology thus understood cannot remain a purely systematic theology. It can no more forgo positive theology than it can dispense with Church history and other, even profane, ancillary sciences. Although in spite of the differentiation thereby established, the unity of pastoral theology as theology remains untouched, there are nevertheless areas very clearly divided from one another by the methods to be used.[4] As a result, the scientific development and deepening of pastoral theology demand on the one hand a greater division of labour. This is achieved more and more through the growing independence of liturgical, catechetical and homiletic studies, through the development of research into pastoral history and the evolution of the various ancillary sciences such as pastoral sociology, pastoral psychology and pastoral medicine, to name only a few. On the other hand, very close co-ordination between all these is also an urgent necessity. The pastoral-theological concept of the *parish* makes it particularly clear that all its aspects must be taken into account if the subject is to be

[1] Only theology among sciences can be practical and theoretical at the same time. Cf. *S.T.*, I, 1, a.4.

[2] On this account pastoral theology is often mistakenly counted as practical theology, since its subject is the activity and working of the Church. But since it is, it must not concern itself solely with action but also with the theory behind the action. Moral theology presents a similar case in also being both speculative and practical, supplying the basis for prudence, which is concerned with individual cases but which as casuistry is no longer scientific knowledge.

[3] Cf. A. Berz, *Der Standort der Katechetik innerhalb der Theologie*; Böhm, 226.

[4] It is rare for anyone to have all methods at his command; here we find one of the reasons why pastoral theology is always reverting to a sort of collection of rules of prudence and conduct. It shares the fate of moral theology which has sunk from the theological heights to mere casuistry and is finding it difficult to regain its former lustre.

dealt with at all thoroughly. And therein lies the main difficulty. For this reason, too, it is impossible to say the last word on the subject here, nor can a truly comprehensive pastoral-theological presentation of the parish be given. All we can hope to do is to contribute one modest stone towards the pastoral-theological edifice on the parish.

This brief sketch of the development of pastoral theology is meant to bring us to the point where we can see that the *parish can really become the object of pastoral-theological study*: and not just the parish as an 'office' but also as *a community*. In the following pages, then, the parish community is treated not as the object of ecclesiastical action but as its subject as far as it is called upon to establish the supernatural kingdom of God through the Church's divine–human functions.

Since the parish is not of divine origin but a human institution and, as we shall see in more detail later, is conditioned by a variety of variable factors, one *important task of pastoral theology will be to* ask to what extent *any given parish structure* helps or hinders the religious activities of the community; whether in a given situation certain parish structures should be modified or replaced in order to further the religious life and apostolate of the community.

II—The Problem

The question to be posed here is, indeed, somewhat narrower and more precise. No attempt will be made to decide whether the organization of today's parish helps or hinders the edification and spread of the kingdom of God. Here we would simply examine whether, and to what extent, the parish of today exhibits the structure of an ecclesial community.[1]

What gives rise to this question is on the one hand the variety of concepts of the parish, witnessed by much that has been written, and on the other hand the discrepancy between certain concepts and the findings of parish sociology.

The kind of pastoral theology that derives its structural principles merely from the *hierarchical Church* is essentially solely interested in the ecclesiastical office with its rights and

[1] It is thus a question of the structure of the parish in general in our time and not an investigation into the vitality or community spirit of this or that parish.

duties, and only touches on the lay community incidentally, in so far as, either as a whole or in its component groups or individuals, it is the object of the cure of souls. With the defeat of individualism there is more room for the cure of souls as a community, while this community remains the object with which the pastoral office is concerned.

An extreme example of this is the position of current Canon Law, in which the word *parish* denotes principally the office and the territory and never directly refers to the community, which incidentally is not recognized as a juridical person. Those who conceive of the parish as an exclusively legal institution cannot from their restricted viewpoint assimilate the idea of the parish community.

Opposed to the idea of the parish as a purely legal institution is the attitude found in the *liturgical movement* which sees the mystery of the Church realized in the parish. In this view the parish is essentially the people of God, a closely-knit community. This movement has produced a considerable volume of literature in which the parish is regarded as the 'family', the original cell or smallest unit of the Church, as an *ecclesiola* or Church in miniature, all of which expressions have found their way even into papal documents (particularly those of Pius XI and Pius XII). The expression 'parish family' has become a widely accepted guiding image—if not actually a myth—linked, in extreme cases, with the so-called 'parish principle' which admits of no pastoral activity outside the parish or at least insists on the strict subordination of any such activity to the parish.[1]

Against the theoretical ideal of the 'parish family' must be set the concrete findings of *sociological* studies of the parish which paint a very different picture. These show that a large part of this 'family' takes no part, or only the very smallest part, in the life of the parish, and that only a very small percentage can really be said to belong to the family.

This brief indication of the discrepancies of opinions and facts forces us to pose the question: does the community

[1] To the extent that it has been realized that the parish is not the last instance, the 'parish principle' has been broadened to become the 'bishop principle'. Today even this principle has been abandoned in pastorally advanced counties.

structure belong to the essence of the parish and must it therefore always be considered the goal of pastoral work; or has the parish a different structure and therefore should a different goal be envisaged?

In order to answer this question we must first show briefly what is meant by *community* in the context of this study. Since it is a complex community having various strata and comprising different viewpoints, the second question that must be answered concerns the methods by which the various strata are approached. Then the main part of this book will study the question whether, and if so to what extent and in what sense, the structure of the parish coincides with that of the community.

1. *The Concept of Community*

Our question is only meaningful if by community we understand *ecclesial* community.

(a) *The Levels of Being of the Ecclesial Community*. The ecclesial community is a very complex reality embracing many levels and correlating them. We are dealing with a supernatural-natural reality, or a supernatural reality which informs and re-forms the natural, and does so in such a manner that certain forms determined by the supernatural are fixed, while others stemming from the natural can be altered or exchanged.

In its inner essence the ecclesial community is a supernatural reality consisting in the union with Christ by grace, which includes the grace-given unity of the members with each other. Its innermost essence consists in this interior, supernatural and invisible unity of life with Christ, the head of the Church, through the Holy Spirit, who 'fills and unifies the whole Church'.[1] The Church is the Body of Christ, beyond space and time, rooted and existing wholly in God. On this plane the community is not yet visible and within the Church as a whole individual subordinate communities cannot yet be distinguished. It is the inner union in grace between individuals and Christ, and among the individuals themselves, regardless of the time and space of the history of salvation. It is indeed the root of all

[1] *De Veritate II*, q. 29, a.4.c. Quoted by Pius XII in *Mystici Corporis* (C.T.S. 1949), § 60.

ecclesial communities appearing in the course of salvation history; but precisely because it is a root, it is invisible.[1]

However, precisely because it is the Body of Christ, the Church is under the law of the Incarnation. Without being of this world, the invisible reality must enter into this world in order to allow its supernatural essence to become visible. A concept of community restricted to the invisible supernatural unity would not adequately express the full reality and community of the Church.

Just as Christ had to enter into mankind in order to allow his divine nature to radiate upon the world, so the Church must take on human characteristics so that her supernatural essence may become a sign 'high-lifted for the world to see it' (Is. 11: 12).[2] 'God willed that that spiritual and supernatural community should appear outwardly and be universally visible.'[3] The supernatural life in Christ which in its invisible root necessarily creates community must equally necessarily bear the characteristics of community in its visible manifestation, in the sacramental union with Christ in the community of faith, hope and charity.

This entering into the world takes place, as it were, in two stages. The Church must assume certain human and earthly forms which necessarily flow from the Church's supernatural essence and its institution by Christ, and which cannot be altered. Among these are, for example, the hierarchical structure, the essential form and matter of the sacraments, of the Body of Christ and of the people of God. In addition, it follows from the nature of the Church that it clothes itself in contingent human, cultural and historic forms which it can and indeed must adopt or lay aside with the changing times in order always to be wholly in the world. Among these are the human juridical institutions, forms of association, culture and spiritual trends. Most ceremonies and Church customs also are of this kind.[4]

These three strata which run through the ecclesial community

[1] Cf. Birou, 26–30, 'Nature intime de l'Eglise'.

[2] Denz, 1794.

[3] Vatican Council. First draft of *Const. de Eccl.* quoted by Neuner-Roos No. 362. Cf. also No. 389a.

[4] Cf. Birou, 48–59; Josef Trütsch, 'Gestaltlose Kirche', in *Civitas* 17 (1961–62), 189–91.

cannot be separated or treated as independent entities. They are grown into each other, dependent upon one another, and together constitute the one essence of the Church as a supernatural community incarnate in a natural society. One of these strata cannot be properly understood except in relation to the others.[1]

The Church is what Birou calls a 'global type' of society, not just in the sociological sense but in the universal sense of the all-embracing history of salvation. Ecclesial community cannot be placed on the same footing as other communities; it follows its own rules.[2] From another angle August Brunner shows very well how faith conditions a community which always embraces the whole of life, with its natural and supernatural dimensions.[3] The Church is built up from above and from below. According to Congar it is the place where the first and the second Adam—ourselves—meet in order to become one.[4] It is in this *global* sense, which embraces all the Church's levels of being, that the notion of community is taken in this enquiry. Not only in the supernatural sense, but in the sense of a supernatural community taking on a living shape in the natural sphere, in the conditioned and changeable here-and-now.

(b) *Community and Society*. This vertical view of the stratified reality of the Church is not yet sufficient for our enquiry. A horizontal view is also necessary to distinguish between the ecclesial *community* in the global sense and the ecclesial *society* (also in a global sense). Both society and community are contained in the global reality of the Church, though not always at all levels nor to the same degree at each level. The deeper one penetrates into the supernatural nucleus of the Church, the more exclusively does community, striving to reach perfection in *communion*, take the leading place; the nearer one approaches to the periphery at the various levels, the more the social structure takes the lead over the community.

[1] 'Thus the entire external life of the Church, even though in certain aspects contingent and limited, interprets and expresses something of her internal life. And every Christian religious fact is situated within the Church.' Birou, 61.

[2] Birou, 37; 60–62.

[3] A. Brunner, *Glaube und Gemeinschaft*.

[4] Cf. Congar, *Paroisse*, 57 f.

So we use *communion* to denote perfection and *community* to denote the supernatural reality on the invisible mystical plane, while the Church in her visible manifestation is denoted by both *community* and *society*. The social structure is internally oriented towards community in order finally to reach its depths, just as community at the deepest level becomes communion.[1]

The present enquiry is restricted on the one hand to the notion of community in so far as it is distinguished from society; on the other hand as ecclesial community it comprises all spheres of the Church. However, community and social structures will not be treated as mutually exclusive or contradictory; we shall simply discuss *whether our concept of ecclesial community embraces the notion of the parish.*[2]

2. *The Method*

Further, a clarification is necessary as to what methods lead to the various levels of being to which this question refers. Without detriment to the inner global unity, both the supernatural and the natural levels have their own laws which demand corresponding methods. It is impossible to treat this problem comprehensively here, and a few indications must suffice.[3]

The supernatural plane is only accessible to faith, on which theology is based. Even as regards the visible Church, theology is the only adequate method, since it alone is capable of establishing the relationships between its visible manifestation and the hidden roots of its essence. Now theology comprises liturgiology[4] also, for 'the life of the Church pulsates above all in the liturgy'.[5]

The naturally visible Church is largely the object of canon law, history, sociology and social psychology, but also of

[1] Cf. Birou, 34; Pin, *Pratique*, 55, note 1.

[2] 'The community is, as it were, half-way between society, which deals with relationships and structures not of our own choosing, and communion, which implies participation and total transparency in a being superior to ourselves.' Birou, 33. Cf. Pin, *Urban Parish*, p. 516 ff., on the concept of religious community.

[3] Alain Birou's book, which analyses these questions from the religious sociological standpoint, is very instructive on this point.

[4] Cf. Vagaggini, Pt. 4. *Liturgie, Glaube und Theologie*, 297–364, partic. 356 ff.

[5] Ib., 326.

liturgiology in so far as the life of the Church expresses itself liturgically even in the natural forms of a given culture or epoch. Finally, on this plane too, theology has an important, even a decisive role, because it must synthesize the different aspects dealt with by its ancillary sciences. Only such a theological synthesis can match the organic global reality of the Church. Theology alone can explain the relation between the visible manifestation of the Church and its supernatural roots, and it alone can furnish the criteria by which it can be decided whether human manifestations of the Church are in line with its essential nature or not. Here theology will have to make use of the ancillary sciences subordinate to it.

3. *Application to the Parish*

Concrete action must be adapted to the essential nature of the parish.[1] Obviously, the parish is an institution of human, and not of divine, law.[2] It belongs to the Church in so far as it is built up from below. It is a human means designed to gain entry into this world for the kingdom of God, and should help from below to introduce this kingdom into a concrete world in a particular place at a particular time. It belongs to the visible, human Church, and is one of those contingent forms which can change and which receive their concrete shape from man.

The parish is primarily a historical phenomenon whose roots reach back to the earliest Christian communities of the New Testament. It has developed under the manifold influences of its temporal surroundings and in the course of history its definite form has been fixed by canon law so that it is even today an accurately defined juridical institution.

To understand the present-day form of the parish it is necessary to summarize its history. Then the structure of the present-day parish must be examined from the standpoint of canon law, where its official legal form is outlined. The law, however, only provides the bare framework which seeks to organize the much richer content of the reality. The juridical institution is like a channel open to the supernatural life of the Church and filled by it, making it available to the members of

[1] Cf. Fichter, *Social Relations*, 153–64.
[2] Cf. Rahner, *Pfarre*, 27; Arnold, *Pfarrei*, 23 ff.

the Church, in fact to the world in general, by bringing it into human society in order that it may become the communion of saints.

Hence the juridical enquiry automatically calls for complementary theological and sociological studies. *Theology*, with particular attention to the liturgy, must show whether, and if so to what extent and in what sense, the parish derives its community structure from the supernatural reality. And finally *sociology* must determine whether, and if so to what extent, the supernatural community is incarnate in the human society and becomes visible as a natural community within the framework of the parish. Some conclusions of pastoral theology will serve to round off the study.

PART ONE

The Historical Development of the Parish

CHAPTER ONE

The Development of the Notion of the Parish

OUR word *parish* is demonstrably linked with the Latin *paroecia*, which in turn developed from the Greek παροικία as has been convincingly demonstrated in spite of various other views.[1] It is worth while to make a short summary of the evolution of the term.[2]

I—THE GREEK Παροικια

(a) *Hellenistic Usage.* Παροικέω means to dwell by, beside or near, or technically to be an alien. The adjective or substantive πάροικος has the corresponding meanings of neighbouring, neighbour and the specialized meaning of non-citizen or alien. The substantive, παροικία, derived from the adjective, appears only in biblical and ecclesiastical usage[3] and means living near or beside.[4] 'The verb and its derivates are then used of immigrants who have settled somewhere and dwell there as aliens without citizenship. Παροικέω thus comes to mean to immigrate, to sojourn as an alien; πάρόικος, immigrating, homeless, and as a substantive, foreigner, denizen, and finally παροικία means living abroad, a temporary sojourn, a limited stay, and abroad.'[5]

[1] In Part I, pp. 425–29, Stolz gives a summary and a critical appreciation of the various views which leads to the conclusion that *parochia* is derived from παροικία. The French *paroisse* has the same origin: cf. Labriolle, 60; cf. also Stutz.

[2] In agreement with Kittel, de Labriolle, Leclercq, Stolz and Stutz.

[3] Kittel, 841.

[4] Leaving out of account biblical or ecclesiastical usage, some authors take the German word *Pfarrei* to derive from this meaning. Cf. *DDC*, VI (1957), 1234 and *DTC*, IV (1911), 1363. Also the French *paroisse*; cf. Louis Rétif, 'Soubassements sociologiques d'une paroisse', in *MO*, 61 (1951), 80; M. Goison, *Mission irremplaçable du sacerdoce*, 76; cf. also Pius XI quoted by Noppel, *Pfarrei*, 82; and *LThK*, III (1931), 341–42.

[5] Stolz, 430.

In Greek *legal* usage the adjective *πάροικος* had a very definite meaning; it was applied to settled foreigners[1] who would remain for some time in the country. They paid a special tax, could not own land nor marry native nationals. They were called *μέτοικοι*, *σύνοικοι*, *ἔποικοι* and, though more rarely, *πάροικοι*.[2] In the *literary* language the idea of transience came to be predominant.

In *Philo* we find a psychological, cosmologico-gnostic interpretation of man's position as a stranger in this world. The pious man lives as a stranger, as an exile in this world.[3]

(b) In the *Septuagint* *παροικέω* occurs frequently (sixty times) as translating the Hebrew גּוּר and its derivatives, meaning to be a stranger, to sojourn, to dwell temporarily,[4] to dwell as an alien.

Παροικος (forty times) correspondingly is used for the Hebrew גֵּר and תּוֹשָׁב in the meaning of immigrant, alien, exile.[5] The Vulgate translates these passages as *peregrinari* or *advena* and their derivatives. *Πάροικος* is also used of the Israelites in a strange land.[6] *Παροικία* hence means exile (גּוֹלָה) or sojourn in a strange land without citizenship or right of domicile (מָגוֹר), or abroad as opposed to the home country. 'All three expressions are also used in the same work in relation to the life of man to characterize it as a brief sojourn abroad, far from his real homeland.'[7]

Israel's attitude to the πάροικος. '*Πάροικος* is then the alien to whom Israel has certain legal and social obligations but who is nevertheless a non-Israelite to be distinguished from residents and members of God's people. . . . In other places the alien is shown as having the same legal status as the Israelite and taking a limited part in the religious life of the people of God. . . . Circumcision is the final barrier keeping him from full community of worship, but it is not an insurmountable barrier for those who desire it and who thereby can become full members of the Israelite religious community.' The *πάροικοι*, however, also represent 'a special legal category'.[8]

[1] As opposed to transients: *ἐπιδημοῦντες, παρεπιδημοῦντες, ξένοι.*

[2] Cf. Labriolle, 60 f.

[3] Kittel, 845.

[4] Cf. Gen. 12: 10; 17: 8; 19: 9; 20: 1; 21: 23, etc.

[5] Cf. Gen. 15: 13; 23: 4; Ex. 2: 22; 18: 3, etc.

[6] Ex. 2: 22; 18: 3, etc.

[7] Stolz, 431; cf. Gen. 47: 9; 1 Chron. 29: 15; Ps. 38: 13; Lev. 25, 23; Ps. 118: 19, 54; 119: 5.

[8] Kittel, 843.

The people of Israel as πάροικος. 'The fact that Israel itself once dwelt as *πάροικος* among strangers reminds it of the fact that before God all nations are not landowners, but only transients.'[1] As a *πάροικος*, Abraham is the type of the people of Israel (Gen. 15: 13). The prophets and the psalmist take this thought up again. 'What am I in thy sight but a passer-by (*πάροικος*), a wanderer (*παρεπίδημος*), as all my fathers were' (Ps. 38: 13).

(c) *The New Testament* clearly follows the usage of the Septuagint (perhaps with the exception of Luke 24: 18 which is a definite and restricted technical term).

Παροικέω (twice) means to be alien, to dwell as a foreigner, or to settle, to take up residence (Luke 24: 18; Heb. 11: 9).

Πάροικος (four times) takes the meaning of immigrant alien (Acts 7: 6, 29; Eph. 2: 19; 1 Peter 2: 11).

Παροικία (twice) is used for Israel's sojourn in Egypt (Acts 13: 17) and to describe man's life on earth (1 Peter 1: 17).

In the New Testament these words acquire a more vivid meaning and a mystical note. The Christian knows that his life in this world is only of a temporary nature. His real fatherland, for which he was born, is heaven. He is on earth as a pilgrim. *Homo viator* was later to become a technical term in the doctrine of grace.

'What was valid for the Old Israel is applied by the Apostle to the new Israel, the *ἅγιοι*, the Church of God in Jesus Christ. They were strangers and exiles, but are so no longer . . . they have become fellow-citizens of the saints and members of the household of God. . . . However, what they have actually ceased to be, they nevertheless remain from another point of view, namely from the point of view of the earth on which they are still wanderers and of the *σαρξ* in which they still live.'[2]

'The New Testament Church is *ἐκκλησία* and *παροικία*, or rather as *ἐκκλησία* it is at the same time *παροικία*. The Church refers to itself the two terms, in legal language technical opposites, according to whether it is looking to God or to the world.'[3]

[1] Kittel, 844 f. [2] Ib., 850.

[3] Ib., 850. Cf. K. L. Schmidt, 'Das Gegenüber von Kirche und Staat in der Gemeinde des Neuen Testaments', in *ThBl*, 16 (1937), 12 f.; 15 f.; Exkurs II, *Die Kirche als Beisassenschaft.*

(d) *The Christian Literature of the First Centuries* follows the New Testament in its use of *παροικέω* and its derivatives. We find it in the letters of Clement of Rome, in Hermas' *Shepherd*, in the letter to Diognetus, in Clement of Alexandria and so on.[1] They describe our world as a place of passage: 'We shall therefore, my brethren, leave the exile of this world (*καταλείψαντες τὴν παροικίαν τοῦ κόσμου τούτου*) and do the will of him who has called us, and not be afraid to leave this world.'[2] 'The letter to Diognetus in V, 5[3] says of the Christians, with 1 Peter 2: 11, that they live as strangers (*ὡς πάροικοι*) in their own country, and similarly in VI, 8[4] that they sojourn temporarily as strangers in the transitory world (*παροικοῦσιν ἐν φθαρτοῖς*) while awaiting the heavenly eternity.'[5]

Besides this more general sense which is used of Christians in general, there is also a narrower technical usage.

First the *verb παροικέω* is brought into relation with the individual Christian community, the *ἐκκλησία*. From the end of the first century the verb is found as 'a technical expression to describe the location of individual churches',[6] but always as complementary to *ἐκκλησία*.[7] Thus the address of the first Letter of Clement reads: *Ἡ ἐκκλησία τοῦ Θεοῦ ἡ παροικοῦσα Ῥώμην τῇ ἐκκλησίᾳ τοῦ Θεοῦ τῇ παροικούσῃ Κόρινθον*.[8] Similarly the address of the letter of Polycarp is: *τῇ ἐκκλησίᾳ τοῦ Θεοῦ τῇ παροικούσῃ Φιλίππους*.[9]

Simultaneously the *substantive παροικία* acquires a technical sense. We meet it first in writing in the letter of the Smyrna community to the church of Philomelium on the martyrdom of St Polycarp (A.D. 155 or 156): *Ἡ ἐκκλησία τοῦ θεοῦ ἡ παροικοῦσα Σμύρναν τῇ ἐκκλησίᾳ τοῦ θεοῦ τῇ παροικούσῃ Φιλομηλίῳ και πάσαις ταῖς κατὰ πάντα τόπον τῆς ἁγίας καὶ καθολικῆς ἐκκλησίας παροικίαις*.[10]

'Here, quite unambiguously, *παροικία* means the individual Christian communities, just as the author of the first translation and also Rufinus in his translation of Eusebius' Church History render the end of the address as *omnibus, quae ubique*

[1] Textual references in de Labriolle, 62 f., and Stolz, 433 f.
[2] 2 Clement V, 1; Funk, I, 188. [3] Ib., 398. [4] Ib., 400.
[5] Stolz, 433 f. [6] Ib., 435. [7] Ib., 438. [8] Funk, I, 98.
[9] Ib., 296; other examples in de Labriolle, 64, and Stolz, 434.
[10] Ib., 314.

sunt, sanctis ecclesiis catholicis.'[1] 'This plural use of the word is one step further in its evolution. Whereas previously *παροικίαι* indicated a state of God's people, or of the New Testament community or even the situation of one or each member of this *ἐκκλησία*, and thereby the existence of this *ἐκκλησία* as the existence of a *παροικία* . . . it is now used parallel to *ἐκκλησία* as an individual community. Thus, whereas in the New Testament *ἐκκλησίαι* is used in the plural (e.g. Gal. 1: 22; Apoc. 1: 20), henceforth the reference will be to the *παροικίαι* of the one holy and catholic *ἐκκλησία*. In this way *ἐκκλησία* comes more and more to be used exclusively for the Church as a whole, while *παροικία* becomes the technical term for the individual communities within the Church.'[2]

In this sense the substantive frequently occurs in Dionysius of Corinth, in Irenaeus and Apollonius, and particularly in Eusebius 'who frequently uses *παροικία* as a synonym for *ἐκκλησία* in the sense of individual church, while as a rule Rufinus translates it as *ecclesia*. Thus by the middle of the second century, the noun *παροικία* has already become a technical ecclesiastical term.'[3]

It is worth noting that in these cases the word *παροικία* is used expressly in conjunction with the universal, catholic *ecclesia*. The sense of all-embracing unity is still very much alive; it is this holy, catholic Church which is present in the individual communities. But just in these individual communities it is most obvious that the present Church has not yet reached fulfilment, that it wanders as a stranger in this world. As a *παροικία* it is indeed tied to a particular place, but nevertheless it is not imprisoned there. This development of the term shows a shifting of emphasis in the view of the Church towards its situation in the world and its transcendence.

The idea is wholly in line with holy scripture. In the Letter to Diognetus (before A.D. 190) there is the following eloquent passage describing the situation of the Church: 'They have a homeland of their own and live there as strangers; as citizens they have a share in everything, yet they behave in all things as aliens; all foreign lands are home to them, and all homelands

[1] Stolz, 435.
[2] Kittel, 851–53; cf. Schlier-Warnach, *Die Kirche im Epheserbrief* 10, 30.
[3] Stolz, 436; cf. Harnack, *Ausbreitung*, I, 421, note 4.

are foreign.'[1] Valesius, likewise, had realized this when he wrote: *Cuius significationis* (*sc.* *παροικία*) *origo ex eo manasse mihi videtur, quod ecclesia in terris dumtaxat inquilina sit et παροικος, eius autem patria et muncipatus in coelo sit.*[2]

This meaning remained for some time in the consciousness of the Fathers. In the middle of the third century Origen is still speaking of the Churches as *ταῖς ὧν παροικοῦσι δήμων ἐκκλησίαις*,[3] as churches being among the peoples as heavenly lights in this world. Eusebius still copied the old formula *τῇ Ἐκκλησίᾳ τῇ παροικούσῃ*.[4] Gregory of Nazianzus (ob. 390) still recognizes the distinction between *παροικία* and *κατοικία*, the vale of exile and the heavenly home.[5] But from then on the original idea progressively disappears from consciousness.

From the beginning of the fourth century the term is also found in official documents: it belongs now to the official language of the Church and has a technical meaning. As was the case in the second century, *παροικία* is now used to denote the individual community, for example by Eusebius in the second edition of his Church history (324–25)[6] and in various conciliar canons.

In many places *ἐπίσκοπος* (in the singular) is used in connexion with several *παροικίαι*.[7] According to Duchesne,[8] Müller[9] and Griffe[10] this denoted bishops at the head of several communities which were under the immediate leadership of a presbyter or deacon. Probably mistakenly, Harnack saw in *ἐπίσκοπος τῶν παροικιῶν* (or *ἐκκλησιῶν*) a regular term for the office of metropolitan.[11] According to him the *παροικίαι* were actually episcopal communities. However, it is well established that in the year 188–89 there was only one bishop (Demetrius)

[1] Funk, I, 398.

[2] In his edition of the Greek ecclesiastical writers, Vol. I, Note on Eusebius, *H.E.*, I, 1, Amsterdam, 1695, quoted in Stolz, 439, and de Labriolle, 71, note 51.

[3] *Contra Celsum*, III, 29; PG, XI, 957; quoted by de Labriolle, 65.

[4] Eusebius, *H.E.*, IV, 23, 5; PG, XX, 385.

[5] Quoted by de Labriolle, 66, note 25.

[6] Eusebius, *H.E.*, III, 4, 5 (PG, XX, 220); ib., V, 5, 8 (PG, XX, 441); ib. V, 23, 3 (PG, XX, 492).

[7] Ib., IV, 23, 5 (PG, XX, 385); V, 23 (PG, XX, 493); VI, 2, 2 (PG, XX, 524); VII, 26, 3 (PG, XX, 705); VII, 28 (PG, XX, 706); cf. also Harnack, *Ausbreitung*, I, 466 f.

[8] Duchesne, *Fastes épiscopaux de l'ancienne Gaule*. [9] K. Müller, *Beiträge*.

[10] Griffe, 'Premières paroisses'. [11] Harnack, *Ausbreitung*, I, 467–73.

in Egypt, and this was the case for some time longer. The communities in Egypt, a country which had no municipal organization, were led directly by presbyters or deacons.[1] Griffe establishes the same as being true of certain towns in Gaul and Germany.[2]

Today it is probably simplest to follow Rufinus and to render the παροικία of this period as Church, individual church, or community.[3]

Thus there is not yet a real change of the meaning of παροικία. This becomes a fact only in the Latin *paroecia*, which shows a completely different development. It is therefore as well to distinguish between the Greek and Latin usages.

So far the term has not yet a territorial connotation. Only later perhaps (influenced by *dioecesis*) with the increasing territorial organization of the Church, does it begin to stand for the territory.[4] It is chiefly used for the episcopal community in the city, but is also applied to the country.[5] According to Griffe,[6] Duchesne[7] and Müller[8] παροικία was also used from the middle of the second century in the west, and earlier still in the east, for individual communities under a priest or deacon. From this it may be concluded that παροικία means simply the individual or local Christian community regardless of its immediate superior. Indirectly a bishop could be at the head of several παροικίαι.[9]

II—The Latin Terms: *Paroecia*, *Parochia-dioecesis*

1. *Paroecia*

Latin made its entry into the language of the Church at a moment when Christianity was spreading very rapidly. This made itself felt also in the organization of the communities and

[1] Ib., I, 370, 457; K. Müller, *Beiträge*, 18–21. [2] Griffe, op. cit.

[3] The proposals of de Labriolle and Dom Leclercq do not correspond sufficiently accurately to the historical facts. Cf. de Labriolle, 67; Hefele-Leclercq I, 1, 320; *DACL*, XIII, 2199; infra pp. 30–1.

[4] K. Müller, *Kirchengeschichte* I, I, 763, note 1.

[5] E.g., Basil, *Ep.* 240 (PG, XXXII, 897); cf. Harnack, *Ausbreitung*, I, 476, note 2; Eusebius, *H.E.*, V, 16, 17.

[6] Griffe, 'Premières paroisses', 229–39.

[7] Duchesne, *Fastes épiscopaux de l'ancienne Gaule.*

[8] K. Müller, *Beiträge*; Harnack would allow this only for Egypt and some exceptional cases in the East; cf. Harnack, *Ausbreitung*, I, 479, 483.

[9] Feine, 85.

resulted in an extraordinary flux of terms, the Latin terms being far more fluid than the Greek ones.[1]

The Latins met *παροικία* as the technical term for the individual community, whether that of a city or rural bishop or one headed by a priest or deacon. It is doubtful, indeed, if they still realized the original etymological meaning of the word.[2] Towards the end of the fourth century, they rendered it *paroecia*: the form *parochia*, which superseded it, is of later date.[3]

The Latin *paroecia* is found quite clearly in the double meaning of individual community (mostly under a bishop) and of a larger association embodying several such communities, more or less corresponding to our diocese, governed by a bishop. Indeed, from the beginning of the fourth century the meaning of diocese prevails very rapidly. By the second half of the century it is current usage.[4]

For the country parish[5] the word *paroecia* was first used in the sixth century, in Gallia Narbonnensis. Until then the generally used term had been *dioecesis*. In the sixth century an extraordinary exchange of terms took place.[6]

This did not take place all at once, but was spread out over several centuries. Alongside the original, biblical *paroecia* the Roman administrative term *dioecesis* was also adopted into Church Latin. This led to confusion: on the one hand, the word *dioecesis* was used in ecclesiastical texts both for the civil province and for the local church.[7] And the term had also evolved in the profane sphere.[8] On the other hand, from the

[1] 'One could write a complete dissertation on the various meanings the word parish (*παροικία, parochia*) had in the ecclesiastical language of the first centuries of Christianity. . . . Generally the context allows one to determine the meaning.' Griffe, 'Premières paroisses', 229.

[2] Cf. Harnack, *Ausbreitung*, 421 f.

[3] Augustine's MSS. have *parrochia*. Cf. de Labriolle, 65.

[4] *DACL*, XIII, 2291.

[5] Not yet in the modern sense, but a baptismal district or organization centred on a baptistery, which still lacked many essential characteristics of the modern parish. Stutz, 241 f.

[6] 'It was only in the sixth century that by a rather curious inversion of words the district of a diocese and that of a country church received the names they have today.' Imbart de la Tour, 5; cf. *DACL*, XIII, 2216. Schnürer seems to have overlooked this development and to have come to a false conclusion—Schnürer, *MA*, I, 188.

[7] For examples see de Labriolle, 69.

[8] Infra, p. 30.

fourth century onwards *paroecia* and *dioecesis* could be used indiscriminately to describe the same thing,[1] which might be the area governed by a bishop comprising several communities or the individual communities themselves.[2]

For centuries both terms were used in this way, a sharp distinction emerging only slowly.[3] Up to the thirteenth century, e.g., *parochia* and *dioecesis* were both used to designate the area of episcopal authority, for which there were also other terms such as *ecclesia*, *territorium*, *dicio* or *fines episcopatus*, and *plebs*.[4] The Council of Toledo (589) uses both terms in the same Canon,[5] and Boniface VIII (1235–1303) 'used *parochia* and *dioecesis* synonymously in one Decretal (c. 3,I, 9 in 6)'.[6]

Nevertheless since the sixth century *paroecia* had come to designate especially the rural community.[7] Finally the Council of Trent had clear terms to deal with, though by this time *paroecia* had long since lost its original meaning.

In the course of the centuries the original theological sense was more and more obscured. From meaning the people and the community, the term came to mean almost exclusively the territory. This usage was so general that it was even taken over into the profane terminology and in mediaeval Latin *parrochia* could still be used for a town quarter.[8] Presumably the term

[1] *DACL*, XIII, 2199.

[2] 'Both served to designate the cell (?) of the Church, the parish, when the parish system began to develop.' de Labriolle, 69. This sentence requires modification since it makes too little distinction between the parish in the modern sense and the episcopal community. One cannot just project our modern terms back into that age. 'In the Merovingian era the two terms are used indifferently for each other and applied equally to the province of a city church or to that of a rural church.' Griffe, 'Paroisses rurales', 48 f. Cf. de Labriolle, 70; *DDC*, VI (1957), 1234.

[3] de Labriolle, 69.

[4] *LThK*², III (1958), 414; cf. Schmid, 41; *Plebs* for its part can denote the community under a priest or under a bishop. Cf. Kurtscheid, I, 277.

[5] C. 20: *DDC*, IV (1949), 1258.

[6] *LThK*², III (1958), 414.

[7] 'It is true that in conciliar decisions from the sixth century onwards *parochia* ordinarily signifies "parish" such as we envisage it today [cf. however Stutz, 241 f.] it being understood that it is always a rural parish, not an urban one.' de Labriolle, 71. The assertion that the modern meaning of the term was established in the sixth century is clearly exaggerated (*DDC*, VI (1957), 1234). It can be assumed, with Griffe, that in the West *παροικία* could be a priest's area in a city, from the second century onwards. Cf. Griffe, 'Premières paroisses'.

[8] du Cange, VI, 178.

then was further narrowed down from the community and the territory to mean only the institution. At least, beside the territorial meaning, if not actually predominating, we find the meaning of presbytery.[1] In any case, right up to the twentieth century there is no proper etymological explanation to be found except that of Valesius who maintains the derivation from παροικέω. Most scholars derived *parochia* from πάροικος = neighbour, or from παρέχω, παροχή = supply, offer.[2] This erroneous derivation has survived here and there to this day.[3] Of the original παροικεῖν nothing more is left. The idea of homelessness and being strangers on this earth has been supplanted by that of being at home in a definite area and that of a permanent institution that has settled into an almost unassailable position. In the same way the original connection with the episcopal community at times gives way to a strongly emphasized autonomy of the parish. In the extreme case of parochianism this reverses the facts and endeavours to turn the parish into a self-contained, independent institution of divine law.[4]

2. *Dioecesis* (διοίκησις)

The Latin term *dioecesis* is also taken from the Greek. Διοίκησις means in the first instance house-keeping and thence management of any sort.[5] It applies particularly to the active administration of an area, later also of money. In the wider sense it applies to the area governed or administered or to the money spent.

In the ecclesiastical sense it can mean: 1. an area coinciding with a civic diocese; 2. the ἐπαρχία (*provincia*); 3. the bishopric (παροικία); 4. the 'parish' (*ecclesia parochialis* or *ruralis*).[6]

These meanings are also found attached to the Latin *dioecesis*, with, however, a more legal flavour. Primarily it means *gubernatio*, *administratio*, *jurisdictio*; thence the place where jurisdiction is exercised. In ecclesiastical writers it can also

[1] du Cange, VI, 178.

[2] For the various meanings see Stolz, 425–29.

[3] E.g. *DDC*, VI, 1234, among others. Cf. note 4, p. 21.

[4] Cf. Denz., 1510 f.

[5] *DDC*, IV (1949), 1257—'Habitation à part'? So *DTC*, IV (1911), 1362.

[6] Lübeck, 175, note 1.

mean the *locus iurisdictionis episcopalis* and sometimes *parochia*.[1]

In contrast to *paroecia* the word was taken over from the Roman administrative language. In ecclesiastical terminology[2] it makes its first appearance in the Codex Theodosianus (368)[3] and then at the Council of Constantinople (381) 'in fact in a sense corresponding to its civic meaning: it denotes the aggregate of Church provinces included within the boundaries of a civic diocese and subject to one head'.[4] The Council, as that of Nicaea (325) had already done, followed the twelve dioceses of Diocletian's Empire.[5]

In the east it is never used for individual communities (not even for those with a bishop at their head) but always for the larger ecclesiastical area divided into eparchies which were in turn divided into *παροικίαι*.[6] This meaning outlived the co-location of civil and ecclesiastical territorial divisions[7] and was noted by Balsamon as late as the thirteenth century.[8]

In the west, however, the situation was different. *Dioecesis* had never really gained currency as meaning a large ecclesiastical area.[9] On the contrary, up to the beginning of the fifth century[10] it could mean an individual country church under a priest or the titular church of a town. Later it came to mean the individual episcopal communities and their territories. Here the influence of Roman law, in which diocese meant an area dependent on a city, is unmistakable. The coincidence of the episcopal diocese with the 'diocese' of a city is of comparatively late date.[11]

The use of the term for the bishop's diocese appeared first at the Councils of Carthage (390 and 397). In the rest of the western Church *paroecia* was preferred for this right into the twelfth century. The use of *dioecesis* for the bishopric became fixed at the beginning of the thirteenth century. Under Gregory IX (1227–39) it was finally accepted Church usage.[12]

[1] Forcellini—de Vit, *Totius Latinitatis Lexicon*, Prati, 1861, II, 726 f.
[2] *DTC*, IV (1911), 1362. [3] Lex 13, *De episcopis et clericis*.
[4] Lübeck, 176. [5] Ib., 176 f. [6] *LThK*², III, 414.
[7] Lübeck, 176. [8] *DTC*, IV, 1363. [9] *DDC*, IV (1949), 1257.
[10] *DACL*, XIII, 2216. [11] K. Müller, *Kirchengeschichte*, I, 1, 762.
[12] *DDC*, IV, 1258.

3. *The Term Paroecia in the C.I.C.*

It is well known that the use of words in the *Codex Iuris Canonici* is unsatisfactory and far from uniform. 'Clearly defined technical terms are used now in one sense, now in another; on the other hand several expressions are often used at the same time to denote one and the same thing.'[1] Further, although the Codex gives innumerable legal definitions,[2] *paroecia* is not among them. Nowhere in the Codex, not even in C. 216, is there a legal definition of 'parish'.[3] Canon 216 is only a clarification, a description of the parish.[4]

Paroecia has various meanings in the Codex. Naz gives four: the people of the parish, the parish church, the benefice, and as the actual meaning the parish territory.[5] Köstler's dictionary even gives only three basic meanings: (*a*) parish territory; (*b*) the ministry or office (by far the most quotations); (*c*) the parish church.[6] Mörsdorf, who seems to be more accurate, gives six meanings: the area, the people, the church, the endowment (mainly), the office, and the benefice.[7] For the meaning of the people of the parish he bases himself solely on C. 2269, §1, where, however, in both cases *paroecia* quite unambiguously means the area and not the people.[8]

It is therefore *negatively* established that nowhere in the Codex does *paroecia* mean the people of the parish.[9] Noser had proved this very clearly in a thorough study of the question.[10] For parishioners the word *paroeciani* is frequently used.[11]

Positively paroecia has in the *C.I.C.* frequently the sense of parish area.[12] 'The places in which *paroecia* is used in a territorial sense can be divided into two distinct groups. In the first group are those canons dealing with people belonging to a parish and placing them *qua* parishioners in relation to the parish. Generally the expression is: *In* (*sua*) *paroecia*. . . .'[13]

'The *C.I.C.* uses a different expression when dealing with

[1] Mörsdorf, 162. [2] Ib., 36. [3] Noser, 15; Hagen, 1.
[4] Noser, 16. [5] *DDC*, VI (1957), 1234. [6] Köstler, 252.
[7] Mörsdorf, 162. [8] Cf. Noser, 29.
[9] Nor in Cc. 216, §4; 1182, §2; 1356, §1; 2269, §1.
[10] Noser, 28–30. '*Paroecia*' does not mean the people of the parish.
[11] Cc. 415, §2, no. 5; 464, §1; 483; 630, §4; 848, §1; 1186, no. 2; 1247 §2; Noser, 30.
[12] Cf. C. 216: *pars territorialis diocesis* = *paroecia*; Noser, 24.
[13] Noser, 24.

things rather than people in relation to the parish area. These are never said to be "*in paroecia*" but always "*in territorio paroeciae*" or "*inter fines paroeciae*". In these cases *paroecia* loses all trace of territorial meaning: it *has* a territory, so it cannot itself *be* a territory.'[1]

We therefore conclude with Noser: 'The territory is of significance to the parish only in so far as it circumscribes the area in which the ministry is exercised. Where there is no direct connexion with the ministry (in the case of inanimate objects and non-parishioners) the territory is specifically indicated as part of the parish. The word *paroecia*, then, is only used in a territorial sense when it is used in connexion with the people of the parish, the parishioners.'[2]

The territory is incidentally not an essential part of the parish according to the *C.I.C.* There are parishes without any territory.[3]

Going one step further, Noser concludes that the term *paroecia*, with the exception of those cases with a territorial connotation, almost invariably means the ministry.[4] 'The ministry represents, not only terminologically but from every point of view, the heart and centre of the parish.'[5] It is 'the most indispensable element of the parish, so that we can identify it as a juridical person (provided it has a juridical personality) with the parish.'[6]

Finally, *paroecia* in the Codex can, and normally but not exclusively does, mean the benefice, or more accurately a beneficed office.[7] The ministry, which is the essential part of the parish, is in most cases but not always beneficed. Canon law, then, normally regards the ministry as a benefice.[8]

In this connexion it should be emphasized that in ordinary, non-legal parlance *paroecia* retains some of its older meaning, to the extent that the Latin *paroecia* can still have among other things the sense of the parish district, and the parish community.

[1] Noser, 25. [2] Ib., 26.

[3] Ib., 26. The parish is not identical with the parish church, which is not an essential element of the parish. Cf. Noser, 46–48. Hagen sidesteps the problem—Hagen, 1.

[4] In the *C.I.C.* usage the ministry is always rendered by *paroecia* (Cc. 192, §3; 389, §1; 147, §2; 451, §1; 453, §2; 458, 459, 2147–2167, etc.). Conversely it should be noted that except where it is to be understood in a territorial sense, *paroecia* always means the ministry.

[5] Noser, 51. [6] Ib., 51 f. [7] Ib., 55. [8] Ib., 56–59.

III—Summary

This rather detailed consideration of the terminology will allow us to follow the broad lines of the development of the institution itself.

The old *παροικία*, deeply stamped with biblical thinking, still meant the people of God, the Church, which has its home and its goal in heaven and as an alien has no citizenship on this earth. It is the entire Church community of a particular place, as far as possible under an episcopus or at least an authorized presbyter. As such it always represents the entire Church on its pilgrimage: *ἐκκλησία ἡ παροικοῦσα*. 'All communities were but the rays of the one sun, points at which the one Church appeared on earth.'[1]

Then the *παροικία* became even more independent, gradually losing its connexion with the one, catholic Church, and becoming restricted to an isolated individual community as it were, whose territory in time became defined. The idea of sojourn in exile was lost when the parish received fixed boundaries, and the idea of a community of people was replaced by that of the governing authority of the bishop.

Whereas in the east the sense of the biblical and theological meaning of *παροικία* remained and was harmoniously absorbed into the necessary forms of Church territorial organization (*diocese*), in the west *παροικία* gradually lost its meaning which was replaced by one borrowed from the secular sphere. The *παροικία* was supplanted by the *dioecesis* where the bishop exercised his rights. It is very significant that the term *παροικία*, based on theology and the Bible, has to compete with the juridical and political term *dioecesis* and that in the west the latter finally prevails.

Once the *παροικία* of the bishop had become a *dioecesis*, *paroecia* was finally restricted to the priest's community within the bishop's diocese. In the meantime, however, the term had lost too much of its meaning, and the Church had become too well rooted in this world for the original meaning to be revived. *Παροικία* must serve for the institution and the territory, which now meant for the Christian 'home' rather than 'exile'.

This evolution, which leads constantly further away from the original meaning, has reached its peak in the terminology

[1] Müller, *Kirchengeschichte*, I, 1, 221; cf. Harnack, *Ausbreitung* I, 447.

of current canon law in which territory, office and benefice have completely replaced the meanings of people, community, the Church homeless in a foreign land.[1] Indeed, the original meaning has been lost so completely that theologians have even found a seemingly valid etymological explanation for the later, secondary sense.

Hence in canon law the increasing narrowing of the term has become complete. It is not even narrowed down to mean the territory so much as the hierarchy, the office and benefice, to the complete exclusion of the people. This evolution of the meaning given to *paroecia* is in line with the development of the concept of the Church as a whole.[2]

This study of the development of the term not only shows a gradual shift of emphasis, and increasing superficiality, it also contributes to a better knowledge of the real nature of the parish, and of its origins. Among these is the derivation from the episcopal community which shows the parish as ordered towards the episcopate: it is a community constituted from above, which may not make itself independent from below. Not only the head, the ministry, is constituted from above, but the whole, the community, the people of God, the Church. And, being the Church, it does not only come from above, it must also always strive upwards: its home and its goal are in heaven. Here below it is a stranger in the land, an exile in this civilization and this age. It may not become naturalized, but must always be on its way, always adapt itself anew, always be on the move through the ages to its final goal.

[1] 'This word "parish", in Latin *paroecia* or *parochia*, comes from the Greek παροικία meaning a group of dwellings. The modern meaning is thus true to the etymological sense of *paroecia* when, with C. 216, §1, it treats the parish as a territorial circumscription established in a diocese'—*DDC*, VI, 1234; *DTC*, IV, 1363 also explains it as a 'group of dwellings'.

[2] 'The parish has generally speaking not experienced the hour of greatness destined for it by the Council of Trent. Besides the general tendencies of the times, the atrophy of the concept of the Church in theology and catechesis due to counter-Reformation polemics has undoubtedly contributed to this. The way, for example, counter-Reformation controversial theology and catechesis under Bellarmine's leadership were concentrated almost wholly on establishing the hierarchical concept of the Church inevitably resulted in a one-sided legalistic view of the parish. Influenced by the deistic spirit of the Enlightenment, in the second half of the eighteenth century Benedict Stattler took this development even further and arrived at a purely sociological natural law concept of the Church devoid of all dogmatic content.' Arnold, 'Pfarrei', 32.

IV—Appendix—*Parochus*

Parochus is certainly not derived from *paroecia* as is often wrongly assumed.[1] It is also not possible to trace it back to the Greek *πάροικος*. This precludes (or at least deprives of its etymological foundation) the interpretation that the priest is not really a member of the community but a sort of alien (*πάροικος*), since he only remains in the community to care for souls.[2]

The term *parochus* gained currency principally through the Council of Trent.[3] 'This much is certain, that even though it was only in the sixties of the sixteenth century that the word was considered suitable to feature in the final form of the council's decisions, it was quite current in the spoken discussions and written exchanges of the preceding twenty years. The use of the word goes right back to the start of the preliminary work for the council.'[4]

In fact, the term had originated earlier. It is met in Spain between 1485 and 1500. There are grounds for believing that it was at the time current in the archdiocese of Seville.[5]

In the German language area the oldest uncontested record of *parochus* is in the so-called *Pfaffenbrief*, i.e. the *concordia inter episcopum Constantiensem et praelatos exemptos et non exemptos vel Clerum Helvetiae*, of 27 July 1493.[6]

U. Stutz, who followed the matter up over a number of years,[7] can produce even older records, as in the first work of Augustinus Tünger, *Facetiae*, which he wrote in 1486, probably in Constance but at all events near Lake Constance.[8] The

[1] E.g. C. Krieg, *Seelenführung*, 462.

[2] Cf. Wetzer and Weltes, *Kirchenlexikon*, 2nd ed., Freiburg, 1895, IX, 1954. Is this false interpretation unconsciously (or even consciously) based on the assumption that clergy and people are separate? What was originally valid of the relationship of the whole Christian community to this world is now suddenly and quite inadmissibly confined to the relationship of the parish priest to his parishioners. The very fact that this derivation is etymologically untenable shows the influence on this interpretation of a definite, false concept of the parish priest.

[3] Cf. Stutz, 'Parochus', in *Savigny*, 32 (1911), 314.

[4] Stutz, loc. cit., 34 (1913), 797.

[5] Stolz, *Parochus*, 196–99; 193.

[6] Stolz, op. cit., 194–96; Stutz, loc. cit., 32 (1911), 315.

[7] Cf. *Savigny*, 32 (1911), 313–18; 33 (1912), 344; 34 (1913), 495 f.; 35 (1914), 497 f.; 37 (1916), 405–12; 40 (1919), 314 f.; 43 (1922), 415 f.; 47 (1927), 332; 55 (1935), 342 f.; 56 (1936), 485–88.

[8] 'Est consuetudo in aliquot locis Germaniae, quod sacerdotes parochi. . . .' Quoted by Stutz, loc. cit., 34 (1922), 415.

objections raised against this by Stolz[1] are shown by Stutz to be invalid.[2]

The origin of the term and its introduction into Spain and Germany are decisively influenced by the humanists. They adopted the *parochus* of Horace and Cicero, undoubtedly influenced alone by the fact that the expression for parish priest current in mediaeval Latin was *presbyter parochianus* or simply *parochianus*, frequently abbreviated to *paroch* or *parochus*.[3] 'The supposedly mediaeval evidence for *parochus* is due to a false reading and should be read *parochianus*. *Parochus* is humanist Latin and first reached wider circles in the sixteenth century, to be adopted into the language of the Church from the Council of Trent onwards.'[4]

Horace's *parochus* comes from the Greek παρέχειν, to offer, to dispense.[5] The Roman *parochus* was the official who dispensed salt, wood, and the necessities of life to strangers, in particular to the Roman legates at his inn.[6] Similarly, the Christian *parochus* has the duty to dispense to the faithful, as strangers on this earth, the food and necessities of eternal life.[7] Despite humanist influence this interpretation corresponds entirely to the original meaning of παροικία as well as to that of the *servus fidelis*.

In canon law (C. 451) *parochus* can also mean a juridical person.

[1] In *ThQSchr.*, 107 (1926), 1–8.

[2] Stutz, loc. cit., 47 (1927), 332. 'A somewhat earlier example in the statutes of the chapter of Reichenau (1454–64) §3 is not entirely certain, since it may have been introduced into the text later by way of a marginal gloss.' Stutz, loc. cit., 55 (1935), 343.

[3] Stolz, loc. cit.

[4] Stutz, loc. cit., 35 (1914), 497 f.

[5] The Greek πάροχος is found in neither the Septuagint nor the New Testament.

[6] Horace, *Satires*, I, 5, 46.

[7] Cf. the article 'Pfarrer' in Wetzer and Weltes, *Kirchenlexikon* (2nd ed., Freiburg, 1895), 1954; *LThK*, article 'Pfarrei', VIII (1936), especially p. 190.

CHAPTER TWO

The Historical Growth and Development of the Parish

THE history of the parish has unfortunately not yet been written,[1] and, what is as significant as it is regrettable, the works available are almost without exception written from a canonical, institutional standpoint, the pastoral aspect being neglected.[2] 'We know all about the juridical system, its origins and forms, all about the roles of prince and bishop, the formalities of transfer of possession, the distribution of revenues, we know everything except the extent to which all this corresponded to religious needs. It seems as if historians have not even considered this fundamental and all-important problem.'[3]

Here only a brief survey can be given which has to rely on secondary sources, and which therefore will not be free from the shortcomings of these, as well as of those of the author.

1. *Early Christianity* (*First to Fourth Centuries*)

Though the knowledge of the primitive communities of apostolic and post-apostolic times is of great importance for the understanding of the origins of the parish, despite a great deal of research information on this subject remains unfortunately rather meagre.[4] From the semantic development,

[1] Cf. Grasso, 297, note 5; Noppel, *Pfarrei*, 17. There do exist monographs on individual parishes, at least over a certain period; there are parish histories of individual areas for a particular period; there is a quantity of short articles on the origins and history of the parish, and on various canonical questions and matters of juridical history. Cf., for German-speaking countries, Homeyer, 'Die Erneuerung des Pfarrgedankens' (a bibliographical summary), in H. Rahner, *Die Pfarre*, 125–28; also the bibliography of this present work.

[2] Le Bras, *Introduction*, Schrott, *Seelsorge*, and Broutin are exceptions.

[3] Le Bras, *Introduction*, II, 21.

[4] Bardy, I, 42.

however, it is clear that no ready-made type of community existed from the beginning, but that in fact right from the start there were communities with different types of structure.

The first Christian communities were formed in cities (Jerusalem, Antioch, Corinth, Ephesus, etc.); for this reason Harnack rightly called primitive Christianity an urban religion. The spread of the Christian faith followed the natural trade routes, largely in conjunction with the Jewish colonies whose eastern communities enjoyed a special status even under the Romans.[1] Christianity therefore largely adopted the outward forms and statutes of a minority sect into which, however, the transforming spirit of Christ was poured.[2]

The foundation of a community[3] probably often started in a small domestic community[4] or families bound together by close ties of love and who, from time to time, gathered together in one house. Such a community might have a hierarchical head from the very beginning (Jerusalem) or might only receive one later (Antioch).[5] It might be established from above by the preaching of an apostle, or it might arise from below (as in the case of Antioch) by the coming together of the faithful (for example, exiles from Jerusalem). In order to become a community in the full sense of the word it was essential that there should be a visible link with Christ through the apostles or their successors—in other words, through the hierarchy. From this results the connexion or the dependence between the communities and the privileged position of Jerusalem.[6]

At first, the organization of the community followed closely that of the Jewish synagogue.[7] As far as possible the apostles themselves were the heads of the communities,[8] assisted by a council of elders (*presbyteroi*) who led the community. Communities with a purely presbyteral structure survived long into post-apostolic times and even later in the country, especially in Egypt.[9] The life of these communities showed considerable variation: socialization was not everywhere, as in Jerusalem,

[1] Duchesne, *Origines*, 4; Kurtscheid, I, 40. [2] Duchesne, op. cit., 1–7.
[3] Kurtscheid, I, 15–20. [4] Harnack, *Ausbreitung*, I, 457 f.
[5] Colson, *Evêque*, 29. [6] Ib., 35 ff.; Feine, 31.
[7] Duchesne, *Histoire*, I, 51. Cf. Schmitt, 'Das jüdische Priestertum und die kirchliche Hierarchie in den Urgemeinden Palästinas', in Guyot, *Das apostolische Amt*, 52–67.
[8] Feine, 33. [9] Ib., 32.

carried as far as the community of goods; in general Christians remained far behind this ideal.[1]

The Christian communities, however, differed decisively from Judaism, above all through the eucharistic celebration on the Lord's Day, which was deliberately opposed to the Sabbath.[2]

On the question of the hierarchical head of the community, Colson distinguishes two lines of development, starting as parallels but later coming together, the monarchical episcopacy remaining predominant. One was the Pauline (western) line,[3] the other the Johannine (eastern) line.[4] Polycarp of Smyrna and Irenaeus of Lyons are witnesses to their unity.[5]

The Pauline line is characterized by the fact that the individual local community was headed by a collegium of priests or 'bishops'[6] with no president or head but depending on St Paul who, as an itinerant apostle was himself the bond uniting all the communities under him. This conception is based on a particular theology of unity[7] which puts the accent on the community as a body. The body, indeed, has various hierarchically ordered members, but these members are only functions of the one body destined to grow into the perfect body of Christ. Thus for Clement the 'bishop' is, above all, the organ of the Spirit in the Church. Paul and Clement were not interested in the organ of unity but in the realization of unity in the communities.[8]

The Johannine line is recognized by the monarchical bishop resident in the community.[9] For John the unity of the Church is embodied in its 'angel', in whom the whole community is gathered.[10] He is the image of their living unity. The loving

[1] Duchesne, *Origines*, 10. [2] Cf. Huber 15–34; 65–70.

[3] Paul, Clement of Rome, Hermas Pastor; cf. Colson, *Evêque*, 47–78.

[4] James of Jerusalem, John, Ignatius of Antioch. Cf. Colson, op. cit., 79–108.

[5] Colson, op. cit., 108–24. Cf. Plöchl, I, 45 f.

[6] There are three views about these *presbyteroi* or *episkopoi*: they were all consecrated bishops; they were all only priests; at least one of them was a bishop. Cf. Kurtscheid, I, 19 f.; Colson, *Fonctions*, 92–112; especially the presentations and well-arranged tables in Bruders, *Verfassung*, 104–13.

[7] Cf. Kurtscheid, I, 12–15: *de unitate ecclesiae*. [8] Colson, *Evêque*, 86.

[9] Cf. Kurtscheid, I, 22–25: *de episcopatu monarchico*.

[10] Cf. de Fraine, *Adam et son lignage. Etude sur la notion de 'personnalité corporative'*, Bruges, 1959; Henrici, 'Bibel-Philosophie und Bibel-Theologie', in *Orient*, 23 (1959), 214 ff.

unity of the faithful with Christ must be a community with someone who can be seen and touched.[1]

After the death of the apostle of the Gentiles, whose powerful personality was able to hold a number of communities together, it was almost a necessity that a resident head should come to preside over the college of 'bishops'.

The local monarchical episcopate was perfected in the person of Ignatius of Antioch, who was also its first and most important Greek theoretician.[2] 'The community of each town symbolizes the vocation to unity of the entire Christian people gathered together in God. It is, in the untranslatable expression of St Ignatius, *τὸ ἐν θεῷ πλῆθος* (the fullness in God). It is the "Church" or community of God, *ἐκκλησία θεοῦ*.'[3] We must not, however, regard these communities as being self-contained. The letters of St Ignatius are evidence to the contrary, for he sent them not only to his own but also to other friendly communities for whom he also felt responsible.[4] The most important element binding the Christian communities together among themselves was the *communio*. This meant first the union of the individual Christian with the eucharist, and through the eucharist with all Christians. This is not just a community of belief and disposition, but equally a mystical and legal bond

[1] Colson, op. cit., 81–87.

[2] Stauffer, *Urkirche*, 303.

[3] Colson, op. cit., 91; cf. Harnack, *Ausbreitung*, I, 447.

[4] So Ignatius of Antioch wrote to the Ephesians on the subject of his warm attachment to their bishop (5, 1); he counts on their prayers, in which he wishes always to have a share (11, 2); he proposes to instruct them (20, 1–2); and even finds the following words for this community which is not his own: 'I offer my life for you and for those whom for the glory of God you sent to Smyrna, where, too, I am writing to you with thanks to the Lord and with love for Polycarp and you. Remember me, as Jesus Christ may remember you! Pray for the Church in Syria, whence I am being led away in chains to Rome, though I am the least of the faithful there. . . .' (21, 1–2). Cf. also *Magnes.*, 12, 1; 15, 1; *Trall.*, 6, 1; 'I merely warn you betimes since you are dear to me' (*Trall.*, 8, 1); 'My spirit is consecrated to you, not only now, but also when I have happily made my way to God' (*Trall.*, 13, 3). 'My brethren, my love for you overflows all bounds, and it is my supreme delight to provide you with safeguards, though it is not really *I* that do it, but Jesus Christ. Being in chains for his sake, I am all the more apprehensive, since I am not yet perfected. But then, your prayer will make me perfect in the sight of God. . . .' (*Philad.*, 5, 1). Cf. also *Philad.*, 6, 2; 10, 1–2; *Smyrn*; 4, 1; *Polyc.*, 6, 1–2. (Transl. by Kleist in *Ancient Christian Writers*, Vol. I, Longmans, Green & Co., London, 1946.)

between the Church and its members.[1] With the bishop, and subordinate to him, are always also the presbyters and deacons.

In Polycarp, and even more in Irenaeus, we find the fusion of the incarnationist and universalist perspectives. The individual churches, with their 'monarchical' bishop or their college of presbyters at the head, together form the greater unity and community of the whole Church with Rome at its head.[2]

It is noteworthy that the hierarchical leaders (bishop, presbyters and deacons) on the one hand themselves constitute a community and lead a common life[3] and on the other are closely linked with the laity, and that their position is determined by their functions.[4] Right from the beginning there exists a healthy tension in the relations between the local church and the Church as a whole,[5] which alone makes true community possible both as regards the local and the universal Church. A local church that isolates itself must die; on the other hand the universal Church presupposes strong local churches.

Thus, in its essential features the evolution of the monarchical episcopate was complete in the course of the second century.[6]

2. *The Episcopal Communities*

In most places there is an obvious tendency for the local community to develop into an episcopal community. Except for Egypt, this obtains right into the third century even in small places with a limited number of Christians.[7]

[1] Cf. Hertling, *Communio und Primat*; Plöchl, I, 40, 57 ff.; Colson, 'Evangélisation'.

[2] As early as the writings of Ignatius there is frequent reference to the Church of Syria, or of Asia, that is of a large association. 'Ignatius is much more than the Bishop of Antioch. He calls himself Bishop of Syria (*ad. Rom.* 2, 2) and writes pastoral letters to the communities in Asia Minor' (Stauffer, *Urkirche*, 303). The bishops themselves feel themselves bound to each other. They are, in Cyprian's phrase, the mortar binding the one Catholic Church together. Cf. B. Botte, 'Der Kollegialcharakter des Priester- und Bischofsamtes', in Guyot, *Das apostolische Amt*, 68–91, especially 76–86: 'Ordo Episcoporum'. Cf. also Rahner-Ratzinger, 78 ff.

[3] Cf. also Colson, *Fonctions*.

[4] The community really is a community and not just a society. Cf. Acts of the Apostles and St Paul's epistles.

[5] Harnack, *Ausbreitung*, I, 446 f.; 473.

[6] Plöchl, I, 51; Hergenröther, I, 238.

[7] Plöchl, I, 47; Harnack, *Ausbreitung*, I, 475; 457.

(a) *In the Towns.* Following the local extension of Christianity, episcopal communities first came into being especially in towns. The bishop was the ordinary pastor of the community: parish priests did not as yet exist; but the bishop had presbyters and deacons to assist him in his pastoral and charitable work. Although there was as yet no clearly defined territorial sovereignty, the bishop of a city nevertheless felt himself as the ecclesiastical authority of the whole area embracing both the *civitas* and the *suburbium.* In the second and third centuries the city area was divided into *regiones diaconales* or *regiones presbyterales* under a deacon or presbyter subject to the bishop in conformity with civil administrative or police districts. These are not yet parish districts, for the bishop was still the direct superior of each district. In the west the bishop's territory gradually spread to include the smaller rural communities which were looked after from the town. So far there is no evidence that the Roman territorial constitution already served as a basis for the Church's territorial organization before the Council of Nicaea in 325.[1]

(b) *In the Country.* Although Christianity spread principally in the towns it extended to the villages (*κωμίαι*) and larger villages (*μητροκωμίαι*) as early as the second or perhaps even the first centuries.[2] According to eastern practice a bishop was installed as soon as a reasonably large group of the faithful was gathered in such a village, which had at first been governed by a presbyter or a deacon; the bishops would be assisted by a more or less numerous clergy.[3]

The rural bishops or *chorepiscopi* (*ἐπίσκοποι τῆς χώρας* or *χωρεπίσκοποι*, *episcopi vicani*, *regionarii*, etc.), were originally equal to the urban bishops; but very soon the greater influence of the towns led to a hierarchical gradation and then very quickly to the subordination of the rural bishops to the urban bishops.[4]

[1] Plöchl, I, 52–55.

[2] *DACL,* III, 1424; Kurtscheid, I, 57.

[3] For some figures see Bardy, I, 46 f. There are canons specifying that a community must number at least twelve Christian males before a bishop could be elected. Plöchl, I, 53 f.; 141 f.

[4] *DACL,* III, 1425 ff. The name first occurs in C. 13 of the Council of Ancyra (314–15) but even here the institution goes back further than its name. As early as 296 there is mention of rural bishops in a synodal letter of the Council of Antioch. Cf. Eusebius, *H.E.*, VII, 30, 10; Kurtscheid, I, 60.

The *chorepiscopi* had certainly received the episcopal consecrations but gradually were not allowed to confer the major orders without the written permission of the urban bishop. Whereas in the conciliar *acta* the urban bishops always added the name of their town to their signatures, the *chorepiscopi* did not add the name of their village but that of the area, since they were not tied to any particular place.[1]

Rural bishops are attested very early not only in the east (especially, Syria and Cappadocia) but also in Africa, Southern Italy and Spain. In Africa bishops were appointed to numerous villages and hamlets. In 397 Aurelius, Bishop of Carthage, said he had an episcopal consecration almost every Sunday.[2] In the struggle with Montanism both parties multiplied the number of their bishops in order to acquire a voting majority in the synods.

In Southern Italy at the end of the second century and during the third there were rural bishops (though not called *chorepiscopi*) who were on the same footing as urban bishops.[3] The same was true of Spain. After the Peace of Constantine so many episcopal churches were established that they were almost able to meet all pastoral needs of the first centuries.[4]

In Northern Italy,[5] Gaul and Germany the spread of Christianity to the countryside began later. In these areas it was still an urban religion so that at this period 'countryman' and 'non-Christian' were synonymous: both were called *pagani*.[6]

The *chorepiscopi*, who had become more and more numerous in the east, gradually had to give way in the villages and small towns where a priest was enough to handle the pastoral work[7] to itinerant bishops who, in the name of the urban bishop, visited and cared for the communities that had become dependent on him.[8] Finally *chorepiscopi* were entirely

[1] *DACL*, III, 1434. The element of mobility, suitable for the needs of the countryside, was already present with the *chorepiscopi* and did not only come in with their successors the *periodeuti*.

[2] Bardy, I, 48. [3] *DACL*, III, 1442. [4] Kurtscheid, I, 263.

[5] Nanni, 477 f. [6] *LThK*, IV (1932), 877.

[7] Synod of Sardica, A.D. 343–44.

[8] The reasons for this development put forward by Kurtscheid are interesting: poor education of the bishops and the danger of heresy and schism. Instead of strengthening unity, the exaggerated multiplication of the number of bishops led to disunity in doctrine and to schism. Besides these pastoral reasons, however, sociological reasons also played an

forbidden[1] or at least limited in number[2] so that each urban bishop was allowed only one. It is not known how long this system prevailed in the east.[3]

3. *Communities under Priestly Rule*

(a) *In the Towns.* Although the general tendency was towards episcopal communities and though the bishops mainly resided in the towns, there were also urban communities governed only by a *priest* or a *deacon*.[4] Both Griffe and Duchesne have shown that at first this was the case in many towns and that the installation of bishops took place only gradually. Griffe believes that in the second century there was only one bishop for the whole of Gaul, with his seat in Lyons.[5] Around the year 250 the number of bishops in Gaul was still very small. The building up of an episcopal hierarchy for the more important towns of Gaul was not completed till towards the end of the fourth century.[6] The oldest 'parishes' (in the broad sense of priest-communities) arose, in the west at least, in the towns and not, as is commonly assumed,[7] in the country. Moreover, this happened very early. In the west they originated in the country only after Constantine.[8] According to Griffe this

---

important part; for example, adaptation to the civil administration in which the country districts were entirely dependent on the towns, and the general contempt for country people. Probably one can discern even here an alienation of the Church from a certain class of people. Cf. Kurtscheid, I, 60; Bardy, I, 47.

[1] Synod of Laodicea, A.D. 343–81.

[2] Synod of Seleucia-Ctesiphon, A.D. 410.

[3] Last mention at the second Council of Nicaea in 787. With the Nestorians it continued into the thirteenth century and is supposed to be still known in the east. Cf. *LThK*², II (1958), 1080; Harnack, *Ausbreitung*, I, 447 f. In a letter to the African bishops Leo I (440–61) forbade the installation of bishops in small villages and demanded that they be satisfied with a simple priest. Cf. Van der Meer, *Augustinus der Seelsorger*, 30 f. The west did not have the chorepiscopal system in its eastern form. They are here first mentioned in 747 and they are a kind of missionary or conventual bishop, of Irish–Scottish origin, without territory or jurisdiction. With a few exceptions they had disappeared by the twelfth century. Cf. *LThK*², II, 1080; Kurtscheid, I, 251–7; Siegwart, 83.

[4] Griffe, 'Premières Paroisses', 229 f.

[5] The community there about the year 150 consisted principally of easterners from the Roman colony.

[6] Griffe, op. cit., 229; 'Paroisses rurales', 23; Daniel-Le Mouel, *Paroisses*, 43.

[7] Zorell, 89. [8] Griffe, 'Paroisses rurales', 35.

development from priest's to bishop's community occurred also in many towns in the east, though even earlier.[1]

(b) *Titular Churches*. Beside these small priest-communities established with missionary interests in view, another kind of priest-community existed, connected with the organization of large urban Christian communities, the so-called *tituli* or titular churches,[2] which were found especially in Rome and Antioch.

From the very beginning, the faithful there were governed by the one bishop of the city; in Rome, by the pope. Nevertheless, in the second century, the Roman community did not present a homogeneous external picture: it was divided into various independent and sometimes even antagonistic groups, and even into different rites.[3] These groups assembled in their own meeting places which, being private houses voluntarily placed at their disposal, followed no topographical plan. The houses were known by the name of their secular owners (hence titular). Later, from the third century on, these houses passed into the possession of the Church and were altered and fitted up as real titular churches with their own baptisteries.[4]

The titles show that the Christian community of Rome possessed churches even before the Decian persecution (249–50). The twenty oldest titles probably date back to the first half of the third century and some even to the end of the second century. In the fifth century they numbered twenty-five.[5]

These titular churches were often quite close to one another and spread over the whole city as it were in pairs, but almost exclusively in the expanding residential quarters. They accommodated only a small number of the faithful.[6]

At least two priests officiated at each titular church. Isolation of priests was contrary to the views of the primitive Church.[7] 'One has the impression that at that time the clergy

[1] Griffe, 'Premières paroisses', 239. [2] Denis-Boulet, 14–32.

[3] Ib., 19 f. Heresies lead even to schisms.

[4] For baptismal purposes private bath-houses were chosen when possible. Up to the middle of the second century baptisms were carried out in the Tiber, probably never in the catacombs. Ib., 29.

[5] Ib., 16, 18; cf. Monachino, *La cura pastorale*, 279–309.

[6] Ib., 19. In the third century Rome numbered some 30,000 faithful. The largest hall then available could accommodate about 400. At the time of Cornelius (251–53) Rome had 46 priests and 108 other clerics. Ib., 16, 20.

[7] Ib., 16 f. Cf. Botte, 'Das Weihesakrament nach den Gebeten des Weiheritus', in Guyot, op. cit., 28.

of the titular churches was, as it were, hereditary, for in the fourth, fifth and sixth centuries it was composed of the same families, from which, among others, St Gregory and St Damasus sprang.'[1]

The *tituli* had as yet no territorial jurisdiction, for they were still spontaneous groups living a genuine community life. This is shown also by the *diaconates* belonging to the various *tituli* which, although very close to each other and having no fixed boundaries, never interfered in each other's works of charity. The division of Rome into seven ecclesiastical districts, which continued into the eleventh century, had nothing to do with the *tituli*: but corresponded to the seven papal deacons.[2]

Perhaps Pope Marcellus (307–9) may have been the first to concede to the titular churches the rights of baptism, confession and burial of martyrs. In any case they had a baptistery and a room where the liturgy could be celebrated. Up to the time the Lateran basilica was built even Easter was not celebrated in company with the bishop but in the individual titular churches.[3]

The individual life of the titular churches did not, however, impair the greater unity centred in the bishop. Even for the Rome of the titular churches the pope, the bishop of Rome, represented the organ of unity. This unity was expressed most strongly in the celebration of the eucharist, although Ignatius' ideal of one bishop and one eucharist did not long remain a practical proposition. Concelebration by all the priests with the bishop in the presence of all the faithful—even if it had ever taken place in early Christian Rome—had become impossible at the time of Irenaeus. In its stead there arose the custom of the so-called *fermentum* which can be traced back to the middle of the second century.[4] In 416 Innocent I gives this explanation: on an ordinary Sunday 'the priests cannot join with us on account of the people in their charge; they receive the *fermentum* from us so that they shall not regard themselves as separated from our community.'[5]

But the single pontifical Mass had already established itself

[1] Ib., 29.
[2] Ib., 24, 32; cf. Monachino, *La cura pastorale*, 327 f.
[3] Ib., 20 f.
[4] Ib., 21. Cf. Jungmann, 'Fermentum'; *DACL.*, V, 1371–74.
[5] PL., XX, 556 f. Cf. Jungmann, op. cit.

by the last quarter of the fifth century for great feasts and obligatory fast-days: the twenty-five priests of the titular churches concelebrated with the pope, who was also assisted by his seven deacons and numerous lesser clergy. The entire people took part and received holy communion.[1] This was made possible by the building under Constantine of the Lateran Basilica, an event that resulted in the most significant changes in the Church in Rome.

Now there was a place available, big enough for the bishop to gather the clergy and people about him on great feast days. In the first half of the fourth century only Easter was celebrated in common in the Lateran basilica. This is also the origin of the so-called 'stations'. The centralization progressed only slowly, not least because the Lateran basilica was too far from the city centre. In the second half of the fourth century several basilicas were built, in the cities, as a kind of local hall, having no clergy of their own, to serve for 'super-parochial' gatherings. Under Innocent I (402–17) the old titular churches were rebuilt and more lavishly adorned.[2]

Although before centralization there was no question of the titular churches being urban parishes in the modern sense of the word, they are nevertheless at the root of our parish organization. Harnack therefore rightly calls them 'parochial churches'. But they possess the characteristics of 'personal' parishes (*paroecia personalis*) rather than those of territorial parishes (*paroecia territorialis*).[3] For they were the actual centres of pastoral work, even still in the time of the great basilicas, which only served as places for worship.[4]

(c) *In the Country*. Many of the episcopal communities in rural areas developed from small communities which had previously been administered by a presbyter or a deacon. Not all communities, however, acquired a bishop; some had to be content with a presbyter, particularly the large villages (*μητροκωμίαι*) which did not develop sufficiently. These pastoral centres of the eastern Church are one of the roots of the later parish churches.[5] The constitution of Egypt, which originally

[1] Denis-Boulet, 27. [2] Ib., 25.
[3] Harnack, *Ausbreitung*, II, 854–60: Monachino, op. cit., 349 f.
[4] K. Müller, *Kirchengeschichte*, I, 1, 487.
[5] Plöchl, I, 53; cf. Kurtscheid, I, 59 (cf. 56 f.); Zorell, 77–80.

had only *one* bishop, is well known. 'Greater Egypt constituted *one* Church with *one* proper episcopal see, that of Alexandria.'[1] With the great expansion of Christianity Demetrius (188/9–231) began cautiously to instal bishops in the most important places, but they remained in practice vicars of the Bishop of Alexandria.[2] The founding of these sees coincided with the introduction of the municipal constitution during the third century.[3]

In the western Church, Africa had such presbyter communities in the villages fairly early. These rural priests were sometimes raised to the rank of bishop.[4]

In Gallia Narbonnensis the first few rural churches under a priest appear in the fourth century, probably immediately after the Edict of Milan (313). The Council of Arles provides certain evidence for their existence.[5]

From Spain there is evidence that, besides the rural bishops, rural communities headed by a priest or deacon already existed by about the middle of the third century.[6]

4. *Summary*

The striking thing about these early periods is the incredible variety in the development of Church institutions and the cure of souls, which were largely able to adapt themselves to existing needs and structures. However, pastoral, apostolic or theological reasons are not alone responsible for this development. Even now the ecclesiastical organization was dependent to a considerable degree on sociological conditions, on national structures and cultural influences which, for their part, are purely relative and determined by the times. The organization of the synagogue, the Jewish colonies, the sociological and political distinctions between town and country, between east and west, the trade routes and Graeco-Roman culture all played a part.[7]

As we have seen, the main tendency of development was

[1] K. Müller, *Beiträge*, 21. [2] Ib., 21. [3] Feine, 40.

[4] Zorell, 91 f. [5] *DACL.*, XIII, 2200: Zorell, 94.

[6] Letter of St Cyprian, Council of Elvira 300. Cf. Zorell, 93.

[7] Cf. Häring, *Macht*, 106: 'If we look at the New Testament, we make an interesting observation: the mission of the Apostolic Age is in the highest degree, one might almost say unscrupulously, versatile in making use of every possible sociological link in order to make contact with man and offer him Christian salvation.' K. Rahner, 'Betrieb und Pfarrei', in *Sendung und Gnade*, 437.

towards a monarchical episcopate. In the course of this evolution the most varied forms of community came into being. Thus from the very beginning, besides the ideal episcopal community, there was a graduated distribution of the full episcopal powers among several persons working closely with the bishop. With this hierarchical structure there was linked a feeling for the principle of subsidiarity which allowed each member to fulfil its function. The isolated cleric was rather exceptional, his state was due to missionary exigencies. Normally the clergy formed a community.

In short, the parish organization goes back both to the presbyter-communities which developed into episcopal communities and to those that reverted from episcopal status. While the episcopal communities were the starting-point or the goal, the forerunners of the parish are in a state of flux, no self-contained whole but always related to the episcopal community.

II—From the Edict of Milan to the Council of Trent (fourth to sixteenth centuries)

Under the Emperor Constantine the Church achieved recognition by the state and under Theodosius I (379–95) Christianity became the state religion. In spite of its predominance, the Church fell in many matters under the influence of its secular surroundings. 'A whole area of canon law was given the Roman stamp, and even today bears traces of ancient Roman characteristics.'[1] The Roman influence in the structure of the Church continued by and large until the beginning of the eighth century. It is characterized by the baptismal churches. The Arab onslaught brought about a change. Later Germanic influences formed a new organization, at first alongside the Roman one, but finally leading to its disintegration. The German influence came in from below and is characterized by the private church system which led to 'the complete replacement of the baptistery church organization and to the setting up of small tithe churches and parish areas',[2] bringing in its train the system of benefices. Only the Cluniac-Gregorian reforms of the eleventh century succeeded in partly freeing monasticism and the Church from these foreign Germanic

[1] Feine, 59. [2] Ib., 136.

elements. The independent Church system deteriorated into a system of patronage and incorporation. The strengthening of the central papal authority in the peak period of the Middle Ages is paralleled by the development of canon law which 'to a basis of ecclesiastical principles added a happy balance of elements of public law (Roman) and civil law (Germanic)'.[1] The Council of Trent was a new turning point.

During this period the parish did not develop equally in town and country. In the city the unity of the episcopal church was preserved much longer. There were also considerable differences in the structure of urban and rural parishes. Only the Tridentine legislation was to achieve uniformity.

A—The Ecclesiastical Organization of the Country

1. *The Origin of the Diocese and the Major Parish*

After its liberation by Constantine the Church took over to a much greater extent than hitherto typical institutions of Roman law, mainly in the sphere of organization and administration (principate and provincial constitution). 'The Church law of this time, conceived from the standpoint of the ecclesiastical community, had entirely the character of an objective, public order, but with a preponderance of the administrative over the constitutional law and with considerable scope for arbitrary decision.'[2]

(a) *The Origin of the Diocese.* The Church now undertook its own *territorial division* in conformity with the civil administration, particularly with the Diocletian division of the empire (A.D. 294). Here we are concerned only with the episcopal dioceses. Till then there had been no properly defined areas. True, there had always been the tendency for urban bishops to extend their influence to the surrounding rural churches. Thus emerged the principle whereby the territory under municipal administration was also ecclesiastically governed by the bishop of the city. In the fourth and fifth centuries this became the rule, although it succeeded in the west later than in the east: at the end of the fourth century in Africa, in the middle of the fifth century in Gaul, and later still in Italy and Spain. In the Merovingian era in the west the urban district

[1] Feine, 242. [2] Ib., 60; cf. Plöchl, I, 115.

and the diocese (*diocesis* and *παροικία*) were identical.[1] In the east the episcopal territory was extended from the urban district to the province in conformity with the civil organization.[2]

The bishop was the sole lord and master in his diocese. He represented the Church. Having the priestly power in its fullness he was the regular minister of solemn baptism (the authority to baptize was only gradually extended to other pastors), the protector of doctrine and law, and the shepherd of his flock. He was the sole law-giver of his diocese and the administrator of all Church property. The clergy was pastorally, personally and economically completely in the bishop's hands (*ad nutum episcopi*); it was called 'ordo' in imitation of the civic decurionate and was more sharply distinguished in status from the laity than hitherto.[3]

Right up to the sixth century, influenced by the Roman law of corporations, the holder of Church property was the diocese. In Roman law local churches could become juridical persons; at first this applied only to the episcopal churches and their pastoral subsidiaries but from the fourth century also to the smaller churches. Church property, however, was still indivisible: it belonged to the Church and in no way to the members of the clergy. Even the bishop was not the owner but, since the beginning of the fourth century, only the head of the administration. Property and administration were still one.[4]

The possession of property by individual churches developed, albeit only gradually. This finally broke up the unity of property in the sixth century and led to a change in the legal position. All that remained to the bishop was a right of supervision of the property of subordinate churches, which under the Edict of Chlothachar (614) was to be administered by the inhabitants of the area concerned. The complete decentralization of the diocese was due to the development of privately owned churches or *Eigenkirchen*; in accordance with Germanic

[1] Feine, 88 f.

[2] Plöchl, I, 142. The insular Church in Ireland and Scotland had its own special organization based not on towns but on clans and kindred, not in the diocese but in monasteries. As a rule every clan had a monastery which it maintained, and which formed an enclave, a sort of abbatial diocese, within the diocese. From 664 onwards Scotland was anxious to adopt the Roman organization. Plöchl, I, 143 f.

[3] Feine, 114, 117 f.

[4] Plöchl, I, 117, 234 f., 242 f.

law. At the turn of the eighth to the ninth century the economic independence of individual rural churches had become complete.[1]

The Archdeacon, who in the fourth century had been no more than the head of the deacons, later became the bishop's agent and administrator of the episcopal household, and in the sixth and seventh centuries rose to be the plenipotentiary representative of the bishop at councils and finally the highest ecclesiastic in the diocese after the bishop. Since priestly orders were incompatible with the archdeaconship, from the fifth century the bishop was represented in his priestly functions by an urban archpresbyter.[2]

(b) *The Origin of Rural Churches* (*Baptistery Churches, Basilicas and Oratories*). While the episcopal sees were more and more being limited to the towns, where the unity of the episcopal community was still preserved for a long time, the country, where since the Edict of Milan (313) Christianity was rapidly spreading, had to be organized for pastoral work. This led to the rise of a whole network of church buildings which called for a new organization to integrate them into the episcopal cure of souls.

The origin of new rural churches was principally due to the initiative of the *bishops*, the laity and the monks. The widening of the bishop's territory and the simultaneous suppression of the rural bishops demanded a new organization. The rural bishops were gradually replaced in their churches by clergy sent by the urban bishop with certain powers for the cure of souls. Besides, the bishop erected in the territory belonging to his see new oratories and baptismal churches.[3] The foundations of St Martin of Tours and his successors are particularly well known.[4]

Furthermore, powerful laymen, the so-called *potentes*, built oratories or churches for themselves and their dependents on

[1] Plöchl, I, 234, 243, 389 f.; Feine, 121.

[2] Plöchl, I, 154 f.; Feine 118.

[3] The Council of Orange (441) provided as follows: If a bishop wishes to build a church on ground belonging to him but in another diocese, he must refer to the bishop in question who will undertake the consecration and retain all rights. The founding bishop may only recommend the clergy who will serve that church. Cf. Griffe, 'Paroisses rurales', 44 f.

[4] Figures in Bardy, II, 45; Griffe, 'Paroisses rurales', 42–44.

their vast territories and appointed a priest whom they had ordained by the bishop.[1]

Monks, too, played a considerable part in the establishment of rural communities. The old monasteries themselves resembled rural parishes.[2] In the fourth century some bishops tried to combine the clerical with the monastic life (Vercella, Hippo: Augustine). Sometimes, with the abbot's permission, the bishop ordained monks for parish work.[3] Sulpicius Severus tells us that in Touraine religious communities liked to settle near a parish church, which certainly contributed to making it more easily possible to solemnize the liturgy in the manner of the cathedral.[4] In the fifth and sixth centuries rural churches were still trying to imitate the episcopal church in the town even to singing the Office.[5]

Above all, monks played an important part in the actual founding of rural churches. This was not so much due to the influence of the large monasteries but to individual monks who lived in poverty among the laity and influenced the pagans by their preaching and example. From their hermitages developed oratories and churches, often even monasteries which then became the centre of a lay community.[6] Particularly in England, which was Christianized by Roman monks, the monasteries played a specific and decisive part in the pastoral organization.[7]

Various circumstances determined the founding of a church. Mostly it was the need of a Christian community for care and, above all, a meeting-place. So churches were built in villages, in forts, in market towns, at important cross roads, on the trade routes. Churches frequently replaced pagan temples that had been destroyed under a law of Valentinian III (425–55),[8] thus giving visual expression to the victory of Christ over Satan.

[1] Plöchl, I, 157 f.; Schmid, 65 ff.

[2] *DACL*, XIII, 2222.

[3] Ib., 2223, 'Clericism and monasticism are incompatible in Italy but compatible in Africa.' Cf. Rousseau, O., 'Priestertum und Mönchtum', in Guyot, *Das apostolische Amt*, 158–71.

[4] Griffe, 'Paroisses rurales', 42, 47.

[5] Ib., 58, 60.

[6] *DACL.*, XIII, 2206.

[7] Cf. Hergenröther, I, 723–31; Bardy, II, 52 f.; Schnürer, *M.A.*, I, 253–58; cf. also note 2, p. 52, supra.

[8] *DACL.*, XIII, 2207 f.

On the other hand pagan temples were simply turned into Christian churches.[1]

After the Peace of Constantine the cult of relics and saints had an enduring influence on the building of new churches. Oratories, churches, monasteries or parishes were established above the graves of saints or on the scene of their activities. Hence, as Leclercq says, the heart of the rural community is to be found in the cult of the dead.[2] From the fifth century, the church was no longer just a place for meeting and worship but had to be provided with the relics of a saint who became the spiritual and temporal patron of the place. The patron saint became the most important personality of the parish and received special honour and gifts: he was even made a juridical person to whom the church's property belonged. He became the symbol of the unity of the parish and the reason for its independence, autonomy and individuality.[3] When Germanic thought gained the upper hand, this led directly to the system of privately owned churches or *Eigenkirchen*.[4] Thus the various churches and church communities came into being, entirely dependent upon and very largely influenced by the existing cultural structure.[5]

The increase in rural churches was quicker in the east than in the west;[6] thus in this respect Spain was behind Africa.[7]

In Gallia Narbonnensis the power of paganism had been broken towards the end of the fourth century. Accounts of the rural parishes there are found in the *Acta* of the Councils of Riez (439: C. 4), Orange (441: C. 10), Vaison (442: C. 3).[8] From the reign of Constantine and his sons, in any case from about the year 400, most places in the coastal area had their parishes.[9]

[1] Cf. the letter of St Gregory to Mellitus (601) on turning heathen temples into churches, quoted in Bardy, II, 48.

[2] 'Thus the cult of the dead is the nucleus of the rural community. . . . Tomb or memory, people believe, will be the necessary guarantee and, as it were, the justification of the rural parish which claims the name of a saint.' *DACL.*, XIII, 2209.

[3] Ib., 2209 f. [4] Cf. pp. 61 ff. infra.

[5] *DACL.*, XIII, 2209 f.; Feine, 135 ff. [6] Plöchl, I, 185.

[7] Council of Elvira, c. 300.

[8] Cf. letter of Pope Zosimus (417) about the parishes of Ceyreste and Garguier.

[9] *DACL.*, XIII, 2202.

Further north development proceeded more slowly. With the invasion of the Goths and Burgundians Arianism had replaced paganism. At the beginning of the sixth century the Burgundians became Catholics, so that most of the Arian churches could simply be taken over.

(c) *The Major Parish System of the Baptismal Churches.* The various churches and the Christian communities associated with them[1] which had grown up without any previous planning were now gradually incorporated into the diocesan organization.

To serve the rural churches, the bishop normally assigned priests 'whose pastoral powers became, in time, more and more independent even where this had not already been the case'.[2] The definition of boundaries between the individual rural churches (the parish system) developed more slowly in the west than in the east. At first the rural churches had no boundaries at all. So long as an area had not been *de facto* or *de jure* annexed by a neighbouring parish, it remained directly under the episcopal church.[3] 'At the end of the fifth and the beginning of the sixth centuries in Italy, there began a comprehensive ecclesiastical organization of the rural areas',[4] but this was not yet a parish system in the ordinary sense.[5] Whether this organization followed the natural boundaries of the *vicus* or *villa*, or the old secular administrative boundaries,[6] is a matter of controversy.

There were now two basic types of rural churches: first, the so-called baptismal churches (*ecclesiae baptismales*, *plebes*) in which services were regularly held and baptism administered and which had at their head an archpresbyter appointed by the bishop. These were to be found in the principal localities and this generally covered a considerable area. They were the central feature of the major parish system of the baptismal churches which came into being in Gaul and Spain in the sixth century, still on the basis of Roman church law.[7] The village (*vicus*) therefore represents the oldest 'parish' centre in the country.[8]

[1] Occasionally under deacons; cf. Kurtscheid, I, 167; *DACL.*, XIII, 2217.
[2] Feine, 90. [3] Griffe, 'Paroisses rurales', 49. [4] Stutz, 241.
[5] Plöchl, I, 160. [6] Stutz, 241; *DACL.*, XIII, 2217; Schmid, 68.
[7] Feine, 90.
[8] The Council of Tours (567) calls rural priests *presbyteri vicani*, and *vicus* often has the meaning of parish. Their area was also called *parochia* or

The other type of rural church is furnished by the numerous basilicas and oratories in smaller places and on estates which sometimes had their own priests or were served from the local church. They had no font and in various matters depended upon the baptistery church in whose area they were situated.[1]

Baptismal churches were the result of decentralization and increasing independence which came about, generally speaking, in three phases.

At first these rural churches were entirely dependent upon the urban bishop, who supplied his own clerics. These belonged to the episcopal 'college' of priests and had their fixed centre in the town.[2]

However, towards the end of the fourth and during the fifth century the baptismal churches tended to become autonomous, owing to the spread of Christianity in the countryside and the need for a more effective cure of souls. The priest in charge became permanently attached to the church and received more and more faculties. He said Mass for the people who before had had to attend the cathedral church on the great feasts. With a few exceptions, even the clergy were no longer obliged to attend the pontifical Mass on feast-days, but conducted the services in the rural churches.[3] However, only in the sixth century did the bishop delegate the right to baptize—at first only at Easter and Pentecost—to the archpresbyters of the rural churches, and in the same century also to other priests. They could, however, baptize only within the diocese and with the consent of their bishop. During Lent they had to report to the bishop on the previous year's baptisms.[4] About the same time in the west the right and duty to preach, too, until then

---

diocesis, since it was analogous to an episcopal area—Kurtscheid, I, 167; the country (*villa*) could not be the seat of a parish until the sixth century. *DACL.*, XIII, 2217; Stutz pointedly remarks: 'Such a major church, in a significant interim usage reflecting the growth of urban episcopal churches into bishoprics, was called *dioecesis* or *basilica dioecesana* as well as *parochia, ecclesia parochitana,* but later specifically *plebs, ecclesia baptismalis* or *baptisterium.* Since essential features and characteristics of the later parish are missing, this institution is best described as a baptismal area or baptistery organization.' Stutz, 241 f.

[1] Feine, 90.

[2] Nanni, 481.

[3] Ib., 481 f.

[4] Plöchl, I, 191; Stutz, 241.

the prerogative of the bishop, was delegated to the archpriest,[1] who was also allowed to give the various Church blessings.[2] In the ninth century the right of burial and the tithe rights were added.[3] Through the institution of the archpriest, to whom the other clergy of the rural church were subject, and above all through the pastoral visitation of the bishop, which dates back to the first priest-churches, dependence upon and unity with the bishop were constantly stressed. The appearance of the bishop in the church of a priest was always a great event.

In the fifth century the bishop's powers over the property of individual churches came to be limited[4] since the patron saint was made the legal owner so that the bishop could not alienate it. The founders, too, claimed their material rights. The eighth Synod of Paris (614) assured the *economic autonomy* of the rural churches. The bishop thereafter had only a supervisory right.[5]

The baptismal churches prevailed in Spain and Gaul from the sixth century, and from the seventh century also in Italy with its many bishoprics, particularly in Tuscany and Lombardy. North of the Alps the majority of the baptistery churches were lost to the bishoprics through secularization in the seventh and eighth centuries; the remainder became episcopal churches. In Italy the baptismal churches (*plebes*) were partly reserved to the bishoprics till the late Middle Ages. Since they owned extensive landed property they were of considerable economic value to the diocese. From the middle of the ninth century the baptismal churches were then leased by the bishop to the *plebanus*, and from the tenth century also to lay persons, for a high rent (up to one hundred solidi). 'There the *plebanus* became a large landholder.'[6]

From the eighth century the number of baptismal churches

[1] Lesêtre, 27. St Augustine was the first priest in Africa to preach in the presence of the bishop (cf. Possidius, *Vita Aug.*, *PL.*, XXXII, 37). In the east, however, any priest present might speak when he felt like it. The bishop always gave the final address. Cf. Van der Meer, *Augustinus der Seelsorger*, 26. Cf. also Monachino, *La Cura pastorale*, 21, 75, 158 f.

[2] *DACL*, XIII, 2218.

[3] Plöchl, I, 323.

[4] Cf. Instructions of Pope Gelasius (492–6), on founding of churches; Feine, 120.

[5] For development of tax-structure and ownership conditions, cf. *DACL.*, XIII, 2219–20.

[6] Feine, 167; cf. 166.

increased considerably, mostly through the acquisition of baptismal and parish rights by already existing dependent rural churches. They freed themselves from their mother church and formed their own parishes. Hence many councils had to define the parish rights.[1] The mother churches often became the seat of the rural deaneries.[2]

The baptismal churches were served by a more or less numerous clergy, after the example of the bishop's church, who under the guidance of an archpriest were living in community.[3] This term occurs first in a canon of the Council of Tours (567), but the function is much earlier. In the middle of the sixth century the archpriest was the 'parish priest' responsible for his community and the immediate superior of his clergy whose conduct he had to supervise;[4] in addition he was responsible for the supply of young priests whom he had to recruit from his own parish;[5] he had further to establish a school for the education of his clergy, his fellow-workers and successors.[6]

'The baptismal churches of the Latin countries were paralleled in the Germanic countries, particularly in Germany,

[1] Plöchl, I, 323. 'Even though from the eighth century the foundation of a parish had juridical significance, it was at this time no definitive institution. It cannot therefore be said that the principles of common law made it necessary to fix a definite parish area.'

[2] Ib.

[3] The wives of the married clergy lived separately with the servants. Only the archpriest—though previously all in major orders—was allowed to live with his wife as brother and sister. Cf. *DACL.*, XIII, 2213 f.; Kurtscheid, I, 174 f. From the middle of the ninth century the clergy of the baptismal churches in many parts of Italy formed an association with a *vita communis* and common property administration (*schola*). With the disappearance of the *vita communis* in the twelfth and thirteenth centuries church property was absorbed into trusts which led to benefices for the rural clergy. Feine, 167, 187. Cf. pp. 83 ff. below.

[4] 'It is worth noting that in the sixth century the increase in the number of priests engaged in parish work led to difficulties since they all had the same rights. The eleventh Council of Toledo (657) therefore made provision that the choice of curates should be left to the permanently appointed priests. This decree may point to the origin of curates, chaplains, etc.' Plöchl, I, 159.

[5] This applied first to episcopal communities, later to parishes. Cf. the Emperor Honorius (398): 'Ecclesiis quae in possessionibus, ut assolet, diversorum, vicis etiam vel quibuslibet locis sunt constitutae, clerici non ex alia possessione vel vico sed ex eo ubi ecclesiam esse constituit eatenus ordinetur'; quoted in *DACL.*, XIII, 2219.

[6] Vaison (529); Merida (666).

Scandinavia and England, by the original churches of the major parishes [*Urkirchen der Grosspfarreien*] which came into being in the Anglo-Saxon-Frankish period and later.'[1] Their expansion followed the great trade routes and they were often erected on the sites of old pagan sanctuaries. As corporation churches of some territorial division (*Gau*, *Zehnt*, *Mark*) they were frequently centrally situated and connected with assembly rooms and courts of justice.[2] The original churches also had rights of baptism and of celebrating the principal services.[3]

Privatkirchen (privately owned churches) (basilicas and oratories), which had a variety of origins, were also subordinated to the rural pastoral system. The relationship of the baptismal church and the private church was analogous to that between the episcopal church and the baptismal church. In Gaul, for example, where the oratories increased rapidly, only the celebration of Mass was permitted, but not on the greater feasts when both clergy and people had to attend the baptistery church.[4] If they could not support their own clergy, they were supplied from the baptistery church.[5] However a great change came about at the end of the fifth and during the sixth centuries owing to the private church system. Many oratories and other privately owned churches then acquired parish rights and became much less dependent on the bishop.

2. *The Development of the Parish under the Influence of the Eigenkirchen*

The eighth century represented an important turning point in the evolution of the parish. The Germanic influence contained elements which were to destroy the Roman baptismal church system. 'The Germanic Church law does not hide its alien origin nor the fact that it comes from below, but bears a conspicuously unecclesiastical and even unchristian stamp. In this law individuals are most important, its strong agrarian and economic tendency gives it the more pronounced subjective character of civil law. The ecclesiastical office becomes a

[1] Feine, 167.
[2] Members were responsible for the choice of clergy and their upkeep. Feine, 184.
[3] Feine, 168 f.
[4] Councils of Agde, 506, Orleans, 511, Vaison, 529, and Clermont, 535.
[5] Nanni, 487 f.

matter of lease where the material endowment, mostly including some land, comes first and the office becomes a negotiable title to the ground ('*Pfarrzwang*'). Individual duty becomes a charge on the property (e.g. the priest's service to the Church). Thus the whole of Church law acquired the stamp not of public administrative law, but of personal case-law'.[1] The social and juridical feudal system also had a profound influence on the life and organization of the Church. What Mitteis calls the 'Rule of the Nobility' was in fact overcome only towards the end of the eighteenth century.[2] The actual parish system came into being under the influence of Germanic law.

(a) *The Eigenkirchen System in General.* The further evolution of the parish can only be understood against the background of the private church through which Germanic law was most firmly integrated into the structure of the Church.[3]

Opinions differ about the origin and nature of the *Eigenkirchen.*[4] Stutz and his school assume common Germanic roots in the Indo-Germanic custom according to which the father of the family was at the same time the priest of his household.[5] Plöchl on the other hand believes that a variety of factors led to the development of the peculiars. 'Pastoral, legal, economic and, not least, social motives, the last due to the social structure of the world at that time, all contributed to the development of the *Eigenkirchen*, the nucleus of which goes back to the early Church, but was variously developed according to local conditions in the different areas. Undoubtedly Germanic legal thinking played a considerable part in this.'[6]

This system of privately owned churches was soon to control the entire Church constitution of Europe, including the British Isles, for many centuries. It also found its way into Byzantine and Slav Church law.[7]

[1] Feine, 136. [2] Ib., 136 f. [3] Ib., 147.

[4] For the various theories cf. Feine, 142–47; Plöchl, I, 238 f.; Nanni, 519–21.

[5] Feine, 148.

[6] Plöchl, I, 241; cf. also 239 f. The Germanic private church system is now being thoroughly studied. Schmid's work gives an interesting glimpse of Slav conditions. It was possible there for an independent system of private churches to develop under direct Germanic influence. Cf. Schmid, 1048–60.

[7] Feine, 147 f.; cf. Schmid.

There is general agreement about the nature of the *Eigenkirchen.* U. Stutz has defined the private church as: 'a house of God so subject to private ownership, or rather private control, that from there resulted not only autonomy in regard to its property but also to its complete spiritual authority.'[1]

The *Eigenkirche* became a legal concept governed by the Germanic idea of *gewere* (lawful possession). 'The centre is the stone altar firmly built into the ground, in which the relics —"the saint"—are kept. . . . Everything belonging to the land on which the altar is built is considered as part of it and in case of doubt shares its legal fate: church buildings and fixtures, churchyard and graves, parish house with garden, land and dependents, tithes, stole-fees, and offerings. The saint, so to speak, signs for everything.'[2]

The Church property became a special property of its owner as distinct from his secular property. It was subject to the processes of civil law. The landlord regarded the church built on his ground, together with all its appurtenances, as his property (*ecclesia propria*) which he could sell, give away or bequeathe. With the revenue from it he had to maintain the priest and bear the other expenses of the church and the celebration of the liturgy. Anything over and above this went to the owner. 'With the acquisition of parish and tithe rights the yield was considerable, and the church could develop into a commercial undertaking in the name of the saint.'[3] Private churches were the most advantageous capital investments of the early Middle Ages (Stutz). Hence they were established not only for religious motives but, just as much, for economic reasons.[4]

They could be the property of laymen, both of individuals (landowners great and small, kings or princes) and of families (family churches) as well as of settlers' associations (corporation churches), who began more and more to erect or acquire churches and monasteries; or they could belong to bishops or monasteries. Among the Franks and Langobards *Eigenkirchen* belonged to small owners; only from the reign of Charles Martel did the larger landowners also acquire them.[5] Thus the

[1] Feine, 147.

[2] Ib., 151; cf. Plöchl, I, 240. *Gewere* originally meant the transfer of ownership of land, but later also came to mean the tenure itself.

[3] Feine, 152.

[4] Ib., 151 f.; Plöchl, I , 392 f.

[5] Feine, 150 f.; Plöchl, I, 392 f.

Church came to be no longer subject to public but to private law.

From the second half of the seventh century the spread of *Eigenkirchen* was rapid, reaching its climax in the eighth and ninth centuries.[1] They multiplied beside existing baptismal churches. At first they remained outside the authority of the bishops, who did not pay much attention to them, but soon the bishops began to campaign against the various forms taken by the private church system in the different areas.[2]

In Spain this struggle began immediately after the country became Catholic in the sixth century.[3] But the bishops' prohibition of privately owned churches was ignored, for in the Moorish era genuine private churches were to be found everywhere.[4]

In Italy, where the baptistery church system continued longer, the baptismal churches themselves were treated as private churches by the bishops from the ninth century and from the tenth century were also given to laymen. As happened north of the Alps, here, too, *Eigenkirchen* multiplied and by acquiring parish rights began to supplant the baptismal churches. In the south, the old system remained longer in force thanks to the smaller dioceses. Two Roman Synods, of 826 and and 835, specifically recognized the existence of the *Eigenkirchen*, which was tantamount to papal approval. This led to their greater extension in the west and to their inclusion into western Church law.[5]

In France the first action against privately owned churches was taken by the Council of Châlons (c. 650). With the secularization under Charles Martel, the baptismal churches, which up to around 700 had remained in the hands of the bishops, passed into lay hands together with many abbeys and even some bishoprics. 'When in 810 Charlemagne separated imperial from episcopal property in Chur, the bishop retained only six baptistery and twenty-five subordinate churches, while the fiscal exchequer received approximately ten and two hundred respectively.'[6]

[1] Plöchl, I, 392.
[2] Feine, 152 f.
[3] Synods of Braga (572) and Toledo (589, 633, 655).
[4] Feine, 153.
[5] Feine, 153, 155; Plöchl, I, 394; Nanni, 486 ff.
[6] Feine, 154; cf. U. Stutz, 'Karls des grossen Divisio von Bistum und Grafschaft Chur'. For the Slavonic and Byzantine private church organization see Feine, 163–65; Schmid.

As a result of abuses, the *Eigenkirchen* system began to disintegrate and decay with the decline of the west Frankish royal power in the ninth and tenth centuries. 'For, owing to the generosity of the faithful and the increasing revenues, the founding and administration of private churches had come to be a profitable undertaking, almost a trade. On large estates, particularly those of monasteries, the number often rose into the hundreds.'[1] The decay was also hastened by the breaking up of estates into smaller independent units.[2]

The outcome of the Investiture struggle, however, put an end to the private churches. At first it affected only the major, but soon also the subordinate churches. 'The legal basis was provided by the decisions of first and second Lateran Councils (1123 and 1139) according to which the grant of even minor benefices was to be reserved to the bishop, and lay ownership of churches was universally forbidden.'[3] This was relatively simple to enforce where an individual or a family owned the church, but much more difficult where ownership was in the hands of an association of settlers. However, from the middle of the twelfth century the fate of the privately owned churches was sealed. It was to be replaced by patronage and incorporation.

Inner development. In the middle of the seventh century the *Eigenkirchen* had gained such a hold on the Frankish kingdom that churches were owned not only by the kings and nobles and also quite small landowners and farmers, but principally by the monasteries. At the same time secularization was steadily progressing. 'Secularized property was mainly used to endow vassals. Since church property was inalienable it was given out in the form of benefices, so that the Church remained the owner and the lessee only had the usufruct. For this secularization the Church received indemnity in the shape of tithes.'[4]

The reform movements of Pepin, Carloman, Boniface and Louis the Pious brought about some improvements but they did not touch the private church system as such. To start with, the selection of lessees was improved in accordance with the

[1] Feine, 156.
[2] Plöchl, II, 369; Kurtscheid, I, 275.
[3] Plöchl, II, 369; cf. Gratian's Decree, 1, 7 (1140).
[4] Conrad, *Rechtsgeschichte*, 167 f.; cf. 149 f.

letter (748) of Pope Zacharias (741–52) to Boniface. Charlemagne gave legal recognition to lay ownership of churches (749) but insisted on the bishops' right to supervise divine service and the maintenance of the churches as well as their right to approve the appointment and removal of the clergy.[1]

The Carolingian church was completed through the great Church Capitulary of Aachen (818–19) of Louis the Pious. He insisted on security of status for private churches in relation to their owner and required an adequate endowment, of which the owner could not dispose at will. He could, indeed, dispose of the whole church and its property by private arrangement, but he could not break up the property. Church property was thus assured of retaining its original purpose.[2]

Until then the *Eigenkirchen* had been served by free, but more often by unfree and probably frequently married, priests who were at the mercy of the owner. 'Their service which consisted in saying Mass and performing other ecclesiastical duties did not differ legally from the service rendered by the landlord's miller or his peasants. . . . The bishop possessed the power to ordain but hardly any right of supervision.'[3]

After the Carolingian reform, however, a priest could only be installed in a private church with the bishop's approval; he must be a freeman and have enough rent-free land to support him. He was permanently attached to the church and could be removed neither by the owner nor by the bishop except by the sentence of an ecclesiastical court. So the priest became economically less dependent upon his landlord and also more independent in relation to his bishop although he was in principle subordinate to him. The bishop had the duty of visitation and the priest had to make regular reports to him and be present at diocesan synods.[4]

In the ninth century the bishops had great difficulty in enforcing this legislation. Once it had come into force, it became customary in France 'for church owners to lease to their priests the office by way of a benefice, or another form of tenure customary in the country. Here is the root of the *benefice system*'.[5] But benefices were not tied up with vassalage.[6] The whole

[1] Plöchl, I, 393. [2] Ib.; Feine, 154. [3] Feine, 184.
[4] Ib., 154 f.; Plöchl, loc. cit. [5] Feine, loc. cit.
[6] Cf. Conrad, *Rechtsgeschichte*, 147 ff.

church property was leased by the landlord who nominated the priest (after examination by the bishop) and who received a rental from him. In return, the priest had to serve the church. In many places his duties were set out in detail and graded according to the character of the church. 'The ecclesiastical benefice in the strict sense developed in the peak period of the Middle Ages from the lease of rural churches, and received its classic form under decretal law.'[1] The benefice, became 'a property, and the title to it exclusively destined for the maintenance of a priest. But this development became possible only after the *Eigenkirchen* system had been essentially defeated.'[2]

Just as the relationship between the office and ordination had been increasingly loosened so that the office could be assigned without ordination, thus office and benefice, too, gradually began to be separated. Originally the benefice was necessarily tied to an office. Later a distinction was made between *beneficia maiores*, which were tied to an office enjoying ordinary governing authority, and *beneficia minora* which were not necessarily tied to an office and hence were divided into *beneficia curata* and *beneficia sine cura animarum*.[3]

The reform movements at the end of the tenth and beginning of the eleventh centuries at least succeeded in clarifying once more the distinction between the church as a *temporale* bestowed by the landlord and the ecclesiastical office which the bishop demanded to confer.[4]

From the end of the seventh century the Church itself had already been trying to get possession of the privately owned churches, and by the ninth century episcopal churches had come to be treated as such. So by devious ways of civil law, more probably as a result of the advance of Roman law, at least part of the diocese came under the direct control of the bishop.[5] True, the establishment by bishops of privately owned churches in other dioceses led once more to confusion. 'Thus

[1] Feine, 186. [2] Plöchl, II, 361 f. [3] Ib., II, 176.

[4] Ib., I, 394.

[5] On this point Schmale sees more clearly. 'From the standpoint of legal and constitutional history this means that we are not dealing here, as has frequently been supposed up till now, with the adoption of Germanic private-church law, but on the contrary with the re-assertion of Roman church law which admitted of no rights to churches other than those of the bishop.' Schmale, 61.

the benefice system as well as the private church system did not only greatly further the decentralization of the dioceses, they also dissolved the diocesan property and weakened the power of the bishop.'[1]

In the eleventh century the private leasing of church property led the Church to adopt the leasing of offices which was already practised in civil law.[2] 'With the leasing of offices and their authority Germanic law had gained a decisive victory in the Church.'[3] The office acquired sovereignty over a certain territory with the rights belonging to it. 'The revenues of the office were no longer the compensation for the duties of office; the latter were rather the burden involved in the territorial sovereignty on account of the office and taken over with it.'[4] From here to the simoniacal conferment of offices was but one step.

(b) *Patronage and Incorporation.* In the course of the Cluniac-Gregorian reforms the Roman authorities had come to realize that 'the right to *Eigenkirchen* was the cause of the subordination of the ecclesiastical office to the *temporalia*',[5] of the much-criticized investiture of laymen and of the whole materialistic view of church matters. At first lay investiture was opposed only in episcopal churches; later, when the investiture controversy had been settled, the problem of the lesser churches was tackled as well. The distinction between the *ecclesia* (*temporalia*) and the *altare* (*spiritualia*) could not be enforced in the lesser churches. The Lateran Councils of 1123 and 1139 ruled that only bishops might bestow the minor benefices and that the laity should not have any ownership of churches. Finally (1140) Gratian transformed the *Eigenkirchen* right into the right of patronage and incorporation.[6]

Alexander III (1159–81) declared patronage to be a *ius spirituali annexum* 'which signified its subordination to Church legislation and in practice allowed the Church to diminish its rights'.[7] Thus, the Church reduced the ancient *ius fundi* and many other rights of the owners of private churches to a right of patronage including certain rights and duties defined by the Church. Beside the most important right of presentation there

[1] Plöchl, I, 395; cf. 394.
[2] Ib., I, 391 f.
[3] Feine, 191.
[4] Ib.
[5] Ib., 233.
[6] Ib., 234 f.; cf. 351 ff.
[7] Ib., 351.

were also certain honorary rights as well as the right to revenues. On the other hand the patron had the duty to protect the church and its property and to be responsible for the upkeep and maintenance of the buildings and outbuildings. Patronage rights were also open to priests; these applied principally to parish churches and minor benefices.[1]

In practice this legislation could only slowly be enforced, and the system continued in the guise of patronage. The patronage, which in Germany was largely tied to real estate, was sold, exchanged, mortgaged, given away or bequeathed. Since the owner still conferred the *temporalia* the bishop was practically forced to comply with his proposals even if the living was to be given to laymen (often even minors) of his family.[2]

Incorporation was closely linked to the system of *Eigenkirchen* and patronage.[3] It became a technical term about the middle of the thirteenth century, though the practice itself had already developed in the twelfth century. There were two kinds of incorporation. The first, *incorporatio in usus proprios*, comprised at least the usufruct of the revenues of the church or benefice and the right of presentation to a permanent vicar. In practice, however, the right of usufruct was largely treated as a right of ownership. The second, *incorporatio in usus proprios et pleno iure*, allowed in addition the appointment of a non-permanent vicar who could be removed without reference to the bishop. Incorporation became widespread, especially in monasteries, chapters, universities and other religious bodies. Its principal effect was to replace the *Eigenkirchen* of the monasteries.[4]

Once the holy see had suppressed lay investiture, it attempted also to curtail the right of presentation as far as possible and to secure for itself the appointment to higher and lower ecclesiastical offices. First, the right of presentation was removed from ecclesiastical owners, and later, in the fourteenth century, from laymen.[5] Under Urban V (1362–70) the holy see had

[1] Plöchl, II, 369–71; Schnürer, *MA*, II, 244.

[2] In 1237–39 in Mainz the age-limit for presentation was set at fourteen. In 1274 the second Council of Lyons considered twenty-five years of age, but did not put it through. Feine, 359 f.

[3] Stutz. Feine, 352. For the two theories about its history see Plöchl, II, 371.

[4] Plöchl, II, 371–75; Feine, 352–54, 361–64.

[5] Nanni, 532.

gathered more or less all such rights to itself. Along with the great advantages, however, this brought considerable disadvantages. In the curia, where ecclesiastical office was largely for sale, there was unheard-of haggling about benefices large and small. The results were pluralism and absenteeism, and consequently neglect of pastoral work, decline in general piety, and the bad condition of church buildings. The popes were too preoccupied with the western schism to pay much attention to this development.[1]

(c) *The Evolution of the Parish.* Among the various elements that determined the further evolution of the parish, the private church system was the most important.

While this developed initially alongside the old baptistery church organization, it all too soon destroyed the system of large parishes. For, first, not only the baptistery churches themselves but also their dependent churches became *Eigenkirchen*, and secondly, towards the end of the fifth century and during the sixth many oratories and lesser churches in Gaul assumed parish rights.[2]

Territorial forms. In the Merovingian era parish churches were almost entirely restricted to the *vici* and were rare in the *villae*, but from the eighth century onwards most *villae* also had a church. Hence the *vicus* ceased to be the religious unit. The *villae* had become as it were the seedbed of the rural Church and the forerunner of the parish unit.[3]

From the territorial standpoint *three types* of parishes may be distinguished: those consisting of a group of *villae*;[4] those consisting only of one *villa* (in Carolingian times particularly in the north); and finally *villae* having several churches and therefore often divided into several parishes, though in general the unity of the *villa* was preferred. The last form appeared towards the end of the ninth century and in the tenth, in both north and south.[5]

Small tithe and parish areas. While missionary activity and the increase of the Christian population had necessitated the

[1] Ib., 534; Feine, 300–4.

[2] Griffe, 'Paroisses rurales', 53.

[3] *DACL.*, XIII, 2226.

[4] Often eight to ten or more, each having a chapel of ease or oratory; Zorell, 268 f. From ninth century, cf. *DACL.*, XIII, 2226.

[5] *DACL.*, XIII, 2227.

division of countries into parishes the payment of tithes especially led to their accurate definition. King Pepin had already awarded the bishops a tithe of the land revenue of their dioceses as a compensation for the secularization of church property. This benefited principally the baptistery churches. Since 818–19, however, the owners of private churches had also obtained this right as a welcome source of income. This made an accurate definition of tithe areas necessary, especially in the eyes of the bishops who were anxious to secure the tithes of the baptistery churches and defined the areas themselves, enforcing their decisions by threatening ecclesiastical censure. 'So from the large parishes covering whole districts or counties there gradually arose numerous small parishes embracing usually only a few villages while the superiority of the original baptismal church remained barely recognizable by the retention of a few special rights.'[1] This division was slower in Germany than in France.

On the basis of the tithe division a new small parish system arose, 'as the infiltration of "Germanism" encouraged and consolidated the division of the diocese'.[2] The present parish systems of France and Germany go back to the Carolingian tithe parishes which were under the control of lay owners of *Eigenkirchen*,[3] but legally fixed parish boundaries were only required by the Council of Trent.

On economic grounds the Church did not approve of the division of parishes,[4] which hardly took place before the ninth century,[5] although pastoral care and real parish community life were often very difficult. 'It is stated of rural parishes that villages were so far removed from the parish church that children frequently died unbaptized and adults without confession or Holy Communion. The division of parishes failed . . . mainly because the parish priests often resisted it since it involved financial loss.'[6] For when a new daughter church was erected in a parish, the tithes remained with the mother church unless the bishop wished it otherwise. But if a baptistery church was erected in a *villa*, it acquired the tithes of the *villa*.[7] This is why parish clergy preferred the establishment of daughter

[1] Feine, 170. [2] Ib., 156. [3] Ib., 171.
[4] *DACL.*, XIII, 2225; Zorell, 269 ff. [5] Kurtscheid, I, 279.
[6] Schrott, *Seelsorge*, 25. [7] Kurtscheid, I, 279.

churches to the division of the parish. Many bishops, however, systematically fostered the division of parishes because this increased the number of clergy who had to make payments to them.[1]

Precisely because the main reasons for the founding of parishes had often nothing to do with religion, the Church insisted time and again on their canonical establishment. Alexander III's constitution to the Archbishop of York (1170) which was embodied in Gregory IX's decretals gave the following grounds for founding a parish: great distance of the people from the existing church, difficult access particularly in winter; an adequate income for the old parish despite the transfer of some of its assets to the new one. The right to erect, divide or amalgamate parishes belonged to the bishop, but was not everywhere exercised.[2]

With the decline in the predominance of the large parish from the thirteenth century onwards the autonomy of the smaller parishes increased. The major parishes continued to disintegrate, being badly affected by the breaking-up of Church discipline during the great western schism (1378–1415). Absenteeism was rife among bishops and archpriests. Chapels and other benefices were transferred and alienated. It was a time of feverish emancipation for the minor parishes which sought to emulate the claims and rights of the major parishes.[3] 'In the fifteenth century the rural parish system of central Europe probably reached very nearly its present state.'[4]

From the thirteenth century onwards the western Slav countries and Hungary also developed their parish organization. Until then the episcopal churches were the only parish churches there, but now succursal churches were erected in important places; in Slovakia and Hungary the same term meant 'parish' and the civil district belonging to a castle.[5] In parts of Croatia, as was the case in the eastern Church, no fixed parish areas came into being in the whole of the Middle Ages.

Revenues of parish churches from Eigenkirchen, *based on private church law.* As a rule, the following revenues were associated with privately owned churches: the *ius regaliae*, i.e. the net

[1] *DACL.*, XIII, 2226. [2] Plöchl, II, 148 f. [3] Nanni, 535 f.
[4] Feine, 333. [5] Ib., 334; cf. Schmid.

revenue of a vacant church until it was again occupied, fell to the owner; the *ius spolii*, i.e. the estate of the priest, particularly if not a freeman, was claimed as a whole or in part by the owner, since the ninth century by prescriptive right. Stole fees also played an important part, for on the one hand the officiating curate was often entirely dependent on them, and on the other the owner of the church had an interest in them. What previously was a matter of custom and free gift was now demanded as a right by the parish priest or vicar and acquired a legal basis in the *Eigenkirchen* system. 'For in the case of private churches the levying of fees was closely connected with their nature as private enterprises.'[1]

'The tithe, taken over by Jerome and others from the Old Testament (the Mosaic levitical tithe) in the fifth century, was made obligatory under pain of excommunication by the Second Council of Mâcon (585), and also by civil law, probably since Pepin, since Tassilo in Bavaria, and throughout the Empire by Chapter Seven of the Capitulary of Herlstal (779). It was probably the price which the civil powers caused their subjects to pay to the spiritual powers to make the reconstruction of the Frankish Church possible without having to restore the sequestrated Church property.'[2] At first the tithe was allotted to the fiscal churches and the episcopal baptistery churches, but in 818–19 it was extended to the privately owned churches encouraging the founding of more churches. Bishoprics and monasteries also benefited. In general the tithe was paid from all produce, but increasingly from grain. In certain places there was also capital tithe on property. Among the Slavs, where the church was originally not provided with any ground, there was a fixed tithe—from which the nobility was exempt.[3]

[1] Feine, 174. Two kinds of stole fees are distinguished. The *pactio* where the fee was paid *before* the spiritual action was undertaken, the latter being thus dependent on the former; and the *exactio*, which was a legal prescription to pay the dues *after* the administering of a sacrament. However, it often happened that the sacrament was refused if the fee were not paid in advance. In 1215 Innocent III condemned the *pactio*, but defended the *exactio* as a *laudabilis consuetudo* against laymen who wished to see stole fees abolished entirely. Since the mendicant orders administered the sacraments free and only accepted free gifts, they inevitably came into conflict with the parish clergy. Plöchl, II, 385 ff.; Feine 174.

[2] Ib., loc. cit.

[3] Ib., 174 ff.; cf. Schmid.

The Bannus Parochialis. With the 'ban' another foreign Germanic element came to influence the organization of the Church, and parish life in particular, for many centuries. The *Bannrecht* was the most important right of the Frankish king. 'Ban'[1] originally meant a state order, and only later the right to give orders and forbid things under pain of punishment. It could also mean the penalty for disobedience to the order. The king ruled his realm by use of the 'ban': he used it as a prescriptive 'ban' which allowed him to punish transgressions of his decrees, as an administrative 'ban' to impose his orders on the army and the administration, also to enforce peace and finally as a juridical 'ban'. Local corporations also had a right of ban which extended over woods and fields as well as trades, to ensure that certain installations existing in the common interest were used to advantage.[2]

The first ban attested for bishops was the peace ban to ensure the security of the tithe area and the revenues of a church. It soon developed into an administrative ban embracing all spiritual and temporal matters.[3]

The parish areas of the tithe churches which broke up the baptistery church organization are a result of the episcopal ban which ensured the revenues of an area under threat of punishment.[4] Within such a parish area the *bannus parochialis* was in force: parishioners had to receive the sacraments and to attend to all other ecclesiastical matters solely in the parish church, above all they had to pay their tithes and stole fees there.[5] The parish priest had the duty, and even more the right, to administer the sacraments to his parishioners; the faithful had the right, and even more the duty, to apply exclusively to their parish priest, and cure of souls became part of the parish 'ban'. From the cradle to the grave the Christian was tied to the *one* church and the *one* person of the parish priest who was responsible for baptism, penance and confession, the eucharist, Mass, anointing the sick and viaticum, and later also for the

[1] 'The word is connected with the Sanskrit *bhan*, to call loudly, with the Greek φημί, φάναι, φωνή, and the Latin *fari*, *fana*, *fanum* (= a place dedicated as a shrine by solemn pronouncement) and originally meant a solemn and binding word, particularly an order from authority where obedience was assured by sanctions.

[2] E.g. mill, bakery, brewery, etc. Conrad, *Rechtsgeschichte*, I, 280.

[3] Feine, 196. [4] Ib., 170, 192. [5] Ib., 171.

publication of marriage banns, for preaching, education, and the care of the poor and the sick.[1]

Mass was primarily celebrated in the cathedral, the parish and monastery churches, but it might also be said in a private house, particularly in the case of illness. The parish prerogative required all the faithful to attend Sunday Mass in the parish church.[2] 'The Council of Nantes expressly prescribed that on holy days and Sundays, before beginning the Mass, the parish priest should ask those assembled if there were present anyone from another parish, *qui proprio contempto presbytero ibi missam audire velit* (who wanted to hear Mass there, despising his own parish priest). If such a person were present, he was to be turned out of the church and required to go back to his own parish. Closely connected with these prescriptions were those forbidding a priest to celebrate Mass outside his own parish church, unless he were travelling.'[3] Even confession had to be made only to the parish priest or bishop.[4] The right to baptize, originally reserved to the bishop but then extended to major churches, was now extended to the minor churches.[5] In the ninth century the cemetery of the parish church was stated to be the obligatory last resting-place.[6]

[1] In many parts of Poland, as a result of patronage rights the nobility might belong to a different parish from that of their peasants although they lived next to each other in the same village. It was considered degrading for a nobleman to receive the sacraments in the same church as the peasants. Cf. Schmid, 822 ff.

[2] The universal Church law obliging the faithful to hear Mass on Sundays dates only from the thirteenth century. There are individual prescriptions of earlier dates. In 797 Theodulf of Orleans urged priests to say Mass in the oratories very early in the morning of feast days so that the faithful would not be prevented from assisting at Mass in the parish church. He censured the abuse of 'quickly hearing a private Mass in the morning and spending the rest of the day in drunkenness'. Zorell, 264; cf. Kurtscheid, I, 280.

[3] Zorell, 265.

[4] Kurtscheid, I, 280. Until the thirteenth century there was no general regulation. The fourth Lateran Council (1215) was the first to prescribe that one must confess once a year to one's *sacerdos proprius*: Plöchl, II, 248. Easter confession and communion, obligatory on parishioners since the fourth Lateran Council, remained a parish prerogative: Feine, 357; Plöchl, II, 235.

[5] In Spain up to the sixth century, in Gaul up to the eighth: Kurtscheid, I, 180. The bishop was no longer the principal minister of baptism, but limited himself to baptizing two or three children on Holy Saturday: Plöchl, I, 350.

[6] Kurtscheid, I, 281.

The parish prerogative was diminished by the privileges of the mendicant orders to whom certain parish rights were transferred with or without exemption. This led to the unfortunate conflict between mendicants and seculars which was stirred up less by zeal for the salvation of souls than by financial considerations. The mendicants entered actively into the cure of souls and built churches and oratories, often quite near the parish church. The parish was thus disrupted, and many revenues were switched to the friaries. Only in 1517 did Leo X legalize the fulfilment of the Sunday obligation in the mendicant churches, except in cases of contempt for the competent parish priest.[1]

The social significance of the parish. With the decay of economic unity, religion remained the strongest bond between men. The villa disappeared, but the 'parish' remained[2] and through its institutions the church became the centre of religious and civic life.[3] Hincmar of Rheims (845–82) wanted to erect a school in every parish to be open to all children and not just to clerics as hitherto.

Next to the school, the care of the poor had an important place. Each parish had its *matricula*, that is an officially registered and supported association of poor people. Only parishioners who were unable to work on account of sickness or age were admitted and various synods legislated on this subject.[4]

The church soon became also the community business centre: purchases, gifts and all public acts took place there. Slaves were freed before the altar. The church served as archive and often enough in the country as barn or threshing floor. It provided sanctuary for fugitives, but was also used for legal processes, banquets, plays and dancing (which had to be forbidden time and again). Religious and profane activities were closely interwoven as are shown also in popular customs.[5]

In the eleventh century the religious play, which grew out of the liturgy, also began to draw people to church, and gradually developed into the fourteenth-century mystery play. Towards the end of the sixteenth century the miracle plays

[1] Cf. note 5, p. 74 supra. [2] *DACL.*, XIII, 2228. [3] Ib., 2233.
[4] Nantes, 658; Aachen, 813; Paris, 829; Mainz, 847. Cf. Lesêtre, 37 f.
[5] Cf. Lesêtre, 77–90.

gave way to profane plays which penetrated into the church.[1]

Besides these attractions there were also means of compulsion to get the people to church. A synod of Toulouse (1229) made it obligatory for the husband and wife of a household to attend Sunday Mass. Absence without excuse was punished by a fine.

Entirely unchristian means of enforcing the Sunday rest were used at the end of the seventh century in England[2] and in the eighth century in southern Germany. Alemannic and Bavarian laws inflicted flogging, fines and imprisonment for breaking the Sunday peace by 'service work'. An incorrigible servant could even have his right hand cut off.[3] The Carolingian reforms were to abolish these measures and restore the Christian spirit of Sunday rest.[4]

The magnificent church buildings of the thirteenth century are evidence of the high religious standards due to the Gregorian reforms. The parish priest was the official representative of this flourishing Church. In the social scale he held an equal or even superior position among magistrates and officials.[5]

There was considerable interaction between the parish and the secular community; on the one hand certain parish rights were restricted and supervised by the local authority, on the other some civil functions were taken over by the parish priest.[6] The co-operation of the people played a considerable part in establishing the legal form of the parish itself, and at the same time the parish influenced the formation of rural communes and corporations.[7] The parishes often formed the basis of the civil constitution, above all through the parish courts.[8]

The position of the laity. Roman Church law tended to exclude the laity and replace them by the civil power. The people often lost the right to vote. Nevertheless, through the *Eigenkirchen* the laity attained a controlling position which was seriously abused to the detriment of the Church.[9] Under Germanic law the laity did indeed lose their influence on the high ecclesiastical appointments, but the right to vote for the parish priest was widely exercised. With the change from privately owned churches to patronage, not only the nobility but also other

[1] Cf. Lesêtre, 77-90. [2] Huber, 136 f. [3] Ib., 140–42. [4] Ib., 145–74.
[5] In Poland the parish priest felt and lived as a great landowner. Cf. Schmid, 826 ff.
[6] Plöchl, II, 150. [7] Ib., II, 148. [8] Feine, 369. [9] Plöchl, I, 164.

laymen were able to retain presentation and nomination rights. The laity also gained influence on the administration of Church property.[1]

In 1278 a synod held at Exeter mentioned for the first time five or six laymen commissioned by the parish priest to maintain the church and render him an annual account. In the same year a synod at Würzburg excluded laymen from the administration of the parish since they had intruded without the consent of the ecclesiastical superiors. In Cologne (1330) laymen administered the temporal property of the church, reporting on it every two years. In France the synod of Lavaur (1386) mentioned for the first time a lay administration of the parish.[2] The Council of Trent presupposed this custom to be universally established.[3]

In the twelfth century the lay officers of the Church (*vitricus*, provost, steward) emerge in England and Venice, in the thirteenth century in Burgundy and Germany, and universally in the fourteenth, especially in places where the parish was of a corporate character. Here, too, Church and civil authorities worked together, for the latter filled and supervised these offices.[4] Otherwise 'the parishioners did indeed have a claim to religious care exercised by the parish priest or his curate, but apart from that they were merely the object of the cure of souls without further rights. Yet they bore the burdens of the parish, paying tithes, oblations, stole fees, etc., and were largely also responsible for the upkeep of the buildings. . . .'[5] The laity, cut off by the rood-screen, no longer took any active part in the liturgy, which had come to be restricted to the clergy.[6]

(d) *Summary*. As has been shown, the undermining of episcopal unity in the diocese reached its culmination under the parish system that had evolved from the private church law. For whereas the centralism of Roman law had favoured unity, Germanic particularism had a fatally disruptive effect. This

[1] Plöchl, II, 160 f., 392. [2] Cf. Synod of Mainz, 1449.

[3] Cf. Lesêtre, 118–24.

[4] Plöchl, II, 392 f.; Feine, 385. To be distinguished from the civil church bailiff introduced by Charlemagne who was also court bailiff. Owing to the many abuses, reform movements (Cluny, Hirsau) opposed the office of bailiff. *LThK*, X (1938), 668.

[5] Feine, 357 f. [6] Cf. Jungmann, *Liturgisches Erbe*, 80 f., 90 ff.

time the attack on unity came from even lower strata than in the case of the baptismal churches; it came from the laity and from an entirely unchristian attitude of mind. The Church did not succeed in assimilating and transforming Germanic law to serve her purposes, but to a great extent succumbed to the secular culture around her.[1] The institution of the parish was so changed that it became itself almost a foreign body within the Church. In the extreme forms we have the paradox that the *παροικία*, which should represent the Church's exile in this world, became a place in which the world had made itself at home in the Church.

Then the tithes determined the territorial division. The parish community became less important than the profitable land of the parish property; the office was separated from ordination and was overshadowed by the benefice. Pastoral duty became a right, selfless service a commanding and even punishing authority, the administration of the sacraments a matter of collecting fees.

Because neither Church nor parish could dissociate themselves from their worldly surroundings, the parish became untrue to its mission. Nevertheless, the authentic spark was never quite extinguished; though even today the foreign elements which largely gave the parish its enduring form are in some measure still present.

B—The Urban Parish

1. *The Ecclesiastical Organization of the Town*

'In the towns the Roman ecclesiastical order, the administrative and economic unity of the diocese under the bishop, continued much longer than in the country, where it was gradually replaced by the system of *Eigenkirchen* and the innovations connected with it.'[2] At first, the bishop remained the responsible pastor of the town. He was assisted by the archdeacon who always accompanied him and represented him in all secular and disciplinary matters (in the Carolingian era, he was actually his Vicar-General), and by the archpriest responsible for the liturgy and cure of souls of the cathedral. Besides,

[1] Cf. Plöchl, I, 389; Schmid, 1058.
[2] Feine, 177.

the bishop appointed town priests who lived *canonice*[1]—according to canonical prescriptions—and thus were called canons. In time the city clergy were formed into a community organization, the chapter, on the model of the monasteries. Thus during the ninth century the cathedral chapters came into being, which lived according to the Rule of Chrodegang and its modified version the Aachen Rule (816), with *mensa* and *massa communis*, under the provost, later the dean. The chapter participated to some extent, in an advisory capacity but also with certain powers of decision, in the diocesan government of the bishop.

In the ninth century collegiate chapters with a provost or dean at their head came into being in the other large churches of the episcopal city. These collegiate churches served the pastoral needs of the city,[2] while the cathedral church remained the centre of worship for the whole diocese. In many places, however, special cathedral parishes originated, and this often led to the building of special parish churches near the cathedral instead of the episcopal baptisteries.

Collegiate churches also came into existence in other towns, giving rise in the ninth century to one or more collegiate parishes. In the larger towns there might also be ordinary parishes as well.[3]

Collegiate life in the cathedral and collegiate church chapters (*scholae*) reached its full glory in the eighth and ninth century in upper Italy where it also spread to the countryside. The provosts —later their substitutes—had the cure of souls, while the canons were responsible for Mass and divine office in choir. Later, however, standards deteriorated and community life was nearing its dissolution.[4]

By the tenth century the old economic unity had disappeared. First the property of the chapter was separated from that of the bishop (*mensa capituli—mensa episcopalis*), partly as early as

[1] 'As opposed to: *incanonice vivere*, as the (from the bishop's point of view) unruly and often married rural clergy generally lived, particularly those of the private churches; and *regulariter*, like the monks, following the Benedictine Rule.' Feine, 177.

[2] In part they were entrusted with the cure of souls, in part they just took it upon themselves. Plöchl, I, 324.

[3] Cf. Feine, 177 f.

[4] Ib., 178 f.

the ninth century. With the decay of community life in the tenth and eleventh centuries, however, capitular property too divided into canonries. 'Thus, the remaining unity of diocesan property fell victim to the decentralizing influence of the Frankish era, the benefice system.'[1]

In the age of universal Church reform many collegiate chapters and a few cathedral chapters adopted the so-called Augustinian rule, gave up personal property and lived a monastic life as canons regular. Other rules of the eleventh century did not attract much interest, and in any case the reform did not last long.

In the twelfth and thirteenth centuries cathedral and collegiate church chapters formed themselves under the influence of canon law into bodies independent of the bishop and responsible for their own government and administration. This now independent cathedral chapter changed from an advisory body to a jointly governing authority in the diocese. In 1139 papal legislation restricted to the cathedral chapter the right to vote for the bishop, which had been guaranteed to clergy and people by the Concordat of Worms. The last vestiges of the common life disappeared in the thirteenth century when the prebendary organization was completed. The life of the secular chapters became aristocratic and feudal, and the prebendary rights came to overshadow the religious duties.

Apart from the government of the diocese, development in the chapters of collegiate churches followed the same lines; parish functions were, however, more to the fore.[2]

2. *The City Parish*

In the eleventh and twelfth centuries, the break-up of the episcopal unity in the city led to the full establishment of the parish system, a process that continued into the thirteenth century. So the city parishes came gradually into being, in some places as a result of a special episcopal order, because pastoral work had become impossible without them.[3] Many sick had to go without the sacraments, and frequent communion was impossible because the parish priest could not

[1] Feine, 189 f. [2] Ib., 313–21. [3] Feine, 366 f.

possibly have coped with the confessions obligatory before communicating on holy days.[1]

Throughout the Middle Ages the division of towns and cities into parishes continued, including also suburbs lying just outside the walls and even some rural districts. The city parish now became a parallel institution to the old rural parish.[2]

As a rule, but not invariably, exact parish areas were defined. Some 'personal' parishes developed from the monastery family parishes on the basis of a special status as in the case of merchant parishes.[3]

As a rule urban parish churches were the *Eigenkirchen*, later the patronage churches of a landowner, though sometimes of the bishop or of a religious institute. In many places the citizens were given the right to the parish vote, but this did not become the general rule any more than in rural parishes.[4]

The parish priest could appoint assistant priests.[5] He had a completely free choice and was not limited to the diocese. The assistant priest could also be dismissed by the parish priest. His legal position was not favourable since normally he had no fixed income but had to come to an agreement with the parish priest about his frequently very poor remuneration. He was more or less the apprentice of the parish priest, who felt himself to be his lord and master.[6] In the larger parish churches (sometimes also in the country) there were moreover chantry priests,[7] who mostly lived on this endowment. From the fifteenth century the larger city churches had also preaching benefices, normally held by academically qualified priests.[8]

As has been mentioned before, from the thirteenth century, inroads were made on the parish obligation, particularly in urban parishes, through the pastoral activities of the mendicant orders, especially the Dominicans, who took no notice of church

[1] Quoted in Schrott, *Seelsorge*, 25.
[2] Plöchl, II, 147.
[3] Feine, 367; Plöchl, II, 137 f.; Conrad, *Rechtsgeschichte*, 455.
[4] Feine, 368.
[5] In common law since the twelfth century.
[6] Plöchl, II, 152.
[7] Constance Cathedral 54; Ulm Minster over 60; the Elisabethenkirche in Breslau 122, etc.
[8] Feine, 373 f.

boundaries. They knew how to adapt themselves to the city mentality and were versatile in their methods.[1]

There was considerable give and take between the urban parish and the civil organization, which had its effect on both. Very often the community life of a town was lived within the parish which supplied the framework for the town: while the emphasis might be either on secular or on ecclesiastical tasks. 'Nowhere in the Middle Ages was the civil community separated from the parish community; on the contrary the city or other community always served both ecclesial and secular interests; it was at the same time Church and civil community.'[2]

In towns even earlier than in the country *laymen* functioned as curators in the administration of collegiate church property. This office which was originally held by a priest became more and more a part of the civil administration which in time also took on the administration of the finances.[3]

The care of the sick had always had an important place in the Church. Hospitals (*xenodochia*) were introduced by monks from the east. They were at first independent ecclesiastical institutes, but were soon replaced by those dependent on a monastery or other religious foundation; these in turn no longer satisfied the needs of the expanding towns and were supplemented and replaced by independent hospitals run by religious fraternities and later by purely civic institutions. With the development of the towns in the thirteenth century hospitals were soon almost completely laicized with the exception of those in episcopal cities where the compromise of mixed administration might be reached.[4]

Similarly cathedral and collegiate schools were replaced, not without a hard struggle, by municipal schools or here and there even municipal universities on the basis of papal privileges.[5] 'Thus, at the end of the Middle Ages the town council appeared as the superior authority of the Church, although not to the same extent as the prince. "The town had become very largely the legal arbiter of Church affairs." (A. Schulze)'[6]

[1] Cf. Chélini, 138.
[2] Feine, 370; cf. Plöchl, II, 147.
[3] Feine, 371.
[4] Ib., 371 f.
[5] Ib., 372.
[6] Conrad, *Rechtsgeschichte*, 456.

C—Clergy and Common Life[1]

Colleges of priests had already been in existence in cathedral churches since the second century. There are accounts dating from the fourth century of the community life of such colleges, and from the fifth century in the oldest parish churches.[2] The centre of the *vita communis* was understandably in the towns, but it was always spreading out to the larger rural churches.[3]

1. *The Rule of Chrodegang of Metz* (760)

In 760 Chrodegang of Metz promulgated a statute based on the Benedictine Rule and on that of the Lateran canons, to be observed by the clergy of his church, who were associated together in a chapter. They lived in *one* house, ate together and slept in one dormitory. They said office in choir and on Sundays had a chapter meeting and reading. On Sundays and holy days there was a general communion, and twice a year confession. They bequeathed their property to the Church, while retaining its use during their lifetime. Differences of rank and status were observed in their conduct and way of life. Those who were still being trained also formed part of the community. This ideal of community life for the secular clergy was soon appreciated and widely copied.[4]

2. *The Aachen Rule* (816)

Charlemagne and Louis the Pious, like Boniface before them, saw in community life for the clergy an important means of reform. They therefore declared the so-called *institutio canonicorum* of Aachen[5] binding throughout the Frankish empire. This rule was based on Chrodegang but was milder and distinguished more clearly between monks and canons. The canons did not wear a monastic habit and could own property.[6] The rule was first introduced into cathedrals and

[1] It was unfortunately not possible to make use of Siegwart's important Dissertation on this subject. We have to be satisfied with a few references to it. Cf. especially Siegwart 231–61 on the apostolic life and the introduction of profession among the clerics regular.

[2] Schrott, *Seelsorge*, 26.

[3] Cf. Plöchl, I, 319 f.

[4] Schnürer, *MA*, I, 382; Feine 177 f.; Siegwart, 64 f.

[5] Cf. Siegwart, 65–68, 162 ff.

[6] 'What caused scandal at the time in the Aachen Rule was that it allowed personal property which was recognized as the real source of laxity and worldliness among the clergy.' Schmale, 43.

collegiate churches, but all Carolingian legislation is permeated with the idea that all clergy should live according to the holy canons, either as monks or as canons. Hence in the ninth century the canonical life was introduced into all the larger churches served by several priests. In spite of zealous propagation, however, it did not become universal in the ninth and tenth centuries.[1]

From about the ninth century the cathedral clergy in some parts of Italy and later also the clergy of baptistery churches led a community life with common property under a spiritual head.[2]

3. *The Gregorian Reform*

One of the main objects of the Gregorian Church reform of the eleventh and twelfth centuries was the reform of the clergy (simony and concubinage) and of the cure of souls. Community life was regarded as an absolutely essential means of reform. The Roman synod of 1059 had already taken up this question. Two trends emerged, one more moderate, the other very strict; the latter, based on the Acts of the Apostles, the Fathers and the early councils, demanded also community of goods. In northern and central Italy the stricter version obtained, but not in Rome. The canonical life spread first in the towns and later also in the large rural parishes. According to Nanni neither Chrodegang's rule nor that of Aachen had gained much ground in Italy, so that only as a result of the Gregorian reform did the canonical life make any appreciable headway there; it flourished from the eleventh to the thirteenth century, particularly in the country.[3]

This form of clerical community life differs in some important points from the Roman and Byzantine *schola sacerdotum*, as also from that of Carolingian times. We are dealing here with genuine corporations with statutory rights. In particular they practised true community of goods—as opposed to the Carolingian institution. The assets of the major parish constituted a common substance *quoad fundos* as well as *quoad fructus*. Rights

[1] Schnürer, op. cit., 381 f.; Feine, 178; Plöchl, I, 320.

[2] 'In 1145 Eugene III was able to count fifty-five such regular collegiate *plebes* in the diocese of Verona. In the next century the number was up to around seventy.' Feine, 170.

[3] Nanni, 530; Feine, 229; Siegwart, 253 f., 256 ff.

and duties applied to the college as a whole. In the thirteenth century the *mensa capitularis* was divided and the collegiate clergy disappeared when the unity of the large parish was lost.[1]

As a result of the Church reforms, many collegiate church chapters, but few cathedral chapters, adopted the Augustinian rule and lived as canons regular. Other rules of the eleventh century had only a very limited following.[2]

4. *Fraternities*

The idea of community life, or at least life lived in close association, was revived by the fraternities which originated in the thirteenth, and developed especially in the fourteenth century. An interesting fraternity was founded at Raulhac in Auvergne in the fifteenth century which almost resembled an association of worker priests. It was started by the parish priest and two curates and in the following century numbered seventy members, although to belong to it a priest must have been born, baptized and resident in that parish. Admittedly the parish of Raulhac at this time embraced forty villages and twenty-five hamlets as well as three chapels of ease, six private oratories and five chaplaincies, so that there was no lack of recruits nor of work. The most important priests in the parish lived in the town, others in the villages and hamlets, with their relations, leading a simple life among the peasants who respected their priesthood. Many also lived the common life. They all practised a handicraft and worked on the land. No one was scandalized by this way of life. On the contrary, people would have been astonished if they had done no work. Naturally they took time off to visit the sick, teach the catechism and in the schools and administer the sacraments. In 1789 this fraternity had dwindled to eleven members.

Such fraternities in the country are reminiscent of the rural presbyterium of the first centuries. In part they went back to the twelfth century; they flourished in the sixteenth and seventeenth centuries, after which the decline set in. On the eve of the French Revolution the diocese of Limoges, for example, still numbered 114 fraternities with an average of eight to ten priests each.[3]

[1] Nanni, 531 f.; cf. Feine, 232 f.

[2] Feine 335; Siegwart, 258 ff.

[3] Lesêtre, 115–17.

D—The Organization of the Diocese

The splitting up of the diocese and of the original large districts served by the great baptismal churches called for a new diocesan organization.

In Italy the older rural archipresbyterate replaced the old baptistery church parish. The archpriest was as it were the parish priest of a large parish and his clergy lived in community (*vita* and *massa communis*).[1]

The more recent rural archipresbyterate, embracing several parishes, developed in Germany from the second half of the ninth century and followed the pattern of the original parish. From the eleventh century it was usually called a deanery. The deanery, which originated in the ninth century north of the Alps, followed the old baptistery parish and embraced all the smaller parishes, the dean being frequently the successor to the archpriest. In the eleventh and twelfth centuries the deanery was replaced by the archidiaconate. However since from the twelfth and thirteenth centuries, the archdeacon used to appoint a deputy the position of the deanery improved and finally acquired its real significance: it normally became a subdivision of the archidiaconate. The rural dean was chosen from among the parish priests by the bishop or the archdeacon and became the intermediary between parish priest and bishop. The archpriest or dean became the bishop's overseer in his diocese, which involved an annual visitation and report to the bishop. In addition he had to arrange monthly meetings of his clergy at which theological questions and diocesan matters were discussed. In the thirteenth and fourteenth centuries these rural chapters became corporations with their own financial administration.[2]

Whereas in the eighth century the one archdeacon, as the bishop's vicar, still supervised the Church discipline in the diocese, in the ninth and tenth centuries the administration became more complicated until the deanery was gradually supplanted and became subordinate to the archidiaconate which embraced it. In some places its starting point was the chorepiscopate, but mostly it represented a new formation in the diocese which sometimes followed the boundaries of the

[1] Feine, 180.

[2] Feine, 180 ff., 328; Plöchl, I, 316 f.; II, 135.

civil territorial divisions. In western Europe they were generally quarters of a diocese, but in the east were smaller and more numerous.[1] Many of the dean's functions were now taken over by the archdeacon. In particular he also deputized for the bishop in his jurisdiction. In the eleventh and twelfth centuries he became an intermediate authority between the bishop and the parish priest with his own disciplinary and administrative powers, so that the bishop was more and more removed from direct control of his diocese. From the ninth to the eleventh century the archdeacon was to have only deacon's orders, but the number of ordained priests steadily increased.[2]

III—From the Tridentine Reforms to the Code of Canon Law

1. *The Tridentine Reforms*

(a) *The Reform of the Diocese.* The Tridentine reform of the Church aimed principally at renewing and consolidating the task and position of bishops. Most difficulties in the Church's organization resulted from the inadequate functioning of diocesan government, which was impeded by exemptions and immunities and made ineffectual by pluralism and neglect of pastoral work. The popes of the twelfth and thirteenth centuries had indeed considerably strengthened the central power in an attempt to remedy these shortcomings, but no closer relationship between the diocese and the bishop corresponded to the closer bond between the bishop and Rome. The object of the council was 'strengthening of episcopal authority in the diocese with the simultaneous assurance of the papal power'.[3] Once more the bishop bore the responsibility for divine service and the cure of souls, for the ideal of the council was the good shepherd. Pluralism was forbidden and the duty of residence was made obligatory under pain of heavy penalties. Emphasis was placed on the religious nature of benefices, which are inseparable from the *cura animarum.* Visitations, diocesan synods and the institution of seminaries were also seen as serving the cure of souls. However, the Tridentine legislation was enforced

[1] In older sources the archdeacon's district is called *parochia,* but after the eleventh century, archidiaconate. Plöchl, I, 315.

[2] Feine, 181 f.; Plöchl, I, 315 ff.

[3] Plöchl, III, 258; cf. 257.

only slowly and with difficulty on account of the many obstacles placed in its way either by the state or by the bishops themselves. 'Tridentine episcopal law, frequently insisted upon and promoted by succeeding popes, became the strongest pillar of the Church's new spirit, and brought forth a rich harvest, the gathering and consolidation of which was finally one of the most important works of Pope Pius X.'[1]

(b) *The Reform of the Parish.* The Tridentine reform also paid attention to the parish, which still bears essentially its stamp. Its guiding principle was again the cure of souls. Nevertheless, the relevant legislation was neither unequivocal nor all embracing, and this had its inevitable results in the future. However, in the twenty-fourth session a solid foundation was laid in *De reformatione.*[2]

The Parish. After the bishop the parish priest was responsible for the cure of souls. Since the shepherd must know his flock, the faithful were to be divided into clearly defined separate parishes each served permanently by its own parish priest. This principle was, however, somewhat weakened by allowing other more suitable measures to be adopted if local conditions required it.[3]

It was not clearly expressed whether the membership of the parishioners should be based on the *territorial* or the *personal* principle. Theory and practice did not agree, but in practice territorial parishes were preferred while allowing the personal parish its right, and this was maintained in future. The personal parish could appeal to older rights. It mostly took the form of urban family parishes which were not restricted to hereditary descendants but could also admit later arrivals.[4] Other forms of personal parish existed for the army,[5] for those belonging to different rites, and for national minorities.[6] Personal parishes are an urban peculiarity and are seldom found in the country. 'Incidentally, the prescriptions of the Council of Trent had also the effect of obliterating the historically different evolution

[1] Plöchl, III, 267; cf. 259 ff. [2] Ib., III, 304. [3] Ib.

[4] Decision of the Congregation of the Council of 1778. Such newcomers, however, once they were there might not change to a second personal parish but only to a territorial one.

[5] Members of the army and their families. Here one can even speak of personal dioceses. Plöchl, III, 221; cf. 224.

[6] Particularly overseas in the nineteenth century.

of the urban and rural parishes.'[1] This is probably also one of the reasons for the inadequacy of the urban cure of souls in the industrial age.[2]

Just as the council on principle refused to accept church people without a parish priest, it recognized the *parishioners* as a constituent element of the parish. Hence the question of how many people constituted a parish body acquired some importance.[3] In 1762 the congregation of the council set the minimum figure at ten families. Already existing parishes with fewer persons were allowed to remain in existence.[4]

An upper limit was not set by the council except for the stipulation that every parish priest must know his people. This question was not discussed before the eighteenth and nineteenth centuries. Thus in a letter to the French bishops of 1791 Pius VI opposed Paris parishes with more than 6,000 members. On the other hand in 1905 the congregation of the council rejected the division of a Capuchin parish of 6,500, but agreed to it in 1907 when it had increased still further. Leo XIII (1823–29) set down the principle for the parish organization of Rome: not more than 3,000 souls per parish, which must be provided with two priests, and two others for confessions.[5]

Although in principle each parish has a church, the Council of Trent did not regard this as an essential element: several parishes may use the same church.[6]

The erection of the parish and any changes in it were reserved to the bishop. At first a verbal decision of the bishop sufficed for the erection of a parish; since 1897, however, the congregation of the council has required a written instrument. The bishop also had the right to divide a parish, even against the wish of

[1] Plöchl, III, 305.

[2] Ib., 304 f.; Even the *C.I.C.* no longer recognizes the terms urban and rural parish. Hagen, 2, note 3.

[3] Ten houses or ten families are mentioned (Barbosa), which include heretics in places where there is a mixed community (Pirhing), or ten persons including those not of the age of reason (Faganus).

[4] Plöchl, III, 305 f. If the number fell to three or four families, they had to attach themselves to another parish. One family was undoubtedly insufficient.

[5] Plöchl, III, 309 f.

[6] Ib., 306, Congregation of the Council decisions of 1895 and 1918 (!), Propaganda 1875.

the parish priest, if he thought it necessary.[1] In this case, some of the assets of the mother church would be transferred to maintain the clergy of the new parish, and if necessary the people had to contribute as well. From the nineteenth century a permanent income including also the voluntary contributions of the faithful could take the place of a capital basis. The bishop was also competent for the merging of parishes.[2]

Rights and duties of the parish priest. The Council of Trent also defined parish rights more accurately. 'After the bishop, the parish priest was accorded an exclusive authority, with few exceptions, over his parishioners, and he was also to administer the sacraments. The parishioners were bound to this authority but they also had the right to pastoral care and the sacraments which could not be refused without just reason.'[3] The right to burial fees was again taken away from the regular clergy and their faculties for hearing confessions were restricted. The exclusiveness of the right to baptize became the subject of many hard struggles, based on older claims, but confession might be made to any authorized priest. Clement X (1670–76) also extended the freedom to the Easter confession and thus settled any former doubts. Easter communion, however, remained a parish right, as did also anointing of the sick and viaticum, but not other holy communions.[4]

The parish priest had the *duty* to preach himself at least on Sundays and holy days of obligation and was allowed a substitute only for a legitimate reason. In addition he was to preach at least thrice weekly in Lent and Advent. He also had to expound the gospel and the catechism.[5] Apart from the parish clergy, neither regulars nor seculars were allowed to preach without the bishop's permission, not even religious in

[1] From the second half of the nineteenth century this was valid also without notification of the parish priest although such notification formed part of the proceedings.

[2] Plöchl, III, 306 f., 311 f.

[3] Ib., 313.

[4] Ib., 313 f., The right of burial normally belonged to the parish priest of the place of death.

[5] The Roman Catechism was, after all, made for the parish clergy. The 1910 decree *Maxima Cura* of the Consistorial Congregation provided that a parish priest might be removed if he neglected the duty of expounding the Scripture and Catechism. This was a sign that the new provisions were not easily applied.

the churches of their order. The Tridentine legislation did not favour an extra parochial preaching apostolate, nor did it make any contribution to popular missions.[1]

Further, the parish priest had to offer his Mass on Sundays and holy days for the members of his parish and could take no stipend for it.[2]

Pastoral duties also included preserving faith and morals, and the supervision of schools was to be supplemented by charitable and welfare work. Breach of the duty of residence was punishable by censure and fine.[3]

The *status animarum*, which goes back to the fifteenth century and was fairly widespread in the sixteenth, was made of general obligation by the Council of Trent (baptismal and marriage registers). Later these parish registers began also to interest the civil authorities.[4]

The accumulation of parish benefices was forbidden. Bishops had the right to transfer simple benefices to other churches at their discretion. Benefices were to be given to qualified persons really able and obliged to exercise their office. On the question of replacing unfit incumbents the council was extremely cautious.[5] Possession of a benefice was once more inseparably tied to the exercise of the office. Tithes were authorized and the care of poor parishes was recommended to the people. The right of patronage was restricted to those who founded or endowed a church. In certain cases it was occasionally linked with the right of presentation. The council wanted to exclude once and for all the economic factors which had come to play such a large part in the parish.[6] New posts were frequently filled by the *concursus parochiales*.

The council by-passed the question of assistant priests. As hitherto, the parish priest could appoint an assistant priest,

[1] Plöchl, III, 316 f.

[2] Ib., 323 f. Session XXIII, De ref. 1; congregation of the council 1670; ib.

[3] Ib., 324 f. [4] Ib., 320 ff.

[5] It said only that the bishop might give an uneducated or inexperienced parish priest a co-adjutor or curate or might '*aliter providere*'. Plöchl, III, 462 f. In the fifteenth and sixteenth centuries there were still cases where the parish priests knew neither the Ten Commandments, nor those of the Church, nor the articles of faith, nor the form of administration of the sacraments. Nanni, 542.

[6] Nanni, 540 f.

either on his own initiative or with the consent of the parishioners. He had to pay him out of his own income, but he could also dismiss him at will. The council only made the validity of an assistant priest's absolution dependent upon an examination by the bishop.[1]

In many places the reforms were applied only with great difficulty. 'In countries that remained Catholic the many benefices remained in the hands of the higher and lesser nobility, and although the clergy were soon once more very numerous, many of them were not engaged in pastoral work.'[2]

The laity. The laity, who had badly misused their influence through the *Eigenkirchen* system and their right of patronage, were given Cinderella treatment by the council. The Tridentine legal concept of the Church 'had one great disadvantage in that it was too narrowly confined to the hierarchy: it condemned the lay element, the people of the Church, too much to passivity. The lay Christian became a mere subordinate, a role which resulted in superficiality and lack of interest. That he should nevertheless be led again away from this passivity was due mainly to the last popes of this period, who saw further than many pusillanimous conciliar Fathers of Vatican I.'[3]

The hierarchical order was regarded not only as the bearer of Church authority but as the Church itself, while the laity were seen as subjects whose first duty—according to rigorous theologians—was obedience.[4] Although this concept was not generally accepted, it did show an attitude of mind. Even in Constitutions of Alexander VII (1655–67), Clement IX (1667–69) and Benedict XIV (1740–58) the most important right of the laity was still their claim to receive the sacraments and pastoral care. Even at the end of the eighteenth century and in the mid-nineteenth many jurists spoke of the right of laymen to an orderly government of the Church as whose subjects they were to be regarded. This view, though not the only one, remained fundamental. In the nineteenth century the Church adopted a very cautious attitude towards the laity so as not to allow them a greater influence. For this reason the

[1] Plöchl, III, 329, 464 f. [2] Schrott, 'Pfarre', 12 f. [3] Plöchl, III, 64.

[4] Ib., 387. Compare with the same development outside the Church. Evolution towards absolute monarchy to the exclusion of the mediaeval democratic structures.

Vatican Council of 1870 came to an impasse on the definition of the mystical body of Christ. Pius X (1903–14) made the distinction between 'laicism' and the laity. At the same time the beginnings of the lay apostolate coincide with a renewal of the Church.[1]

Summary. The Council of Trent aimed at giving pastoral work a sound legal basis. Although there were at the time a few isolated big cities,[2] their meteoric development in the industrial era could not have been foreseen. There were also, both within the Council and outside it, very great difficulties in the way of reforming the structure of the parish and thus the cure of souls. Nevertheless, the subsequent development of the parish followed the lines laid down by the Tridentine legislation, though the reform of the episcopal and parochial cure of souls was a long and painful process.[3] At first its place was taken by the free missionary activity of the various 'reform' orders, which were not yet co-operative with the parish. Even Charles Borromeo, for example, who reformed his own diocese with such zeal, invited regulars to make foundations everywhere and made use of them for the training of his clergy and for pastoral work.[4] Thus the reforms of the Council of Trent, which was by no means favourable to extra-parochial cure of souls,[5] were in fact carried through by extra-parochial means. A significant part in this work was played by the various 'Oratories',[6] where evangelical community life was the basis of pastoral success.

The Council of Trent did succeed to a large extent in cleansing the parish of worldliness, returning it to its pastoral duties and, as far as possible, bringing it back into the unity of the bishopric.

2. *The Parish under the Influence of Enlightenment and State Absolutism*

In Germany and Austria[7] at least, the enlightenment brought

[1] Plöchl, III, 387 f.

[2] Paris, which in the middle of the sixteenth century had over 300,000 inhabitants, Rome and Venice.

[3] Plöchl, III, 307 f. [4] Schrott, 'Seelsorge', 88, 90, 106. [5] Plöchl, III, 331.

[6] E.g. Philip Neri (1515–95) or Bartholomew Holzhauser (1613–58).

[7] The English scene, so drastically altered by the Reformation, would require a separate study; but in any case, Catholic parishes in this country did not again come into existence until the hierarchy was re-established in 1850.

about a radical, rationalistic and therefore highly double-edged reform which nevertheless had its good points, for it gave rise to a rich pastoral literature even though tainted by rationalism, and moreover[1] made the parish the starting point of far-reaching reforms. These were not, however, based on Tridentine principles but on ideas that came from the state (Josephinism) as well as from movements within the Church (Gallicanism and Febronianism).

As the rights of the bishops in relation to the pope were exaggerated, so also were those of the parish priest in relation to the bishop. Besides, since the state claimed absolute sovereignty over the Church, the parish priest became a civil servant whose task was 'as friend and teacher of the people to work for the greatest possible happiness for mankind'.[2]

Joseph II (1765–90) established above all many new parishes, thus opposing a conservative trend in the Church, which was against the creation of new parishes. Although the Council of Trent had provided that a parish could be divided even against the wishes of the parish priest, the older conservative school preferred to increase the numbers of assistant priests and chapels of ease to the division and multiplication of parishes. This attitude was also largely shared by the Rota and the Congregation of the Council who were guided by consideration for the existing parish organization rather than by pastoral requirements. The influence of the enlightenment also affected doctrinal but even more practical matters through the state legislation of Josephinism.[3] Between 1783 and 1787 a very large number of new parishes was established, largely at the expense of the monasteries.[4]

A more positive achievement was the first admission of the laymen to the pastoral activity of the parish, especially in the

[1] Schrott, 'Seelsorge', 113–25. [2] Schrott. [3] Plöchl, III, 309.

[4] 'Monasteries were destroyed by being forced to undertake parish work; this meant that many members had to leave their monasteries; other monasteries were abolished in order to found new parishes by means of their assets; other monasteries were forbidden to accept novices. Joseph II abolished more than seven hundred monasteries in his territories. No doubt there was a great disproportion between the large number of monasteries and the small number of parishes, but the way of adjusting this disproportion was dictated neither in principle nor in the methods used by a genuine pastoral spirit, and it led to a weakening of the Church instead of to an inner strengthening.' (Schrott, 'Pfarre', 13.)

'Sunday Schools', an idea which goes back to the Empress Maria Theresia.[1]

The renewal of the parish idea was a great step forward. Only, the interior renewal of priest and people had not kept pace with the external organization, and thus did not produce the fruits necessary for a real reconstruction of the parish.[2]

France. 'At the end of the *ancien régime* the French Church was still outwardly impressive as an organized Estate with an imposing number of members, vast property and great privileges.'[3]

In accordance with the Concordat of 1516 the king still filled the bishoprics, which were reserved for the higher nobility.[4] Many parishes belonged to religious orders, but these appointed a secular priest whom they paid a normally very small *portio congrua* for his services. 'As a rule, parish priests in towns were expected to have a theological degree. Rural parish priests, whose education had been improved since the end of the seventeenth century through the seminaries, generally enjoyed a well-merited regard in the country if only because most countrymen could still not read or write. They kept the registers, were at the head of all organizations, specifically charitable ones, themselves distributed much in the way of alms, undertook many social activities, and worked for peace, reconciliation and mutual understanding.'[5] The people were personally attached to their parish priest.[6]

Although the clergy was the richest estate in the country,[7]

[1] 'This role of the laity in the Church during the decline is the distant signal of a change. The urge to freedom also had a positive side. The emphatic opposition to the Church was fundamentally but the youthful departure from the paternal home destined to end in the return of the mature adult who would himself take over duties in the house of the father. So we find here already the first starting points of Catholic Action.' R. Müller, 'Die Heiligung des Sonntags in der Kirche der Neuzeit', in Peichl, *Der Tag des Herrn*, 89.

[2] Schrott, *Seelsorge*, 146.

[3] It numbered about 120,000 religious: 130 bishops, 60,000–70,000 secular priests, 20,000–30,000 men and 35,000 women in religious orders. Schnürer, *18.Jh.*, 377.

[4] In 1789 the lesser clergy numbered about 80,000 parish priests and curates.

[5] Schnürer, *18.Jh.*, 381.

[6] Le Bras, *Introduction*, II, 30.

[7] The Church's property at this time was estimated at between a third and a half of the whole country.

there was considerable poverty among the lesser clergy, owing to uneven distribution and the inequality of benefices. The most glaring difference was between the 'beneficiaries' who lived on the benefice and the tithes of the parish, and the 'congruists' or curates who lived on a fixed sum, the usually very low *portio congrua*, allotted by their employer.[1] These differences led to a fateful division in the clergy which was to come into the open during the Revolution.

Until then parish life followed the established customs. In the larger parishes the divine office was sung daily, in the smaller ones at least on Sundays.[2] In the country high Mass and vespers brought the people together. From the pulpit the parish priest kept his flock up to date with the latest events. The parish was organized so as to facilitate the fulfilment of religious duties and the reception of the sacraments.[3]

The religious fraternities that had flourished in the sixteenth century still continued in places. Care of the poor of the parish received a new impetus in the seventeenth century from the widespread influence of St Vincent de Paul (1581–1660). In the eighteenth century taxes were so high that life became very difficult for the peasants and artisans. Even the charitable activities of the parish no longer sufficed to combat poverty, for the whole social order in Church and state was rotten.[4]

In France, schools were still the concern of the parish. The edicts of 1695 and 1724 maintained the authority of the parish priest over the school and demanded teachers of both sexes for the parish. At the end of the eighteenth century primary schools were functioning in 25,000 out of 37,000 parishes.

The school was run by the parish priest. Teachers had to be confirmed in the exercise of their profession by the respon-

[1] Town clergy were often poorer than the rural clergy who lived on tithes. Urban clergy were thus more dependent on stole fees. The cult of the dead was probably the best source of income. Lesêtre, 109 f.

[2] Up to 1790 the Parish Cathedral maintained sung Matins at midnight! There was even a confraternity whose object was to assist at nocturnal Matins. Lesêtre, 125.

[3] In the Parisian parish of St Sulpice measures introduced by Olier in the seventeenth century were still in force in 1777. He had divided the parish into eight 'quarters' with one priest responsible for each. Ten other priests were there to help them. Such an organization was obviously only possible where a numerous clergy was available. Lesêtre, 129 f.

[4] Lesêtre, 141 f.

sible canon, and the parish had to provide their accommodation. School property, like all parish property, was administered by laymen. In principle, poor children had the right to free schooling, and in the country this was indeed the case, but in the towns most poor children were excluded because they were not able to pay. In order to avoid this evil, urban parish priests, particularly in Paris, established poor schools (*écoles de charité*) which were only under the authority of the Church. St John de la Salle (1651–1719) made himself especially responsible for providing suitable teaching staff for them.[1]

The French Revolution had devastating effects on the parish. In 1790 the Church was completely subordinated to the state which aimed at its annihilation. Parish boundaries were made to coincide with those of the *arrondissements*,[2] the parish priest became a civil functionary who had to take the oath of loyalty to the civil constitution. Then, from 1794 to 1802, the Church was completely separated from the state. In 1794 there was hardly a parish left in France in which divine service could be publicly celebrated. Those churches that were not completely ruined were requisitioned by the state. On the basis of the Decree of 30 May 1795, which proclaimed religious freedom, parishes on all sides demanded the return of their churches. With the most primitive means divine service was once more held in the badly damaged churches. The priests lived in poverty among a ruined people, but in spite of everything parish life was once more beginning to stir. The clergy who had had to flee abroad came back to the dioceses and parishes between 1795 and 1801.[3]

Summary. Previously, the privately owned churches had made the parish clergy dependent upon the influential laymen and had robbed them of their freedom. Now the state made use of the Church and the clergy for its own purposes. 'Even in the constitutional state, the parish remained imprisoned by it. The appointment and payment of the parish priest were in

[1] Lesêtre, 142 f.

[2] The National Assembly decided to tolerate no parish under 6,000 souls in the big cities, but above that number . . .! Swoboda, 327.

[3] At the time of the Concordat (1801) the French clergy numbered 28,000–30,000 including 6,000 constitutional priests, of whom only one half exercised their parish functions. Cf. Lesêtre, 147–55; Dansette, *Histoire religieuse de la France contemporaine. De la Révolution à la IIIième République*, 7–158.

the hands of the state. This was even more so in the matter of erecting new parishes where the state was responsible for providing the buildings, or at least had to decide about them and about parish property.'[1] In France the Concordat of 1801 officially recognized the Catholic faith as the religion of the great majority of the population. Bishops were allowed to nominate parish priests, but their choice had to be approved by the government.[2] The *concursus* method of the selection of parish priests prescribed by the Council of Trent (Ses. XXIV Cap. 18) was finally reintroduced into many French dioceses in the course of the second half of the nineteenth century.[3] With the approval of the government, the bishops were to fix the dues for the administration of the sacraments, so stole fees were once more officially introduced. This resulted in pastoral work being largely replaced by administration.

The interior reconstruction of the Church was difficult everywhere. Among the European clergy rationalist, Josephinist and Gallican ideas were still rampant, and they were, moreover, quite unprepared for the difficult situation which the social changes were to bring about for the cure of souls. In addition their numbers were decimated in almost all countries. Religious instruction was too antiquated, too naïve and negative, in no way adapted to the new demands of the times, and therefore ineffectual. The life of faith was progressively weakened and a generation of sceptics was growing up. 'Even before the Church had rebuilt her ruined house at great cost, far-reaching changes began to take place in town and country, arising from the removal of all barriers to personal freedom, from the break-up of a community life based on estates and the emergence of isolated individual existences, and the freeing of all personal and economic forces. Groups upon which the Church had previously based her work were submerged and new ones rose to the surface. Community forms in

[1] Schrott, 'Pfarre', 14; cf. Schwer, 8 f.; Dansette, op. cit.

[2] To start with only those who disposed of an annual income of at least 300 frs. could be ordained priest. Not until 1810 was this law repealed by Napoleon, so that the priesthood once more became accessible to poorer people. Lesêtre, 157.

[3] Lesêtre, 158. Whereas under the monarchy there had been 30,000 immovable parish priests and 2,500 movable temporary appointments, under the Concordat the immovable parish priests had sunk to 3,425 and the movable country parish priests had gone up to 34,041.

which the Church had been at home shrivelled up, giving way to entirely new institutions. The ground which had supported the cure of souls for more than a thousand years was shaking, for its organization had been woven into the whole social structure. . . .'[1]

3. *The Parish in the Light of Industrial Development*

In the country the traditional parish idyll was to remain, for a comparatively long time at least, in the smaller and remoter parishes. Even in 1846 in his *Entretiens de Village*, de Cormenin still draws a romantic picture of the village whose centre is the church steeple.[2] There the parish remained identical with the village community at least for a time.[3] In a small village the parish priest was still the most important person who could exercise a powerful moral influence on the inhabitants.

From such parishes comes a large, if not the largest, proportion of priests who have then to work in quite different conditions; and the continued existence of these country parishes explains at least in part the enduring nostalgia for and the unconscious clinging to a kind of parish organization which, in different sociological conditions, is bound to end in fiasco.[4]

But this 'ideal' is for a variety of reasons no longer realized even in many country parishes. In the last quarter of the nineteenth century anticlericalism and freethinking had penetrated also into the villages. Local authority, the schools, and the country chemists in particular, spread anticlerical thought.

[1] Schwer, 32.

[2] Lesêtre, 176–80.

[3] 'Where the church is, there is the village; the church, one might say, gathers its children like a mother. It is the focal point of parish life, it binds the community together. . . . But the church is not only the expression of the community, the seat and centre of its existence, and the heart and soul of the religious encounter, it is also the best vehicle of civilization. When they leave church, the inhabitants gather in groups in the public square, meeting and finding each other, coming to agreement on sales and exchanges, and discussing family alliances. One is sure to meet officials before or after Mass. After Mass the Mayor will stand on the stone bench by the church tower and read out government regulations about harvests and taxes and make all sorts of announcements. In the church porch he pins up the voting lists and the community notices . . .' Quoted by Lesêtre, pp. 177 f.

[4] In a lecture at Freiburg (Germany) University in November 1959 Fr Motte drew attention to the still existing tendency among parish priests to try to build rural parishes in cities.

However, the medium-sized parishes of the cantons and small towns of France, for example, show a different picture. There the parish priest could no longer fulfil his multiple duties single-handed. He was helped by the notables who exercised as much influence as he did, if not more. He was no longer the village pope. Various organizations were to help the people in the church. The confidence of the young people had to be won, but many succumbed to anti-religious influences which were supported by the rising press. Parish and village were no longer synonymous; as a sociological institution the parish had changed. The clergy were frequently no longer adequate to their heavy tasks.[1]

While in the country the parish appeared at least outwardly still to meet pastoral requirements, in towns and industrial centres it became completely ineffective.[2]

In 1844 the pastoral periodical *Der Seelsorger*[3] dealt for the first time with the problems of the care of souls in the city. Everywhere urban parishes were growing beyond all bounds and a real care of souls became impossible on a parish scale, but was confined to a small percentage of the souls entrusted to the parish priest. In spite of the considerable changes in the

[1] Cf. Lesêtre, 175–98.

[2] The concentration of the population in towns and industrial areas rose rapidly. In 1850 there were ninety-four towns in the world with more than 100,000 inhabitants. In 1900 there were 291, and in 1950, 720. The quickest growth, with the exception of Soviet Russia and certain areas of the United States, occurred between 1870 and 1914. Today in the greater part of Europe, N. America, Australia, Argentina and Russia, more than 40 per cent of the population are town-dwellers. At the top of the list comes England with 80 per cent. The 20,000,000 increase in Germany's population since 1875 all accrued to concentration areas, and fifteen of the twenty million to the large cities. After the second world war there were sixty-four cities with over a million inhabitants, and twenty of these were in Europe. Cf. Motte, *Le prêtre et la ville*, 147 f.

[3] Sixth year, vol. 1, pp. 319 ff. 'While everywhere and in every way we do our best to speak for and promote the Catholic Church, to renew our religious conditions, to arouse piety in the people and to repair and improve the highways and byways of spiritual life, we allow parish conditions to drag along the old worn-out ways as best they can. While we are deeply impressed by the religious and moral poverty of our time, and wishing with the best will to renew religious science, want to found monasteries and set up spiritual institutions of all sorts and expend a great deal of noise and energy on various external works, we hear very little said about the setting up of new parishes, the division of those that are too big, of redrawing awkward boundaries, improving bad benefices, or the increase in numbers of assistant priests!' Quoted in Schwer, 40.

social structure of town and country, there was no corresponding change in the structure of the parish, probably for the first time to this extent in the history of the parish. It was necessary to wait for the new *C.I.C.* which was to introduce a few changes after the First World War.

Dr. Heinrich Swoboda, who can be said to be the pioneer of modern religious sociology in a broader sense, has gone more closely into the problem of the cure of souls in large cities and in an impressive survey has thrown light on the alarming situation at the turn of the century.[1]

The problem is clearest in Paris. In 1861 sixty-three parishes had an average of 26,923 souls,[2] though there were individual parishes of over 35,000.[3] In 1877 the average for the whole of Paris had risen to 28,823, by 1886 it was 33,978, by 1896

[1] An extract from Swoboda's Table A.

Town	*Year*	*Parishes*	*Number with more than 10,000 people*	*Largest*	*Smallest*	*Mean*
Paris and Suburbs	1766	39	19	90,000	100	15–20,000
	1908	160(443)	115	96,200	260	22,629
Budapest	1908	17 (62)	11	89,862	40	27,990
Vienna	1858	30	21	35,800	805	15,200
,,	1901	68(209)	41	72,892	30	21,200
London (part)	1907	62 (0)	0	5,000	146	—
Rome	1822	91	1	10,800	204	1,680
,,	1908	60 (23)	20(27*)	19,000	550	8,300
Munich	1907	20 (54)	16	43,000	2,673	22,248
Brussels	1907	34 (54)	23	28,000	2,500	14,446
Milan	1907	44 (41)	19	46,800	300	11,700
Turin	1907	42	13	36,463	328	11,070
Oporto	1907	21	7	20,046	1,058	10,440
Berlin (postal district)	1907	30 (23)	14	31,402	892	10,427
Cologne	1905	41 (17)	15	25,600	1,013	8,520
Essen	1907	12	4	22,272	2,722	8,470
Liverpool	1907	37 (0)	1	11,716	308	4,100
Birmingham	1907	14 (0)	0	4,900	450	1,880
Ravenna	1906	15	0	6,400	137	1,569

Figures in brackets under *Parishes* indicate the number of additional parishes needed to achieve an ideal mean of 6,000 souls.

* From 10,000 up.

[2] Daniel-Le Mouel, *Paroisses*, 136.

[3] Daniel, 'L'équipement', 33.

36,765, and by 1906 it had reached 39,477![1] The record was reached by Notre Dame de Clignancourt which in 1906 had 121,034 souls.[2]

Conditions in Vienna were also extremely grave. Had the court decree of 26 April, 1783 been implemented the pastoral situation would have been very much better.[3] The Vienna synod of 1858 laid down the ceiling figure for an urban parish as 10,000.[4] Another synod in Vienna at the beginning of the twentieth century demanded a minimum of 172 parishes for the 1,720,000 inhabitants of the city. In fact there were only 76.[5] In 1907 there were on the average 3,000 schoolchildren in each parish alone. In contrast to the 76 parishes with 440 priests there were in the secular sphere 454 schools with 6,844 teaching staff.[6] On purely material grounds it was physically impossible in the sixteenth district for all Catholics to fulfil their Easter duties.[7] An indication of the existing religious ignorance is the fact that in one suburban parish 53 per cent of future spouses lived together before marriage largely because of a widespread belief that engaged couples *had* to live together so that the banns could be published.[8]

The situation in Rome[9] and in Brussels[10] was also very dis-

[1] 1957: 2,850,189 residents, 95 parishes, 29 chapels of ease, 30,000 souls per parish, 22,985 per church/chapel. Daniel-Le Mouel, 'Paroisses', 136.

[2] Ib., 137. In this parish there were 15,000 souls to every priest (Swoboda, 76). The overall average for greater Paris 4,340 souls per priest (ib., 70). About 10,000 attend Sunday Mass (ib., 76). For a parish of 26,000 souls the parish priest of N.D. des Victoires reckoned 720 communions for the year 1835. (Schwer, 90.)

[3] The decree laid down that the greatest distance from the parish church should be half-an-hour and the suburbs were accordingly divided into nineteen parishes. In the city there were to be two priests for every thousand souls, and in the suburbs one for every seven hundred. (Swoboda, 127; cf. 335.) Decrees of 1792 and 1783 provided that 'in the country owing to great distances and other difficulties a community of 900, or in diaspora conditions as few as 500, should have a new parish or chaplaincy!' (ib. 334). Leopold II in 1790 cut down these generous regulations (Plöchl, III, 309).

[4] Swoboda, 330. [5] Ib., 133. [6] Ib., 144. [7] Ib., 133. [8] Ib., 145.

[9] An enquiry just before the first world war produced the following figures for the parish of St Saba: of 287 families (1,473 persons) 86 (34 per cent) were practising, 138 (48 per cent) were indifferent, and 59 families (18 per cent) (262 persons) were anti-religious. De Rossi, 'Ciò che possono dire i dati statistici di una parrochia', in *Vita e Pensiero*, 1915.

[10] In the terms of the Concordat eleven parishes were erected in 1803 for a population of 67,000. Of the 400 pre-Revolution priests, 40 remained. By 1846 the population had increased to 180,000 and the number of parishes

couraging. The care of souls seemed better organized in diaspora cities.

In Berlin, where Catholics accounted for only about 9 per cent of the population, care was taken to found new parishes in time. The majority of these started from flourishing Catholic associations.[1] Mixed marriages, however, were an even more vexed problem here.[2] Another worrying fact was that many children were now not baptized.[3] The care of souls depended principally on house visiting and the various associations.

In London, where Catholics were only 4–5 per cent,[4] conditions were similar. The religious development of the parish, however, kept incomparably better pace with the expansion of the metropolis.[5] In spite of the great distances involved—in those days London was the largest city of the world in area[6]—monthly house visits were made regularly in all parishes.[7]

In Birmingham the Church authorities first acquired a good site in time and built a small temporary church, following it later with a bigger one. 'If enough sites had been acquired soon enough in all large cities, how much better would the pastoral situation have been.'[8]

---

to 23, more or less keeping pace with developments. However, between 1864 and 1886 the population increased by 200,000 but no new parish was founded. From 1943 to 1954 there was also no new parish founded. From 1803 to 1951 the population increased 1,426 per cent while the number of parishes increased only 818 per cent and the number of priests only 762 per cent. Today greater Brussels has about a million inhabitants looked after by 305 priests in 90 parishes. For the 900,000 in the centre, there are 74 parishes and 273 priests, which means that the working class quarter is noticeably neglected. Houtart, 'L'évolution', 457.

[1] Swoboda, 110 f. The parish of St Pius, for example, was started in 1888 with about 20,000 souls and by 1911 had been divided three times (ib., 113). Although the average is 10,427 souls per parish, the figure for the individual priest is 3,143 (ib., 115 f.).

[2] 60–70 per cent of Catholic marriages are mixed. Ib., 117.

[3] Ib., 119.

[4] Ib., 110.

[5] Between 1829 (11 churches or chapels) and 1907 about 130 new churches were built: between 1900 and 1906 alone, 26 churches or chapels. 'But the history of this archdiocese since the restoration of the hierarchy in 1850 shows only great names: Wiseman, Manning, Vaughan' (ib., 103).

[6] Greater London 160 sq. m., Greater Paris about 115 sq. m., Vienna 100 sq. m. (ib., 94).

[7] Ib., 100.

[8] Ib., 108.

Milan provides a telling example of the sudden and enormous increases in suburban parishes.[1]

In Germany, owing especially to the Krupp works, Essen rose from 6,000 inhabitants in 1846 to 240,000 in 1900. Corresponding figures for Catholics are 5,000 and 144,000. Up to 1889 there were only two parishes with immense numbers of parishioners—the *Kulturkampf* prevented the founding of new ones. Between 1889 and 1907 thirteen new parishes and four new rectorates were founded to make up for lost ground.[2]

In South America the authorities were helpless in the face of similar problems.[3] In North America national parishes provided a relatively happy solution.[4]

Swoboda considers the 'ideal' size of an urban parish around the 6,000 mark and would in no case go beyond 10,000. He is guided by an over-emphasis on the role of the parish priest

[1]

Parish	*Numbers in:* 1800	1850	1900	*Number of places in church*
S. Francesca Romana	1,600	3,600	43,000	2,500
Calvairate	2,600	2,720	20,000	4,500
S. Rocco	1,300	1,920	20,000	600
S. Gottardo	4,200	5,600	22,000	3,000
S. Pietro in Sala	2,000	5,120	32,000	1,000
Ss. Trinità	3,000	10,000	35,000	3,200
S. Maria al Naviglio	—	4,000	28,000	2,000
S. Maria alla Fontana	—	2,800	26,000	2,500

(Swoboda, 162).

[2] Ib., 200 f.

[3] Buenos Aires may serve as an example. When it became the capital it had 270,708 inhabitants. By 1914—in 34 years—the population had increased sixfold. Fifty per cent were foreigners, but there was not one national parish. Numbers continued to increase rapidly: 1936, 2,400,000; 1947 with suburbs 4,532,000; 1955 with suburbs, 5,700,000. Parish organization did not keep pace. Whereas in 1855 the average number of souls per parish was 7,500, in 1869 it was 13,678; in 1906, 49,278 and 1911, 56,683. In 1928 as a result of the founding of twenty new parishes, the figure sank to 54,000. Although between 1928 and 1936 the number of parishes increased from 39 to 96, there were still more than 25,000 souls per parish on the average. Today the average figure is 27,000 parishioners per parish, which works out at more than 10,000 per priest. Amato-Houtart, 'La démographie paroissiale de Buenos-Aires', 70–73.

[4] In Chicago, for example, the parish adapted itself much better to current needs. In 1850 there were 29,900 inhabitants in five parishes each with 10 priests. In 1953 the 45 per cent Catholics of the city's 5,500,000 inhabitants were cared for by 144 territorial and 140 national parishes (Houtart, 'L'evolution', 50 f.). In 1948 there were 1,535 national parishes in the U.S.A. (Harte, 'Racial and National Parishes in the United States', 162 f.)

who, as the bishop's 'delegate' for the cure of souls, should have personal contact with all his parishioners. He is against 'sharing' the parish authority with curates,[1] so that for him the only viable solution lies in increasing the number of parishes and parish churches,[2] as Winninger also recommends.[3]

On the basis of his research, Swoboda sets out four main requirements: first, contact with every parishioner as a matter of principle; second, the real pastors are the bishop and the urban parish priests; third, numerical limits for all pastoral work; fourth, the true, living spirit of Christ which should guide every pastor.[4] 'Reduced to the simplest terms, individual contact and a normal-sized parish are the two badly undervalued but indispensable conditions for all pastoral work in large cities.'[5]

The figures recorded above show that the problem of pastoral work in big cities has not been solved. The necessary division of parishes, and the even more necessary co-operation in attacking the evils of the times, are prevented by an exaggerated individualism.[6]

Thus the problems were not met by adapting the parish to the new conditions, but rather by the now flourishing Catholic Associations and sodalities, which were, however, principally defence mechanisms, a flight into the ghetto.

Only towards the end of the nineteenth century did pastoral work begin to be both deepened and centralized. But not until the twentieth century was the parish once more seen as a sacramental community of life. This new outlook was due principally to the liturgical movement, although at times this led to theologically untenable exaggerations of the parish principle. Through a gradually developing realization of the Church's missionary character, the idea of the parish has changed. This missionary task cannot be fulfilled by the clergy alone, but by the whole Church, clergy and laity together. Today the parish has once more the chance to revive the original spirit of the *parochia*.

[1] It is understandable that he is against the parish system whereby the 'first curate' has all the 'good' jobs and the 'second curate' is responsible for anointing the sick and burying the dead, because this is a form of false specialization in which the individual pastor no longer deals with the whole man but, as it were, with only a part of him.

[2] As Lesêtre, 187 f. [3] Winninger, *Construire des Eglises*.

[4] Swoboda, 246 f. [5] Ib., 345. [6] Cf. Schrott, *Seelsorge*, 180–92.

when, at the bishop's request, [illegible] the greatest [illegible] the parish [illegible] not the only [illegible] the number of [illegible] and parish churches [illegible]

[illegible] first [illegible] with every [illegible] second, the [illegible] parish [illegible] Fourth, [illegible] guide every [illegible] and [illegible] [illegible]

Though [illegible] work [illegible] parishes and the [illegible] the [illegible] of the [illegible] are [illegible] [illegible]

Thus the parish [illegible] not only by adapting the parochial [illegible] new conditions, but rather [illegible] Association [illegible] a flight into the [illegible]

Only towards the end [illegible] work began to be [illegible] not until the twentieth century [illegible] principle [illegible] gradually developing [illegible] of the Church's [illegible] character [illegible] The parochial [illegible] clergy alone, [illegible] the whole Church [illegible] Today the parish has [illegible] original [illegible] purpose.

[illegible]

[illegible]

PART TWO

The Modern Parish as a Community

CHAPTER THREE

The Parish as a Community and Canon Law[1]

I—The Community Structure derived from the Term Paroecia and the Nature of the Parish

The desire to interpret the parish of today once more in terms of the historical origins of the *παροικία* has led to various attempts to discover the community structure of the parish in current canon law or to derive it therefrom.

1. *Derivation from the Juridical Notion of* Paroecia

Some scholars consider that the parish as a community is contained in the notion or at least in a further determination of the *paroecia* of canon law. This opinion is supported by certain definitions which preceded the *C.I.C.* Marianus de Luca, for example, describes the parish as follows: '*Paroecia designat coetum fidelium, cui praeest presbyter ad curam animarum intra certos limitos ex officio exercendum.*'[2] Here, in conformity with the best tradition, the people is the centre of the definition of the parish. The same line is followed by modern authors who, although they ought to be bound by the legal description of the parish in the *Codex*, nevertheless define the parish as 'a community of the faithful for which one special parish priest with the customary powers is assigned for pastoral purposes',[3] or 'a parish is a eucharistic community of a number of Catholic Christians in a certain area headed by a priest and permanently united by

[1] In this chapter the term 'parish' is used in the strictly canonical sense.

[2] de Luca, *Praelectiones Iuris Canonici*, II, 459, quoted in Hagen, 1, note 1.

[3] Bouscaren and Ellis, *Canon Law. A Text and Commentary*, Milwaukee, 2nd ed., 1951; quoted by Fichter in *Social Relations*, 183, note 7. For the Protestant concept, cf. Böhm, e.g., 141–5, 172, 197 ff.

canon law'.[1] Hagen sometimes simply equates parish and parish community, basing himself quite incomprehensibly on C. 2269, paragraph 1, which specifically distinguishes the *populus* from the *paroecia*.[2]

In our discussions of the term *paroecia* in the *C.I.C.*[3] we have shown sufficiently that the word is never used in the *Codex* for the people of the parish. *Paroecia* always means the (beneficed) parish ministry,[4] except in those cases where it is used territorially, where it is also quite distinct from the people.[5] Hence, no community structure of the people of the parish can be derived from the mere juridical notion of *paroecia* since this affirms nothing at all about the people.

For this reason the definitions quoted above are untenable since they bring the people directly into the concept of *paroecia*. When Noser considers the parishioners as a necessary element of the concept of the parish[6] he unconsciously changes the meaning of the term parish from that given by the *Codex* to the word *paroecia*. For according to his own opinion the canon law of *paroecia* can legally continue to exist even if there are no parishioners left.[7]

2. *Derivation from the Nature of the Parish according to Canon Law*

The *Codex*, and specifically C. 216, contains no legal definition of the parish[8] but only a description, and even this is not of the superior genus 'parish' but only of a particular species.[9] This is perhaps why in the *C.I.C.* *paroecia* is not the equivalent of what we normally understand by parish, but only signifies one of the subsidiary meanings of the comprehensive term, namely, the office or ministry—or else the parish territory. Nowhere in the *Codex* is the word *paroecia* used in the comprehensive sense, embracing the two constituent elements of minister and people: there is not even a word for this in the *Codex*. The English word parish, on the contrary, is normally

[1] From the report of a lecture by J. Pascher, quoted in Roth, 'Pfarrei', 16, note 9.

[2] Hagen, e.g. p. 4 f.

[3] See pp. 32–3 above.

[4] In the *C.I.C.* the parish is mostly mentioned in connexion with the parish priest. It is only mentioned indirectly in passages dealing with the laity.

[5] See p. 33 supra; Noser, 24, 51.

[6] Noser, 33.

[7] Ib.

[8] Ib., 15 f.; Hagen, 1.

[9] Noser, 16, note 12.

used in the comprehensive sense containing the constituent elements.

This difference in the meanings of *paroecia* in the *C.I.C.* and of parish in normal usage inevitably leads to confusion. This becomes evident when Noser investigates the nature of 'parish' in canon law. First he distinguishes between those elements which normally belong to the parish and those which are its essential constituents.[1] He follows and clarifies Mickells[2] in placing the ministry and the people among the essentials. This leads him to the following definition: 'By parish (*paroecia*) in the legal sense we understand the office of the parish priest, normally a benefice, embracing the cure of souls of a particular group of the faithful. In the improper sense, "parish" often means the territory over which the parish priest's powers of office extend'.[3] In the Latin of the *Codex*, the parochial ministry must be rendered *paroecia* and not for example *officium paroeciale*.[4] Thus *paroecia* figures at least twice in each of the definitions, once as the comprehensive and once as the subsidiary term.[5] Only *paroecia* in the comprehensive sense that Noser gives it just does not exist in the *C.I.C.* Thus the Latin *paroecia* he adds in brackets is doubly confusing since it does not correspond to the terminology of canon law. Keeping the comprehensive and subsidiary meanings distinct helps to solve many difficulties. This distinction will be maintained in the following investigations.

(a) *The Essential Elements of the Parish and their Relationship.* Noser arrives at two elements that are absolutely essential to the nature of the parish (as superior genus): the ministry and the people. The ministry constitutes, 'not only terminologically but in all respects, the heart and centre of the parish'.[6] On the other hand the people are, according to him, such a very

[1] Noser, 60.

[2] A. A. Mickells, *The Constitutive Elements of Parishes*, Washington, 1950.

[3] Noser, 61.

[4] This means 'duties of the office'; Noser, 51.

[5] Paroecia = paroecia (office) cum cura animarum pro populo determinato; or Paroecia = paroecia (territorium) in quam se extendit paroecia (office).

[6] Noser, 51. The *Codex* was produced at a time of exaggerated clericalism when the laity had no significance.

essential constituent that the office of ministry is entirely directed towards them, is there to serve them and becomes meaningless without them.[1]

There are two main schools of thought regarding the relationship between the parish ministry and the parish community. The one considers the church people as essentially a subject of the parish,[2] the other regards the community or parishioners 'merely' as the object of the parish.[3]

From the point of view of canon law the lay parish community as such has no rights or duties: according to the *C.I.C.* it is no juridical subject or person.[4] Individual members do, indeed, have juridical personality, but the concept of a community as such is hardly recognizable in the *Codex*.[5] 'The parishioners are assigned as objects to the parish and to pastoral care. Nowhere in the whole of the *C.I.C.* is there a single passage that would change or weaken anything in this perfectly clear legal position.'[6] True, as this object assigned to the ministry the parishioners are, indeed, an element of the parish (as superior genus).

The other concept, that the people are the subject of the parish, can either mean that they are the legal subject, which is not acceptable, or simply emphasize the fact that the parish does not consist solely of the ministry and certain officials but embraces all the faithful.[7] Those who regard the parishioners 'only' as objects assigned to the parish understand the latter in the narrower sense of ministry, such as it is mostly taken in the *C.I.C.* The others, who want to 'elevate' the people to be the subject of the parish, use the term in the larger sense. True, this sense does not occur in the *Codex*, but results from the very nature of the parish. In this sense the people is a constitutive element or subject of the parish.

(b) Now it may be asked whether the *populus determinatus* as a constituent element of the parish shows a community structure

[1] Noser, 65.
[2] E.g. Arnold, 'Pfarrei', 24 f.; *SchwKZ.*, 116 (1948), 262 f.
[3] E.g. von Nell-Breuning, 'Grenzen', 107 f.; Noser, 32 f.; K. Rahner, 'Pfarrprinzip'.
[4] Noser, 30; von Nell-Breuning, 'Grenzen', 107 f.; Hagen 12 f.
[5] Noser, 32 f., 35.
[6] von Nell-Breuning, ib., 107.
[7] Cf. Noser 33.

in itself, or in its relation to the ministry or to the parish area.

The *Codex* uses a variety of terms for the people of the parish. In C. 216 it is stated that a *populus determinatus* is to be assigned to each parish territory. Normally the *C.I.C.* uses the word *populus* (which does not figure at all in the official index) as opposed to *clerus*.[1] The term therefore does not necessarily signify a self-contained community but simply 'the people' as distinct from the clergy. Now a part of this mass of people is allocated to each parish without any decision as to whether this part constitutes a community or not, nor whether the individual members have any interest in the life of the parish. The parish people should on no account be equated with the practising parishioners: it embraces all baptized Catholics.

The term *fidelis* is just as indefinite. It is used in a narrow sense for Catholics and more widely for all baptized Christians.[2] It does not signify a particular attachment to the parish, but rather to the Church into which the believer has been incorporated by baptism. The resulting supernatural community of the faithful extends to the whole Church and knows no parish boundaries. This supernatural community is an essential prerequisite for a genuinely ecclesial parish community, since membership of the Church is a necessary condition of membership of the parish *populus*.[3] It is not, however, by itself sufficient to establish a specific parish community, but requires additional elements.

(c) In the *C.I.C.* members of the parish are often called *paroeciani*.[4] Whereas *populus* and *fidelis* imply only a direct connexion with the Church and its hierarchical structure, the term *paroeciani* expresses a direct relation to the ministry: it designates the individual faithful in so far as they belong to a particular parish. In contrast to *populus* which is a collective term, *paroeciani* envisages the individuals in their relation to the parish ministry or the territory. The term itself says nothing about the parishioners being a community; but it still has to be examined whether they can become one on the basis of the relationship to the *paroecia* implicit in the term *paroeciani*.

[1] Cc. 250 §1, 369 §1, 1209 §1, 1329; cf. Mörsdorf, 128.
[2] Mörsdorf, 129 f. [3] Noser, 27.
[4] Cc., 464 §1, 483, 630 §4, 848 §1, 1186 no. 2, 1427 §2; cf. Noser, 30 who in note 22 refers in error to C. 415 §2.

Indeed, the parish priest is thereby bound to care in the first place for the salvation of the individual immortal souls and not for the general good.[1] From both sides, then, it is principally a personal relationship, not a collective one.

The relation between the parish priest and the individual parishioner is not simply reciprocal, but rather one-sided, in that the priest's duties correspond exactly to the parishioner's rights, while the priest's rights correspond only to certain limited duties of the parishioners.[2]

Thus parishioners have the strict right to demand from their priest or clergy spiritual goods, and chiefly the means necessary for salvation (C. 682). Correspondingly the parish priest has the strict duty to care for the souls confided to him.[3] This obligation extends not only to the well-disposed[4] and to those who claim their rights but to all inhabitants of the parish.[5] Hence the obligations of the parish priest can be said to be the backbone of the parish.[6]

The parish priest has also the right to the care of souls in his parish, but relatively few rights are reserved to him,[7] that is to say there are others besides himself delegated by the bishop or the pope who have certain pastoral rights. Since the parish is given to the parish priest *in titulum*, it belongs to him, as his parish. He therefore exercises his office in his own name by virtue of his ordinary powers, yet subject to his bishops: for his parish remains a part of the diocese. The bishop has the right to allow also other pastors to work in his diocese, and the extra-parochial cure of souls is also provided for by canon law.[8]

Corresponding to the limited rights of the parish priest parishioners have only limited duties. The principle of individual freedom is largely preserved and the old parish prerogative (*Pfarrbann*) has little space in modern canon law. Even attendance at the parish Mass on Sundays and holy days is no longer obligatory but only recommended.[9]

[1] Jone, I, 352.

[2] von Nell-Breuning, 'Grenzen', 108.

[3] Cf. Cc. 464–69 and the useful summary of the parish priest's duties in von Nell-Breuning, 'Pfarrei als Zentrum der Seelsorge', in *SchwKZ* 116 (1948), 362. [4] As von Nell-Breuning wrongly implies, loc. cit.

[5] In a certain sense, non-Catholics as well; cf. C. 135 §1; Michonneau, *Paroisse*, 33 f.

[6] Cf. von Nell-Breuning, op. cit. 461b, 462b.

[7] Cf. Cc. 462, 263. [8] Cc. 1349, 608 §1. [9] Cf. Jone, I, 369; C. 467 §2.

In current canon law the ties between parish priest and parishioner do not have to be at all close. On the other hand the law provides a basis for closer relationships. Yet a legal basis alone is not enough to translate possibilities into facts, for the legal relations remain in force even when they are seldom or never realized as for example in the case of non-practising parishioners.

But however close these bonds may be, they remain between the individual parishioner and the parish priest. The relationships of all the individuals to a third person can, but need not be, the basis of a community of the individuals among themselves; in any case they do not constitute 'a personal association of the parishioners with one another'.[1]

(d) To signify an actual community, the *Codex* uses terms such as *coetus*, *communitas*, and *collegium.*

Coetus, which again does not figure in the official index, can either mean gathering, meeting, session or committee, or an association of persons, a community, a society which may or may not be a juridical person.[2] In the old canon law *coetus* was also used for the parish community, but in the *C.I.C.* it is no longer directly used in this sense, but for smaller groups or sections of a parish.[3]

Communitas and *collegium* are both used in the *Codex* in the sense of corporate association: *collegium* is usually also a juridical person, whereas *communitas* means simply a community without reference to its juridical character.[4] Neither of these expressions is used in the *C.I.C.* of the parish community.

Hagen, whose view is adopted by Noser, believes indeed that the parish community may be regarded as a *communitas*,[5] but his line of reasoning is not conclusive. Though earlier canonists (before the *C.I.C.*) used the term *coetus fidelium* where *populus* is used today and though *coetus* can also have the meaning of community in the *Codex*, it cannot be concluded that the *C.I.C.* really regards the parishioners as a community. True, Noser adds that it is in no case a question of a community with juridical personality, but 'merely of a sociological fact'.[6] Apart

[1] von Nell-Breuning, 'Grenzen', 108.
[2] Mörsdorf, 125.
[3] Cf. Cc. 1188 §2, no. 2, 2003 §1.
[4] Mörsdorf, 123 f.
[5] Hagen, 13 f.; Noser, 35. Floristan also finds this 'evident' on natural and theological grounds: *La Parroquia*, 129.
[6] Noser, 35.

from the fact that this reasoning is inconclusive, in this case sociology would have to decide whether the necessary conditions for a community are fulfilled or not.

Hagen understands community as 'a plurality of physical persons joined to one another by any tie. . . . This can consist also of living in the same area.'[1] In fact normally[2] a person is assigned to a parish because he lives in a particular place.[3] Today the permanent domicile[4] is probably rather rare,[5] but the temporary residence,[6] too, involves the actual parish domicile. Hence membership of a parish is based on the relationship of the individual to the parish territory. This relationship may be stable, or it may be rather loose, and it can vary very much from person to person. The relationship of several individuals to the same locality does not necessarily involve their own direct relationship. Hagen's assumption does not hold water; his concept of community is sociologically unsound.

It remains to consider that residence has the canonical effect of determining one's parish priest and bishop.[7] Thus a twofold relationship follows from a man's domicile: one to a common locality, the other to a common parish priest. Nevertheless, it always remains a relation to a third party, not involving any direct relationship between the first two. As sociology shows, this double relationship is scarcely sufficient to create a real parish community.

Thus it seems that the parish as a community cannot be derived from current canon law alone. This does not mean that the opposite could be read into it: only that the *C.I.C.* itself offers no basis for a positive statement on the parish as a

[1] Hagen, 13.

[2] That is, in territorial parishes: what follows does not apply in the same way to personal parishes.

[3] C. 94 §1.

[4] This includes settling with the idea of remaining permanently in a (quasi-) parish, or *de facto* living there at least 10 years. Cf. C. 92 §1; Jone, I, 103; Hagen, 5.

[5] Since only about 5–10 per cent of people in towns remain 10 years in one place; Bruhin, 8.

[6] Settling with the intention of spending the greater part of the year there, or by *de facto* remaining there for such time C. 92 §2.

[7] C. 94 §1. As a man may have more than one residence, so he may have more than one parish priest and more than one bishop; Jone I, 106; Hagen, 6; Schurr, 92, disagrees. It is also possible to be resident in a diocese without being resident in a parish; Jone, I, 105.

community, and thus we can speak of it only in a non-technical sense. Even less can the notion of the 'parish family' be found in canon law.[1]

But the very example of domicile makes it clear that canon law starts out from the sociological conditions of the inhabitants of a certain locality. Where these form a community, its structure will influence the canonically erected parish. But in this case the principle of this community is not canon law but the already existing social structure. This ability to build on natural conditions is part of the wisdom of Church law. Today's lack of genuine ecclesial communities is probably due not least to a failure to adapt to the available sociological structures which have altered considerably in the course of time.

On the other hand it is quite conceivable—in fact very desirable—that canon law should also give juridical expression to community structures,[2] for the *C.I.C.* does in fact recognize communities whose structure has a legal basis.

II—Canonical Communities

Precisely because canon law does not give the people of a parish community status, it is all the more striking that it recognizes organizations to which it consciously wants to give this. It cannot therefore be said that the *C.I.C.* withholds it from the parish simply because it does not know such a concept. For it legislates for the communities of religious orders and the associations of the faithful.

In the present context only the associations of the faithful are of direct interest. While the section dealing with the laity hardly mentions the parish at all[3] it deals generously, in fact almost exclusively, with the associations of the faithful. Canon law provides for legally constructed communities among the people, not within the framework of the parish, but in connexion with these free associations embracing certain groups within a parish or extending right across several parishes.

In contrast to the people of the parish as a whole, these

[1] von Nell-Breuning, 'Grenzen', 108, 110 f.; cf. Böhm, 347–53.
[2] Cf. Noser, 34. For the corresponding Protestant view see Böhm, 343 ff.
[3] Cc. 682–725. It is dealt with mostly in connexion with the parish priest.

associations can have juridical personality in canon law.[1] There is even mention of 'organic' corporations, the sodalities[2] in which there is statutorily regulated authority and elected heads and counsellors.[3] Laymen who join such organizations are praised.[4] Their object is the furtherance of the Christian life among their members (Third Orders), works of piety and charity (*piae uniones*), and the furtherance of public worship (fraternities).[5]

In canon law these associations are directly under the bishop[6] who also appoints their moderators and chaplains[7] and supervises their temporal possessions. The parish priest has no right to interfere even if an association is established in his parish.[8] The only limitation placed on the activity of associations by the parish is that they may not prejudice its cure of souls. Whether this is the case has to be decided by the bishop.[9]

Owing to their canonical status these lay associations are able to form real communities. Free choice and the large numbers of associations with a great variety of legally established forms and aims make it possible to create communities with common interests, which moreover may in certain cases also build on the class principle. Naturally the fact that these lay organizations are based on canon law does not mean that they will necessarily develop into genuine communities; nevertheless their legal structure—in contrast to the parish—makes this possible. In addition the principle of association offers far more opportunities to make use of already existing (profane) community-building factors than does the local principle of the parish.

According to sociologists a common goal, common interests and professions are far more effective in building up a community than a common territory. It might be expected that Church legislation could aim at strengthening weak communities, but in fact the opposite is the case. The already weak territorial principle of the parish is in no way supplemented by any legal measure designed to strengthen the community. But where, as in the lay associations, the relatively strong

[1] C. 687. [2] Cc. 693 §3, 707. [3] Cf. Jone, I, 602.
[4] C. 684. [5] C. 716.
[6] Except associations under exempt orders.
[7] Or the appropriate Superior, C. 698.
[8] C. 691 §1. [9] C. 716.

bonds of common interests already exist they are strengthened by legislation.

True, to the extent that they are incorporated in the parish, these associations are community-building factors within it, but they do not by themselves make the parish into a community.

It seems as if the parish (ministry) were meant to guarantee the absolute essentials for the salvation of the individual[1] while the associations were to foster whatever went beyond this;[2] life according to the gospel, in accordance with the evangelical counsels, is legislated for in the religious institutes (orders, etc.). While the community life of the religious institutes, and to a lesser degree that of the lay associations, is given a legal basis in the *C.I.C.*, this is not provided for the people of the parish, who are simply left to a ministry entrusted with the salvation of the individual.

Though canon law itself makes no statements about the parish as a community, it nevertheless contains all the elements necessary for the creation of one: the people, the clergy, the lay associations and the communities living according to the evangelical counsels. The more the representatives of authentic ecclesial community work as a leaven in a parish, the more this will itself become a genuine community.

[1] Cf. Cc. 216 §1, 682; von Nell-Breuning, 'Grenzen', 106, 111; Congar, 'Paoisse', 53 ff.

[2] C. 707; to foster a more perfect Christian life.

CHAPTER FOUR

The Parish as Community from the Standpoint of Theology

Introduction

BEFORE discussing the theological foundations of the parish it should be made clear in what sense the word parish is to be taken in this context. The legal meanings of parish ministry and territory must be excluded since they have no direct connexion with the community, which is what concerns us here. The formal legal term must be broadened to the comprehensive term towards which the law itself points. In fact most of those who theologize about the parish take it in the sense of the local body[1] which probably corresponds most nearly to general (non-canonical) usage. Here we would first accept this sense. It should, however, be remembered that for this reason our statements are limited to a particular kind of parish and are not necessarily true of the parish in general. Above all we must not forget the difference from the formal canonical term which does not necessarily embrace the locality.

Efforts to produce a theology of the parish have led to a variety of results and schools of thought. That called *Parochianism* which wanted to make the parish an institution of divine law may here be disregarded. In the course of history parochianist tendencies have appeared quite frequently.[2] Parochianism was condemned by Pius VI.[3]

Fr Grasso gives a good survey of the contemporary position

[1] K. Rahner, 'Pfarre', 35.

[2] The Sorbonnists in the thirteenth and fourteenth centuries; the Jansenists in the seventeeth and Josephinism in the eighteenth.

[3] In the Bull *Auctoritas fidei* of 28 August 1794. Cf. Denz. 1510 f.

and trends of the theology of the parish.[1] He distinguishes two groups: one represents the theological thesis and sees in the parish above all something supernatural, the mystery of worship and of the Church. This group is made up chiefly of liturgists who, according to Congar,[2] have written most on this subject.[3] The other group defends the canonist thesis; its adherents dismiss most of the statements of the theological thesis and regard the parish as a creation of purely human law. Grasso wrongly accuses Fr von Nell-Breuning, the chief proponent of the canonist thesis, of rejecting the mystical character of the parish.[4]

Grasso considers both theses correct in their basic concept, but incomplete.[5] But he rather gives the impression that the difference between them is due to two ways of looking at the same reality, and does not emphasize sufficiently that the two theses fundamentally represent two different realities, although these do in part, but only in part, coincide. Only if this is made clear can an understanding be reached. Briefly, one group considers the parish from the strictly canonical point of view, while the other understands it as the Church in so far as it appears as this community here and now. These are not just two ways of looking at one and the same reality; they are two different realities, as should become still more evident in the course of this discussion.[6]

[1] Grasso. Cf. also the *Materialsammlung* and the *status quaestionis* in Roth, 'Pfarrei'; ib., 13. A short summary of the development of the discussion on the theology of the parish in Wagner, 'Kult', 218 ff.; Monzel, *Parish Research in other countries. Germany*, in Nuesse and Harte 333–40: Fischer, 'Pfarrei zwischen gestern und morgen', in *Seelsorge,* 80–84. See also the Protestant appreciation in Böhm, 355–64. Floristan gives the most detailed and best genetic survey of the latest 'parish theology' but this unfortunately only came to our attention during printing. It is a pity, however, that he does not give a critical analysis of the various positions. See also Floristan, *La Paroquia*, 88–106.

[2] Congar, 'Paroisse', 48.

[3] Grasso, 300. On this Roth says, 'The basis of these thoughts on the parish is taken from the liturgy rather than from the direct deposit of revelation'. ('Pfarrei', 14.)

[4] Cf. p. 147 infra.

[5] Grasso, 312.

[6] Cf. K. Rahner, 'Pfarre', 34, where he makes an objective distinction between parish and local community. Thus, too, von Nell-Breuning wants to distinguish between parish and parish-body in 'Pfarrei als Zentrum', 462.

I—The Theological Theses

Grasso reproduces in outline the most important arguments of the defenders of the theological thesis. He rightly remarks that the theology of the parish is very closely linked with the development of ecclesiology and above all with the rediscovery of the dogmatic concept of the Church. They all regard the theology of the parish as a consequence of the theology of the Church.[1]

Complementing Grasso we shall distinguish five groups who proceed somewhat differently in their reasoning.

1. *The Parish as a Juridically Established Form of the Primitive Community*

First there are those who derive their theology of the parish directly from the original community in Jerusalem.[2] Spiazzi believes that the essential elements for a theological treatment of the parish are to be found in the Acts of the Apostles and other New Testament texts which describe Christian community life and especially the spirituality which inspired it.[3] He regards these communities as local churches within the universal Church.[4]

The parish is especially compared with the community of Jerusalem. Like this, it is the Church in miniature.[5] In this view the parish today is the juridically established form of the Christian community of which the cenacle was the type.[6]

The parallels between the cenacle and the modern parish are very closely drawn. In addition to the flourishing life and the full unity of belief under the influence of the Holy Spirit, he finds in the cenacle also the juridical structure and the spiritual content of a parish: a determined area (the city of

[1] Grasso, 299 f. This connexion is strongly emphasized and well worked out by Floristan.

[2] Jozefcyk, *A modern parish as modelled on the life of the Cenacle*, Fribourg, 1951; Spiazzi.

[3] Spiazzi, 26.

[4] Ib., 28.

[5] 'A "church in miniature"; or better, the cell of the Church, as the family is the cell of the State.' Ib., 31; cf. 33.

[6] 'As one can see, the parish, resulting from a sub-division of the diocese, comes to constitute the modern form—juridically established and organized—of that "Christian community" which has its type in the Cenacle.' Ib., 31 f.

Jerusalem), its own church (the upper room), its own pastor of souls (St Peter), a body of believers who constitute an organized group and a real community, the care for the salvation of souls, the necessary means (preaching and the sacraments), and the works of charity. Moreover, the mutual acquaintance of the Jerusalem Christians with each other is stressed as a particularly important factor.[1]

From these considerations, certain conclusions are drawn for the parish as a community:[2] mutual acquaintance between the parish priest and the faithful, which leads to the demand for small parishes.

The argument from the primitive community is found in most representatives of the dogmatic thesis.[3] 'The district of the bishop's church, originally identical with the diocese, is accepted as the original "parish". There are even some isolated statements alleging that, the parish in its original form being of divine law, certain sayings of the Fathers about the holy greatness, the priestly dignity and the royal significance of the episcopal office and of the primitive community, ought to be applied to the parish.'[4]

This thesis is open to certain criticisms. It undoubtedly disregards the difference between parish and diocese. For the Jerusalem community was quite clearly a bishop's community and the modern parish priest cannot simply be equated with St Peter in Jerusalem.[5] The territory of the Jerusalem church was not restricted to the city, the powers of the bishop of Jerusalem extended over other cities, especially those of St Peter. And there were very soon a number of meeting-places.

In this parallel the parish is simply equated with the local church, even though Peter was certainly not merely the head of a local church.

Further, it is clear from the whole argumentation that the term parish is used in a twofold sense. On the one hand it is taken to mean the modern, canonically defined parish to which belong also the lukewarm and non-practising Christians, on the other it is simply taken or claimed to mean the community of the faithful and the family in the religious and sociological

[1] Ib., 34 f. [2] Ib., 34–42; *parrochia comunitaria.*

[3] Among others, A. Wintersig, M. Schurr, J. Pinsk, Kienitz.

[4] Roth, 'Pfarrei', 14. [5] Spiazzi, 34.

sense. These two views of the parish cannot be put on the same plane.

The primitive community or cenacle can at best be the starting point for a theology of the diocese or of the Church itself. Only a second and quite explicit step could allow conclusions for the specific parish community.

The practical demand to create from or at least within the parish a living Christian community, is, indeed, extremely important, but cannot be established on these grounds.

2. *The Parish as the Church in Miniature*

Another thesis might be characterized as *Ecclesiola in Ecclesia*, the Church in miniature,[1] the parish in the Church like the family in the state, the cell of the Church.[2]

This thesis has certain points in common with the preceding one, where these expressions are also used. It also starts from the fact that the universal Church always appears concretely in a local church, and that these particular churches bear the essential characteristics of the universal Church: the parish is simply the universal Church in miniature.[3]

This thesis differs from the first less in its conclusions than in its argumentation. For it does not argue directly from the local and episcopal church of the New Testament to the parish, but starts from a consideration of the structure of the Church. In this view the organism of the Church is 'constructed concentrically. As a collapsible cup is made of separate rings which fit closely into one another and only form a drinking vessel when they are properly assembled: so it is also with the structure of holy Church which consists of four concentric communities constituting the visible organization of our Lord's Body. First there is the outermost ring, the unity of the all-embracing universal Church. The second ring is the episcopate: though founded by divine law its concrete form is defined by canon law. The third ring is the parish, also[4] created by the

[1] Thus Vagaggini, 197, and Fischer, *Seelsorge*, 82. Cf. Floristan op. cit., 90–92.

[2] Thus also Card. Montini (now Pope Paul VI) in a letter of 14 August 1953 to the Social Week in Canada, in *M-D*, 36 (1953), 10 f. Also Floristan, op. cit., 97–99, 105 f. Cf. Noppel, *Pfarrei*, 2 f., 68; Klostermann, 954.

[3] Spiazzi, 28–31; Roth, 'Pfarrei', 13; Grasso, 299–303. Floristan, op. cit., 105.

[4] 'Only' would be better.

law of the Church. The fourth ring, finally, is the divine institution of the family sanctified by the sacrament of matrimony and itself consisting of individual Christian personalities.'[1]

The bridal relationship to Christ as represented by bishop and parish priest is analysed against the background of this concentric structure. The relation of Christ to the universal Church is represented by the relationship of the bishop to his diocese and of the parish priest to his parish, on the principle that what is true of the whole is also true of the parts.[2] This line of thought is followed by Wintersig, Pinsk and Schurr.[3] It is a reaction against an external, purely sociological and organizational concept of the Church and against the idea of the diocese and the parish as merely administrative organizations. Hence the starting point is the supernatural reality of the Church, the mystery of the mystical Body of Christ, and the Church as the Bride of Christ.[4]

We fully agree with what the authors say about the *relationship of Christ with his Church*. It is in line with the general teaching of the Church, confirmed by Pius XII's encyclical *Mystici Corporis*.

Their views on the relation of the bishop to his diocese and indirectly to Christ and the Church, however, are more questionable. The starting point is the real, mystical and visible representation of the relation of Christ to his Church in that of the bishop to his diocese. The arguments collected from the liturgy are best reproduced in Pinsk: 'The Church receives her divine life from Christ her bridegroom, and Christ renders her fruitful and forms his life in her; and this relationship is the type of that between the bishop and his diocese. For this reason he is called the anointed, the Christ, the *summus sacerdos*, the highest priest. For his consecration, he has received the generative powers which Christ exercises in his bridal relations with his Church, and he thus has firstly become the spouse of his church, of his diocese. The Church, in the form of his diocese, is wedded to him, he receives the ring[5] because he is

[1] Schurr, 84.

[2] Pinsk, 340; Roth, 'Pfarrei', 13.

[3] Schurr, presumably basing himself on Pinsk without naming him, is the most detailed, and Pinsk the clearest, in developing this line.

[4] Pinsk, 399; Wintersig, 137.

[5] Cf. *STh.*, III, Suppl. q.40, a.7c.

married to his diocese: "Receive the ring, the symbol of faithfulness, so that adorned with inviolate faith you may preserve the bride of God, the holy Church incorrupted" (*Pontificale Romanum*). In early Christian times therefore, no bishop was ever consecrated unless a diocese awaited him. The bishop was also bound for life to his spouse and was not allowed to leave her. In accordance with this bridal relationship between the bishop and his diocese the latter was called *viduata* (widowed) after his death. A translation from one diocese to another was only possible with the greatest difficulties in Christian antiquity.

'Thus through the power of Christ the bishop gives his bride, the diocese, the being of Christ, the divine life. And as the religious reality of the universal Church is based on the facts that she is truly the bride as well as the body of Christ, and that Christ in his generating act becomes one with the Church in the spiritual Body of Christ, so also the bishop with his diocese. Because he gives the real life of Christ to the faithful of his diocese the bishop grows into a unity with them; as man and wife on the physical level, so he becomes *una caro* with them on the spiritual level. Hence the bishop and his diocese represent not only the bridal relationship between Christ and his Church, but the bishop and the faithful together are also a concrete form of the Body of Christ. That such is the view of the Church is proved among other things by the rite with which the bishop is received when he comes to a parish for a visitation or confirmation.'[1]

Pinsk rightly does not say that the diocese is a member of the mystical Body. He is content with the vaguer phrase 'the bishop and the faithful together are also a concrete form of the Body of Christ' which can probably still be interpreted correctly. The caution of the papal encyclical suggests that it is better not to describe the diocese as part of the mystical body.[2] Actually, the notion of 'representation' includes all the essentials, if it is fully and correctly understood. In Pinsk's discussions the 'sacramental' structure of representation has not been worked out with sufficient clarity. He sees Christ and the bishop, Church and diocese, too parallel to one another as separate entities. This seems to be the weakness of his argument.

The real difficulties of the argumentation appear when it is

[1] Pinsk, 341. [2] Cf. von Nell-Breuning, 'Grenzen', 106.

applied to the parish priest and the parish. It is asserted that the parish is an organic cell of the body of Christ reflecting and embracing the life of the whole even though not so perfectly as the diocese;[1] further, between parish priest and parish a similar supernatural relationship is supposed to exist as between a bishop and his diocese, and between Christ and his Church: 'As all life in the Church comes from the one Christ, so all truly religious life in the parish comes from the one parish priest.'[2]

The exponents of these views attempt to prove their assertions first from the historical evolution of the parish, secondly and above all from the functions reserved to the parish priests.

The historical proof points to the fact that the parish communities were modelled on the episcopal communities in that the parish priest's relationship to his parish came to be similar to that of the bishop to his diocese.[3] The mediaeval parish 'ban' is mentioned again and again, it being silently and unfoundedly presupposed that this was the ideal which should be re-established at all costs.[4]

The historical view is superficial and inexact. The dependence of the parish priest on the bishop is indeed mentioned,[5] but its theological consequences are not drawn out. No account is taken of the fact that an essential difference between bishop and parish priest consists precisely in this relationship. The

[1] Wintersig, 137.

[2] The extreme formulation of the case runs something like this: 'The parish is a small mystical body in which under the visible head, who is the parish priest appointed by the church to govern it, all the individual members stand and live and must function. In the parish, in fact, all Jesus is present, but on a smaller scale.' As proof of this eccentric notion the way in which Christ is present in the eucharist is invoked. 'In one consecrated particle there is the whole of Jesus, not only in the whole particle but in every part of it. A person who receives the smallest fraction of a consecrated host communicates as perfectly as one who receives a whole particle. In the same way in every parish there is the whole Jesus as there is in the totality of the universal Church.' F. Chiesa, *Parrocchia e parrocchiani*, Alba, 1936, 48 f. quoted by Grasso, 301. The parish is here regarded as a kind of sacrament. The difference between the eucharistic and the mystical Body of Christ is not perceived.

[3] Wintersig, 138.

[4] Cf. Pinsk, 343; Schurr, 96.

[5] Cf. Schurr, 87 f. Floristan works out the theological relationship bishop–parish very well and thus clearly detaches himself from the older concepts. Cf. *Parroquia*, 81–88.

parish priest is only an assistant, a representative of the bishop whose duty it is to establish unity between the parish and the bishop.

However, the main arguments are taken from the functions reserved to the parish priest in canon law and the liturgy. Wintersig believes that these functions indicate 'what the life of a parish is in essence'.[1] The parish priest's duty of applying the Mass to his parishioners is regarded as an expression of the bridal relationship between him and his parishioners.[2] But this view disregards the fact that any non-member of the parish can also attend the parish Mass and be absorbed into the unity of the Church.

One of the important functions reserved to the parish priest is the solemn consecration of the font. According to the rite of this consecration the font is the maternal womb of the Church, indeed of the actual parish community; through its consecration by the parish priest as Christ's representative, it is to be made symbolically fruitful, so that 'a heavenly offspring, conceived in holiness and re-born into a new creation, may come forth from the stainless womb of this divine font' (from the Preface). In the font thus made fertile the parish priest must solemnly baptize all children born to parents living in his parish. 'Thus he exercises his office of bridegroom and his fatherhood creatively in Christ while the community rejoices in becoming a mother.'[3]

This argument suppresses the fact that solemn baptism was formerly reserved to the bishop and that even today the holy oils necessary for it must be consecrated by him. The parish priest is only the agent of the bishop who alone is the 'father' of the community.[4]

This demolishes also another assertion, according to which in confirmation the spiritual fatherhood of the parish priest is assumed by the higher and more comprehensive fatherhood of the bishop, confirmation being the sacrament which integrates the parish into the diocese through the individual faithful.[5]

[1] Wintersig, 138.
[2] Cc. 306, 339, 466; Schurr, 95.
[3] Wintersig, 138 f.; cf. Schurr, 97.
[4] Cf. Siemer, 43–47; Grasso, 307–10.
[5] Wintersig, 139 f. Even Floristan loses himself occasionally here in untenable constructions; cf. op. cit., 161–65.

Incidentally, this assertion shows clearly the latent false premise that the parish and the fatherhood of the parish priest exist *natura prius* before the diocese and the fatherhood of the bishop; that the parish is a complete unit which has to be welded into the larger unit of the diocese.[1]

A little further on, however, this fatherhood is limited in a way based neither on the liturgy nor on canon law. 'Finally a parish reaches only so far as its parish priest, helped by no more than two or three assistant priests, is capable of integrating men and women into the supernatural community of the parish, of knowing each individual as a father knows his children (1 Thess. 2: 11) and of understanding and caring for them personally. Where this personal contact ends, there is the true boundary of the parish.'[2] From this remark it becomes clear that two different concepts of parish are being used, one canonical, the other emotional: this leads to a parish within the parish.

The weakness of this thesis seems to lie in this that the parish is conceived as independent, as a closed, concentric circle, as an *ecclesiola in Ecclesia*, and that as such it is in fact placed on the same plane as the diocese although it is a creation only of human and not of divine law. This is clear from the image above quoted of Schurr:[3] as one of the concentric rings, the parish is placed on the same footing as the Church, the diocese and marriage, all of which are of divine law.

Grasso's work is especially valuable because it shows that the parish and the parish priest are essentially open to the diocese and the bishop and are not self-contained. The parish is only a *pars dioecesis*: the bishop is from the dogmatic viewpoint the father of the *Pfarrkinder* (children of the parish = parishioners).[4]

L. Siemer had attempted to demonstrate this before.[5] He attacked the false basic principle on which the *ecclesiola* thesis is

[1] 'The *first* task of Church discipline is to maintain the parish unit, as it is organized by the ecclesiastical authorities. The faithful belong *first* to the small organism of the parish community and should be vitally conscious of belonging to a *complete* religious community of God.' Krieg, *Seelenführung*, 462.

[2] Schurr, 98 f.

[3] Cf. p. 124 above.

[4] Grasso, 305–10, 313 f.; Dupont, 'Überlegungen', 25, 28–31.

[5] Siemer, 34–37.

built, namely that what is true of a whole is also true of its parts. But what can be said of the Church as a whole 'cannot simply be said about its parts, neither about the diocese nor about the parish'.[1] 'A bishopric is by no means the mystically living Christ, and the parish even less so, for only in the Church as a whole does the full power of the Lord live on. Therefore the use of *ecclesiola* for the parish is not only misleading, it is false.'[2]

Moreover, in the mystical concept of the thesis of bishop and parish priest the two 'fatherhoods' come into conflict. The diocese must be divided into parishes. Now either the diocese becomes a mere organization of already existing parishes, an *ens rationis*, or each member of the faithful is twice begotten by different fathers since he belongs to both parish and diocese. The parish, too, would be twice wedded, once as a *pars dioecesis* to the bishop, and once as parish to the parish priest.[3] If the 'monogamous' marriage between the bishop and his diocese is emphasized so much, what need is there of the parish priest as another partner? The strict parallelism between Church, diocese and parish leads to the conclusion that there are three religious realities side by side, that is two parallel representations and concretizations of the Church in the diocese and in the parish respectively. Basically, the proponents of this thesis fail to understand the hierarchical and essentially sacramental structure of the Church. In addition they confuse priesthood and parish ministry.

The Church has a hierarchical structure in which the bishop is above the priest. Admittedly both bishop and priest represent Christ, each is a 'type of Christ' but not on the same level. St Thomas distinguishes two aspects of order: one is the direct relation to the eucharist (order as a sacrament), the other is its connexion with an ecclesiastical office (order as ministry).[4] If order is considered as a sacrament, there is no difference between priest and bishop, since the episcopal consecration is

[1] Siemer, 44.

[2] Ib., Grasso will not accept this expression as it could be misunderstood, Grasso, 304, 307. Fichter rejects it also, on sociological grounds, *Social Relations*, 143.

[3] The liturgy itself speaks against this. There is nothing in the ceremonies of installing a parish priest that could be compared with the presentation of the ring at the consecration of a bishop. Cf. Grasso, 310. Incidentally it is not the diocese but the Church as the Bride of Christ that is in question here.

[4] *S.T.*, III, Suppl. q 40, a.5c.

not a new sacrament.[1] The sacrament of order is related to the eucharist, the sacrament of unity which is to build up the Church. This includes a relation to the whole Church as such and not just to a certain diocese or parish. And this is true of order, of the priesthood as such, not only of the bishop or the priest.

If order is considered as an office, the episcopate is above the priesthood[2] and can to that extent be regarded as a new order since the episcopacy possesses higher powers concerning the mystical Body of Christ than the priesthood.[3] This is why bishop and priest do not represent Christ in the same way. The priest represents Christ in so far as Christ in his own person exercised a 'ministry'. The bishop represents him more perfectly in so far as Christ appointed other ministers and founded the Church. For this reason the bishop like Christ himself is called the Bridegroom of the Church.[4]

So it is precisely the parish relationship which subordinates the priest to the bishop and places him entirely at his service. Because the episcopate includes order both as sacrament and as office, Ignatius of Antioch's emphatic statement is true: the Church is where the bishop is. He is the principle of unity round whom priest and people must gather. The supernatural reality of the parish is therefore nothing independent, but the mystery of the Church is alive in the parish in so far as it is a part of the community assembled round the bishop.[5]

It is also incorrect to describe the parish as the 'basic cell'[6] of the Church, or to compare it with the family in the state. At most the parish could be said to be in the Church what towns or villages are in the state. But even this is no correct comparison, for the state is constituted and grows from below, whereas the parish derives from the diocese. Families and secular communities exist before the state, but the parish after the diocese.[7] Fr Grasso tries to explain the metaphor of the cell by means of

[1] Ib., a.5, ad 2.

[2] Ib., a.4. [3] Ib., a.5c.

[4] Ib., a.4, ad 3. On the discussion on the episcopacy cf. 'Was ist ein Bischof? Beiträge zur Kontroverse über den Episkopat', in *HK*, 12 (1958) 188–94; Dupont, 'Überlegungen'.

[5] Cf. Grasso, 305; J. Pascher, 'Die Hierarchie in sakramentaler Symbolik', in *Episcopus*, 278–95.

[6] Michonneau talks of a 'mother-cell' in *Paroisse*, 30 f.

[7] Cf. Grasso, 306 f.; Siemer, 37–43; Floristan, op. cit., 144.

the biological division of cells.[1] But this is not right either, for if the diocese is taken as the original cell which divides, the result would have to be other dioceses, which has indeed sometimes happened in Church history, particularly in the early centuries and in the east. Thus the parish cannot really be called a cell either of the diocese or of the Church.

3. *The Parish as a Supernatural–Natural Family Community*

The arguments of the *ecclesiola* theory are taken mainly from the liturgy and pay one-sided attention to the functions of priest and bishop while neglecting the people. Fr Congar sees in the liturgical view of the parish a genuine interest, but considers it nevertheless insufficient for a valid theology of the parish,[2] for parish and Church are in his view more than simply, or primarily, communities for worship and one should not restrict Christology to the priesthood and the *satisfactio Christi*.[3] Congar fears, and not without grounds, that such a narrow and in part false theoretical concept of the parish may lead to a wrong attitude in practice in parochial work.[4]

Congar tries to complete this one-sided view by looking at the parish in its relationship to the social structure of human life and of the Church and doing this in terms of the following pairs of concepts: family and *civitas*; community made from above and community made from below.[5]

In the first part Congar makes an analogy between family: *civitas* and parish : diocese. Since the duality of parish and diocese does not come from the nature of the Church, he sees the form of the parish as corresponding to a certain structure of human life, to a certain structure of the spiritual needs of the faithful.[6]

The term 'family' is used in the old, wider sense embracing the whole household including servants, etc., and meaning unity of table, hearth and housekeeping. The father is at the head of the 'family' but not sovereign. This community suffices

[1] 'A cell, yes, but in the biological sense, in the sense, that is, that it comes from the division and differentiation of the original cell, the diocese, and on that account is generated by the organism of which it is a part, and that only in that organism and in reference to it does it realize its true nature and the reason for its existence.' Grasso, 305; cf. 307.

[2] Congar, 'Paroisse', 49. [3] Ib., 62 f. [4] Ib., 50. [5] Ib., 50.

[6] Ib., 50 f.

to meet the elementary human needs, but the domain of full human development is the town (*civitas*). The *civitas* is where civilization first becomes possible, and as a major community the *civitas* is capable of making differentiations viable and bringing them into place in the whole. The *civitas* is self-sufficient.[1]

Before applying this analogy to the parish-diocese pair Congar makes one important comment: in everything which she is, the Church is simultaneously family and *civitas*. She is family not only at the parish level but at all levels right to the top: she is also *civitas* right down to the individual Christian who is also 'Church'. And though there is an analogy in the Church of the functions of the family and the *civitas*, this does not come from the nature of the Church but from the importation of human social structures into the Church. Hence the parish has a predominantly family structure and the diocese a predominantly *civitas* structure.[2]

The parish is the maternal womb whence the Christian as such is born and formed without any distinctive marks, as man as such is born in the womb of the family.[3] The parish is where the font is, the place where the Christian conscience is formed, where instruction is given and the normal sacramental life is lived. The powers of the parish priest are appropriate to this; he has a fatherly rather than a governing role to play: the hierarchical head of the parish is not the parish priest at all, it is the bishop.[4]

Whereas in the parish the Church exercises only her maternal role, in the diocese, through the bishop, she exercises her sovereign power of government. Bishop and diocese are responsible for everything which differentiates the individual Christian and gives him his place in the great tasks of the Church. The parish—like the family—belongs in the domain of private things (in the juridical sense) while the diocese—like the city—is in the public domain.[5] This is applicable

[1] Ib., 51. [2] Ib., 52 f.

[3] '. . . the parish engenders and forms men simply according to this new existence and this character as a member of the Second Adam, with no special qualifications. . . . The parish is the locale of the generation and basic training of the Christian.' Ib., 53.

[4] Ib.

[5] 'When Christian action, be it in the domain of the apostolate, or in

equally to apostolate and organizations. Thus Catholic action, although organized at the parish level, is logically a diocesan affair.[1]

Fr Congar then observes that this idea of the family and the parish which he took as starting point, today no longer exists at all in this form. The self-sufficient family household hardly exists any more. Today everything is so differentiated and specialized that the neighbourhood community no longer supplies our daily needs any more than the parish does.[2] It would, however, be wrong on this account to give up the parish in favour of a specialized pastorate based exclusively on *milieux*. To demand this of the parish would be to let the structure of the Church become too exclusively involved in the sociological structures of human life and in their changes.

The Church as the mystical Body of Christ, as the supernatural community, cannot be entirely wedded to the differences and structures of the natural sphere. The parish must retain a certain undifferentiated general validity which is above the human differences of class and sex and profession. The simple fact of finding oneself in communion with the Lord represents from the Christian standpoint a value in its own right. The communion is above the means: it is the realization of the Church herself.[3]

Although the mission of the parish is simply making a Christian *sine addito*, there remains the necessity to train him

---

that of organizations, or in that of thought or instruction, passes from the private order to public order—I use these words in their juridical sense—then one passes from the family plane to the city plane, from the parish to the diocese or to some organism at a comparable level.' Ib., 54.

[1] Congar, 'Paroisse'.

[2] Fichter, *Social Relations*, 126, 159, 189 f., 44 f.

[3] Congar, op. cit., 54 f. 'The Church . . . is the meeting place of the first Adam and the second Adam, where the first passes mystically, spiritually into the substance of the second. It exists not only by a communication of the common good of divine life realized in Jesus Christ its heavenly head, but also by human co-operation. It cannot entirely wed human differentiations and structures, because it is the second Adam. As a place in which Christian being is generated and formed, the parish must retain, in a sort of indifferentiation, a transcendence in relation to human differences whether between man and woman or Greek and barbarian, freeman or slave. The pure and simple gathering, together in communion with the Lord, represents from the Christian point of view a value in its own right. This is not just a *means*: it is the *realization* of the Church.' Op. cit., 55.

to his appropriate vocation, in and for the real situation in which he is, and for his real responsibility. But the priest who has the task of producing and training Christians as such, *sine addito*, cannot at the same time be leader and support of the Christians in their material situation, in the specific tasks and responsibilities they will from time to time receive.[1]

Congar does not conclude from this that the parish has outlived its usefulness, but he does draw the concrete recommendation that there must be separation between priestly tasks and the parish system. Specialization in the apostolate does not affect the parish but the priestly apostolate. This specialization in the apostolate is, however, only possible with teams of priests who must necessarily overstep parish boundaries.[2]

On the exposition of this first part the following comment is to be made. The theological statement[3] is strictly speaking limited to the fact that the Church must embody herself in quite definite human conditions already existing and that these conditions to a great extent, but not entirely, establish the structure of the Church. One may ask whether the analogy with family and *civitas* is suitable for making a theological statement about the parish which goes beyond this general observation. Congar himself admits that the Church's realization of both elements, family and *civitas*, is from above, and that in consequence one can only be dealing in terms of 'more or less'. This 'more or less' does not derive from the nature of the parish or the Church but from the contingent historical

[1] 'The priest whose mission it is to generate and train Christians *sine addito* cannot be a guide, a support and a spiritual inspiration to these Christians in terms of the actual conditions of their life and their actual responsibilities if his ministry is to remain common and universal. The loss of faith in a great many individuals and circles . . . is principally due to a lack of realism and effort on this point, personal Christianity cannot remain lively except in a specialized Christianity.' Ib., 56.

[2] 'If there is specialization, it will not be in the parishes but in the priestly ministry, the local spiritual organisms, adapted to the local residential unit, to the neighbourhood community, repeating itself to some extent in spiritual organisms chosen according to the occupation and the type of people. The organism appropriate to the Christian life of a population will remain in the parish; but it will also be, it seems, more and more the team of priests acting as the spiritual inspiration of the various sectors of life. I emphasize: the team of priests. This is of vital importance.' Ib., 56.

[3] And this is what Congar is dealing with: '. . . en vous proposant une sorte de théologie ou d'ecclésiologie de la paroisse', op. cit., 48.

decisions of the Church, which could have been different, and at other times were different, and from the Church's adaptation to the social structure of mankind.

Thus, for example, the maternal character of the diocese was originally much more pronounced: for a long time baptism was reserved to the bishop, as was preaching. The Christian *sine addito* was fashioned by the diocese. The fact that nowadays a cathedral does not have a baptismal font unless it is also a parish church may have organizational and historical grounds, but as a theological argument it contradicts the original practice of the Church. In any case the maternal womb of the Christian is neither the parish nor the diocese but the Church.

Precisely because the Church as a supernatural community cannot simply take over the structures of human society, the parallels between family and *civitas* cannot be carried through. Apart from that, in this comparison the part and significance of the Christian family as a genuine religious community is overlooked.

The Christian *sine addito* which the parish is supposed to form does not in reality exist, he is a mere abstraction. Man is not to start with a Christian *sine addito* and then later *cum addito*, but from the moment of his baptism he is in an entirely real and specific position with his own tasks and responsibilities. The simple Christian St Paul describes to the Galatians (3: 28) is described in terms of his becoming a member of the second Adam; he cannot be taken as the norm for the structure of a parish since the parish is a human institution and must therefore accept the structures of the first Adam[1] precisely in order to incorporate him in the second.

Of course, union with the Lord has value in itself and is above any means thereto, for in this union the Church is realized; but this union does not happen solely or in the first place in the parish. The parish is not this union, but as a human institution is a means to it.

The ideas put forward by Congar, valuable and interesting in themselves, contain no more than a very summary statement on the parish; that it does not stem from the nature of the Church, but is a structure freely chosen by the Church. Perhaps that is all one can really say. The extent to which the

[1] Cf. Congar, 'Paroisse', 50 f.

present-day structure of diocese and parish shows any analogy to *civitas* and family household is less a theological than a sociological question which will be discussed later. The practical consequences for parish pastoral work and for the super-parochial specialized apostolate derive in any case not from theological necessity but are matters of appreciating the situation concerning adaption to existing human conditions.

In the second part Congar shows how the Church is built up from above and below at the same time, because it is the place where the first and the second Adam meet and join.[1]

In so far as the Church is from above, it shows a hierarchical structure down to the parish—indeed, one should add, down to the family. The hierarchical element is a part of the essential structure of the Church.[2]

But the Church is not only hierarchical. It must also be built up from below, by the faithful, the *plebs sancta*, who make the Church. This building up from below is possible only when the parish is a community.[3] 'Less than any other religious reality can the parish be adequately defined outside this community value. Canonical provisions are certainly necessary, but a purely canonical concept of a parish as a territory within which the parish priest exercises certain rights and duties is obviously unrealistically inadequate. The parish is a community and what it retains of strength and vitality comes principally from conformity with a human reality, from the contact which it has with its basis of human life as such. Let us not underestimate the value of this trump we have in our hands . . . so that we can build up from below on a human soil, on a solid basis of reality and understanding. I said that the Church was not articulated from below like the body politic. It is something other than a union of parishes consisting for their part of individual believers. But there is a meaning and a point of view according to which the Church consists of parishes, a little like the way a nation consists of families.'[4]

The parish would thus be characterized as a community of prayer, of spiritual life, of mutual service and apostolic activity; a liturgical, fraternal, missionary community; what we find in the original community of Jerusalem. The active principle of religious activity would be not just the priest, but

[1] Ib., 57 ff. [2] Ib., 58. [3] Ib., 59. [4] Ib., 60.

the priest with the people and in the people, and the people with him.

Finally Congar observes that within a parish which seriously tries to apply the idea of community small groups and communities arise for various reasons. This entails the danger that in a large parish small 'parishes' may arise. Leaving aside the danger of splitting, they are the source of great vitality and correspond to the same logic: the awareness that the Church must be built up from below.[1] These groups constitute in the first place cells of the Church which have a priest with them or in charge of them.[2]

This second part, which particularly develops the build-up of the Church from below, quite unequivocally requires the parish to be a community. Certainly the formal canon law concept of the parish as territory or as office does not suit this demand; on the other hand neither the canonical term nor the comprehensive term excludes the people.

The concept of the parish put foward here by Congar corresponds to the comprehensive term 'parish' to the extent that it includes the people as a constituent element, but he goes beyond this term when he gives the people a community structure. In this the community structure does not result from the theology of the parish, but is demanded as a necessity for the Church's apostolate (the Church's, not the parish's!) but without any proof. It is to a certain extent presupposed by the build-up of the Church from below, from the existing human basis. Whether it actually exists or not is a matter for sociology to decide. Community is a form, in fact, which the parish does not automatically have but which people want to give it on pastoral grounds. One may often succeed in giving the parish

[1] 'I believe, to start with, that these small communities are real communities if they are inspired by a spirit which is really worthy of the name; if they live on the contribution and placing in common of the people themselves, they will be a support and a source of energy for a parish which wishes to form a real community. I am not alone in thinking this; this, it seems to me, is the conviction of the Abbé Michonneau. In addition it could be shown that in ancient times parishes attached men to themselves by groups. I think that these two things, the parish as a real community and these groups based on affinity of interest, correspond to the same profound logic; that of an awareness of the Church from below and the building up of the Church from below.' Congar, 'Paroisse' 61.

[2] Ib., 62.

this form which it does not naturally have, but in the case of most large parishes it will not come off: the community will probably not be a community of the parish as such, but—as Congar quite clearly brings out—of small groups and cells within the parish.

On the other side, Congar's concept of the parish is narrower than the canonical one in that he limits it to the one parish community or to the several groups out of which the parish is composed. The lukewarm, non-practising and those separated from the Church are logically excluded since they are just not part of the community. But if in this connexion the parish is seen as a family household which is built up simultaneously from above and from below, this expression can apply only to a restricted concept of the parish, namely only to those who, within the canonical parish, sociologically and religiously constitute this community.

The observation that precisely because the parish must be built up from below smaller communities exist within it leads to the result that in many cases the parish is not the last unit or cell or household but that it is rather made up of smaller 'cells' or 'families' or communities which taken together probably constitute not a community but a society. So the concept of the parish as a family household once more is put to the question.

There is no doubt that both the apostolate and the nature of the Church demand communities like the original community of Jerusalem. But these communities do not necessarily nor in fact coincide with the parish. The parish can be, but need not be, a fully human religious community.

Congar's exposition gives above all a very valuable basis for the starting point of pastoral theology. He shows very well that the forms of community in the Church are explainable not only by their supernatural nature but also in terms of the human structures which penetrate them. From his exposition it becomes clear that a theological view of the parish necessarily leads to a sociological view of its human basis. Therein lies perhaps the greatest value of this thesis.

4. *The Parish as a Local Actualization of the Church*

Karl Rahner probably has examined the question of the possibility and conditions of a theology of the parish more thoroughly than anyone else.[1] In his discussions he has always been at pains to preserve the theological viewpoint, differing in this from many other writers on this subject.

Rahner bases his whole argument on the theological relationship between the Church and the parish, which he sees in the local actualization (*Ereigniswerden*) of the Church. 'If there is to be . . . something like a theology of the parish as such, and if such a theology is not merely to be simulated by studying canon law or making statements about the parish which simply apply to the Church in general, then such a theology must obviously show a relationship between the Church and the parish. For it can at once be assumed that the parish as such can only be the subject of a truly theological statement (i.e. subject of a salvific (*heilsgeschichtlich*) statement by Christ or of a revealing Word of God) if the Church as a whole is involved, since clearly only the Church can primarily be the object of such a statement. If on the other hand something other than just general ecclesiology is to be meant by the title "Theology of the Parish", then the parish itself must be involved. Now these two conditions can only be reconciled if a theological relationship between the Church as a theological object and the parish be discovered, a relationship that expresses more than a mere canonical establishment of the parish by ecclesiastical authority, otherwise we should get no further than canon law.'[2] Thus the problem is made clear.

An adequate solution requires on the one hand an accurate statement of what the Church is theologically. On the other hand, the canonical meaning of the parish must be accurately defined and related to the Church. Now Rahner expresses the essence of the Church in such a way that its relationship to the local community already appears, for the Church as an event (*als Ereignis*) is necessarily local community.[3] He proves this

[1] Cf. Karl Rahner: 'Friedliche Erwägungen über das Pfarrprinzip'; 'Betrieb und Pfarrei'; and 'Zur Theologie der Pfarre'.

[2] Rahner, 'Pfarre', 28 f.

[3] Ib., 29. This line of thought occurs again in Rahner and Ratzinger. Cf. also op. cit., 24, note 8.

statement by showing that the Church is not only a 'perfect society' in the legal sense, but also that the Church as a visible society where it acts 'reaches a higher degree of actuality than it has through mere continuing existence'.[1] 'It becomes most fully an actual event perceptible in space and time when it becomes an event as the communion of saints, as a society.'[2] Because the Church continues the Incarnation, this happens in the sacramental perceptibility of the eucharist. Here the Church is most intensely event because the union of the faithful with Christ and with each other is most perceptibly realized both visibly and most intimately.[3]

Rahner continues: 'Despite its universal destiny and its relation to all men, the Church is essentially destined to be localized . . . ; the Church itself only becomes most wholly and intensively event in the local celebration of the eucharist.'[4]

According to Rahner the starting point for a theology of the parish is this local materialization of the Church and not a 'derivation of the parish from the monarchical head of the Church via episcopal territories to locally limited parish areas'.[5] According to him this is the reason why the New Testament also calls the individual churches *ἐκκλησίαι*.

In his theology of the parish Arnold starts from this double meaning of the term *ἐκκλησία* without, however, examining the reason for it. Supported by Wikenhauser and Albert Schweitzer, he comes to almost the same result as regards the relationship between the universal Church and local Christian communities.[6] Only the Pauline churches were quite definitely bishop's or house communities, whereas Rahner wants his statement to apply to any congregation gathered round the altar and not just to special cases.

The actualization of the Church in the local community does not really go beyond general ecclesiology. It does not say anything specific about the parish. Rahner is fully aware of this, hence he wishes to demonstrate in a second step that the parish 'is the primary realization of the Church as an event'.[7] This presupposes that the local community as previously discussed is not identical with the parish.[8] Accordingly the parish

[1] Ib. 30., [2] Ib., 31. [3] Ib., 32. [4] Ib. [5] Ib., 33. [6] Arnold, 'Pfarrei', 31.
[7] Rahner, 'Pfarre', 34; cf. Floristan, op. cit., 167 f., 192. [8] Ib.

is not as such the realization of the Church as an event, but only the primary realization among other, secondary ones.

Rahner gives as a reason that the parish is '*de facto* and *de jure* the primary, normal and original form of the local community, simply because it subsists on the local principle alone'.[1] This is not the case with other communities: 'Other communities which are kept together by bonds other than simply the common location do not show this other factor of their unity so clearly, because this reason for their unity is not identical with the local unity of the eucharist.'[2]

It should be noted that in this reasoning 'parish' is not taken in its formal canonical sense. Rahner points this out himself: 'In this statement, parish . . . is taken in a loose, simple, and not yet strictly canonical sense: a union of people who live together as neighbours in the same place.'[3] He cites the example of a succursal church which for this reason should be called a parish church although it is not so canonically.

Rahner's theological statement thus applies neither to the canonical concept of the parish as ministry or territory, nor to the canonical essence of the parish consisting of ministry and people. Nor does it apply to the purely personal parish since in that case the local principle is neither solely nor primarily effective. It applies to a union of men and women who live together in one place. It is not easy to see how this description differs from local communities in general. The statement is meant to draw a distinction between parish in this wide sense and a local community pure and simple, but the distinction does not seem very apparent.

It would seem that the second step, namely from the theology of the local community to the theology of the parish, is not successful, since the concept of the parish is itself taken in the looser sense of local community. The theological statement applies to the parish in so far as it may in certain cases also be identical with the local community. But it says nothing specific about the parish, since the diocese, for example, can also be a local community.

True, the statement is made more precise by saying that the parish is the primary, normal and original form of the local community. Grasso contests this. He shows that the localized

[1] Rahner, 'Pfarre', 34. [2] Ib., 35. [3] Ib.

manifestation of the Church was originally and primarily realized in the episcopal community. Instead of the parishes, episcopal communities, too, might have been multiplied, and this did indeed happen to some extent.[1] His suggestion, however, that the parish belongs only to Church law, does not really affect Rahner's concept since he uses 'parish' in the general sense of local community and not in the canonical sense.

Today the parish is probably the most frequent and normal, but not the primary or original form of the local community.

It seems that Rahner shares this view. He wrote recently: 'The local church does not come into being through an atomizing division of the territory of the universal Church, but through the concentration of the Church into its own actuality (*Ereignishaftigkeit*). This is probably why the very first local church was a bishop's church, and in this connexion it should be noted that the *presbyteroi* (parish and other priests) were originally not those needed for many local communities, but members of the local bishop's senate (which always had several members), so that the original (episcopal) local community contained only elements of divine origin: Christ's holy community of worship, with an apostle, or his successor, at the head.'[2] We shall have to come back to the significance of this pluralist senate later.

It may further be asked whether the parish really subsists on the local principle alone. Very often the local principle presupposes or at least embraces other principles, as for example family or economic ties. It must, however, be admitted that the 'parish' disregards these other principles and only considers the common locality.

Since the parish is not the primary local manifestation of the Church, its specific theology cannot be developed from here, and so this starting point is not very fruitful for the question of the parish as community. For a common locality may, but need not, weld the inhabitants into a community, as will be shown in more detail in the sociological part of this book.

However, since the locality has something to do with the

[1] Grasso, 311. Dupont also conceives the local church essentially as an episcopal church embracing the priest-churches belonging to it. Dupont, 16. He makes a distinction between 'larger' and 'smaller' local churches; op. cit., 33.

[2] Rahner and Ratzinger, 28.

nature of the eucharistic celebration, the question of the parish community may be approached from here. The local principle, which can hardly build up a community by itself is elevated by the eucharist, the sacrament of unity. It is thus impregnated with a supernatural reality which not only tends to community on the supernatural level but will also have an effect on the natural relationships among men. This subject will be treated in greater detail in the liturgical section.

5. *The Parish as Part of the Diocese*

Grasso proposes a method of his own. First he makes a clear distinction between the supernatural reality of the parish and a theology of the parish[1] and thereby dissociates himself from the *ecclesiola* theory which neglects this distinction. But he thus hopes particularly to overcome a purely juridical view of the parish.[2] Yet this distinction does not help him to avoid an ambiguous concept of the parish, which he uses in the course of the enquiry in different senses. To avoid all ambiguity one would have to distinguish accurately between the supernatural reality in the parish and the parish in the canonical sense, and further between a theology of this supernatural reality and a theology of the juridical parish.

Nevertheless, Grasso's distinction leads him to demand special conditions for a theology of the parish. He is not satisfied with a purely theological or primary relationship between the parish and the Church—here he differs from Rahner—but he requires a specific relationship belonging to the parish alone.[3] If this condition be accepted the road suggested by Rahner will not lead to the goal. Hence Grasso concludes that the parish can only be the subject of theology

[1] Grasso, 305. [2] Ib., 305, 310.

[3] 'For a true theology of the parish to be possible, it is necessary not only to show the existence of *some* relationship between the Church and the parish, but also that this relationship is proper to it. This means that a theology of the parish in a true sense is possible only if there exists between the Church and the parish a relationship at least in some way different from that between the Church and the diocese, or that between the Church and any other ecclesiastical institution. So a theology of the parish seems possible only if it succeeds in showing that the genesis of the parish from the diocese was in obedience not only to contingent and particular facts but also to an intrinsic necessity of Church activity which the diocese, the community assembled round a bishop, could not satisfy.' Op. cit., 305.

in so far as it is an 'extension' of the diocese.[1] In his article Grasso is principally concerned to show that the parish[2] is not a self-contained entity but open to both diocese and Church.[3] His argument is based on the statement that the parish is a '*pars dioecesis*'. 'Surely we ought to give its full significance to the definition of the *Codex* as "*pars dioecesis*" and regard the parish only as an extension of the diocese, and consequently as an essentially relative reality.'[4]

As a result of this ambiguous use of 'parish' Grasso arrives at equally ambiguous conclusions. '*Pars*' in the *Codex* means a geographically defined area. But it is impossible to argue from this geographical partition of the canonical parish territory to a supernatural 'participation' in the mystery of the Church.[5] We are dealing with two different meanings of *pars*, on two essentially different planes.

But might not '*pars*' be taken in a deeper, mystical sense so that the parish (in the large sense) would be 'part' of the diocese and the Church?[6] Is it at all permissible to speak in this mystical dimension of the parish as a 'part' of the Church? It has already been pointed out that the parish can hardly be regarded as a 'member' of the mystical Body. The 'part' of the individual communities in the universal Church can scarcely be theologically adequately expressed by '*pars*' or '*membrum*'.[7]

It belongs indeed to the deeper essence of the Church that it is actualized in certain geographically definable places. But this local actualization does not result in any locally conditioned mystical division of the Church. It is always the whole Church (the undivided Christ who, since his resurrection, has in his human nature a new relationship with time and also space) which celebrates the eucharistic sacrifice, which in baptism engenders a new member to eternal life, etc.[8] This is not to deny that the supernatural reality of the parish is related and

[1] Ib., 311.

[2] And this applies in fact to the parish in both the canonical sense and in the wider sense.

[3] Ib., 310. [4] Ib., 305. Cf. Arnold, 'Pfarrei', 34. [5] Cf. Grasso, 304.

[6] 'However one may understand its more intimate nature, the parish is a part of the diocese and, therefore, of the Church. As a part it cannot but participate, even if only in a relative way, in the qualities of the organism of which it is a part. . . .' Grasso, 304.

[7] 'Concentration' is the better expression. Cf. Rahner and Ratzinger.

[8] Cf. Chapter Three; and Dupont 'Überlegungen'.

open to the diocese and to the whole Church. But this relationship and this openness are of a different kind and cannot be expressed in the terms we have just rejected.

A fruitful theological introduction to the relation between priest-community and bishop-community seems to be offered by Rahner's remark that 'parish and other priests were originally not those needed for many local communities, but members of the local bishop's senate (which always had several members)'.[1] The local community is integrated into the worshipping community of the bishop through the priest, who belongs to the bishop's senate, has his powers from the bishop, and can celebrate the eucharist only in union with him.[2]

Thus it once more becomes plain how important it is to distinguish between the parish as an institution of canon law and the manifestation and presence of the supernatural reality of the Church. This supernatural reality is not tied to the canonical institution as such.

Yet the Church will always have to fashion its human institutions in such a way that the supernatural reality can develop in them as well as possible. They should help the working of grace, though they can do no more than that.

Since Grasso sees the possibility of a theology of the parish in the specific relationship of the parish, as a part, to the diocese and to the Church as a whole, it stands on rather uncertain ground. He is, indeed, partly aware of this and therefore wants the term 'parish' and the term 'theology' to be understood in a broad sense and thus ends up in vagueness.[3] The result would be something like this: there exists a theology of the Church, indeed a theology in the real sense. This theology allows statements about the 'parish' in a wider sense in so far as the supernatural reality of the Church is manifested in it, or, otherwise expressed, in so far as the Church becomes localized in the

[1] Rahner and Ratzinger, 28.

[2] Cf. Dupont, 28–35.

[3] 'From what we have said in the foregoing pages it can be concluded that if the parish is the object of theological reflexion, it is so not in itself but as a part of the diocese and ultimately of the Church. Therefore if one wants to talk about a theology of the parish, one can do so, provided the term is not given too technical a sense. There is not a theology of the parish as there is a theology of the episcopate, or of the sacraments, revealed truth. But there is a theology of the Church which throws its light on the parish.' Grasso, 313.

'parish'. But, this would in the end once more be a theology of local communities in general, without any specific reference to the institution of the parish.

6. *Conclusions*

From the foregoing considerations the following conclusions can be drawn: there is no specific theology of the parish as parish, but there is a theology of the parish in so far as it is a local community and the fullness of episcopal power is effective in it through the diocese.[1] The theological statements made in this context do not apply specifically nor primarily to the parish but to the episcopal community and hence to every local community in which the Church is actualized.

The parish has no supernatural reality from itself, but from Christ through the Church. The supernatural reality of the Church becomes certainly apparent in the parish but precisely *in* the parish, and not *as* the parish, but as the Church, just as the Church as Church appears in every ecclesial community: *sit tibi in tribus ecclesia.*

The parish as parish has its concrete form from the human law and practice of the Church. There is no theology of this concrete form of the parish as such except for the wholly general statement that the Church must become localized and to a large extent adopt human social structures. For the concrete form of the parish as such has no specific or essential relationship with the supernatural reality of the Church apart from the necessary localization and incarnational structure, neither of which necessitates just this particular form of parish.

II—The Canonical Thesis

Grasso opposes to the theological thesis the canonical thesis. He blames especially its main representative, Fr von Nell-Breuning, for overlooking the mystical aspect of the parish.

According to canon law the parish is no supernatural, mystical reality but represents a space within the diocese and as such is of purely human, not of divine law.[2] It is consequently a purely juridical institution and as such has neither the traits of a community nor of a family.[3] This thesis agrees largely

[1] For wherever the parish is, the diocese is also, effective and real, not just as a Platonic idea.

[2] *Iure stricte ecclesiastico*; von Nell-Breuning, 'Pfarrgemeinde', 257.

[3] Ib., 258 ff.

with what has been said in the chapter on canon law but with the difference that it regards the juridical form of the parish too one-sidedly from the territorial angle and pays too little attention to the two essential elements of ministry and people. On the other hand, it emphasizes against the family and *ecclesiola* concepts the fact that the parish consists not only of the well-disposed and the devout but also of the lukewarm and non-practising members. It does not exclude the possibility of there being communities, even super-parochial ones, within the parish. But 'the community building force in the parish is not of a juridical-organizational kind, but resides exclusively in the attitude of the loyal parishioners, and in the action resulting from their attitude'.[1] The fact that those who are estranged from the Church also belong to the parish gives it a missionary note.

The canonist thesis can be understood only if it is realized that its representatives do not use 'parish' in a loose, inaccurate way but in its formal juridical sense. By the term parish they do not mean an individual parish but the parish as described in the law books. Canonists and liturgists talk at cross-purposes, because they start from a different concept of the parish. Their notions differ in scope and content, hence the reality they indicate cannot be the same either. The supporters of the *ecclesiola* and family concepts especially apply the statements of the canonists to their own concept of the parish, which was not what the canonists intended.

The supporters of the canonical thesis have no intention of denying the supernatural reality *in* the parish, nor the mystical aspect of the parish (in the non-canonical sense). They too would subscribe without hesitation to the sentence *sit tibi in tribus ecclesia*, Church here taken in the mystical sense. But they deny with good reason, the mystical aspect of the parish *as* parish (in the strictly canonical sense) because this is an entirely human organization, an institution '*iure stricte ecclesiastico*'.[2] This they must do all the more if they regard the parish one-sidedly as merely a section of the diocesan territory. But apart from this one-sidedness, there will always be a difference between the parish as a canonical organization and the supernatural reality which comes into play within this organization.

The parish is certainly no sacrament, as opposed to the

[1] *Iure stricte ecclesiastico;* von Nell-Breuning, 'Pfarrgemeinde', 261. [2] Ib., 257.

Church which can quite properly be called the original sacrament (*Ursakrament*).[1] Because the Church is *Ursakrament* there is a supernatural, mystical reality behind every one of its visible manifestations that is not purely human, and this in the typically sacramental relationship between outward sign and inward grace. Because the parish is not a sacrament no supernatural reality is linked with its outward appearance.

By contrast the diocese shares in the sacramental character of the Church, not indeed because it, too, has a canonical form, but in so far as its visible nature as such is of divine law.[2] As Colson rightly remarks: '. . . the union of the faithful with the bishop is the visible image, the effective symbol, the "sacrament" of the invisible and vitalizing union of their souls with God in Jesus Christ through love.'[3]

It may be disappointing that the idea of community is so unsatisfactorily expressed in the canonical concept of the parish. This may perhaps be due to a clerical view of the Church. On the other hand, a theological consideration of the Church, the diocese and the parish will lead to the realization that canon law has theological reasons also for not forming the members of a parish into a juridical corporation. For this would give the parish an undue independence not in keeping with doctrinal considerations.

The strictly canonical concept of the parish points in various ways beyond itself: as territory the parish is only a part of the diocese, humbly taking its place in the supernatural structure of the Church. As parish ministry it has a share in the episcopal cure of souls. It is thus precisely the supernatural reality of the Church and the diocese which is taken into account by canon law and the proponents of the canonist thesis.

The bishop, not the parish priest, is in and after Christ the principle of the unity of the faithful. Around him the (mystical) community is formed. His priests and his faithful crowd visibly round him. He is the effective symbol of the union of the faithful

[1] Cf. Semmelroth, *Die Kirche als Ursakrament.* It is unfortunate and misleading at the least, if not actually wrong, to speak of 'parochial' and 'diocesan' sacraments as Floristan does: 'Confirmation, like Order, is a diocesan sacrament' (op. cit., 160). '*Strictly parochial* is the sacrament of love, the sacrament that constitutes a family' (op. cit., 163). 'Because baptism is parochial, so is matrimony as well' (op. cit., 164). All sacraments are *of the Church.*

[2] Cf. C. 329. [3] Colson, *Evêque*, 94.

with Christ. This union embraces that of the clergy and of the faithful with the Lord, as well as that between clergy and people. If the term *ecclesiola*, the Church in miniature, be used at all, it can at most refer to the bishop's church, the diocese[1] namely in so far as the bishop is the principle of unity, the direct representative of Christ founding and building up the Church, and in so far as the eucharist must be celebrated in union with him (or with the pope). The bishop's church, in its turn, remains open to the universal Church.[2]

III—Parish Community from the Theological Viewpoint

The statements about the parish which can be gained from theology remain very general. There are no specific statements applying exclusively to the parish; but they are related to various aspects of the Church which the parish shares with other church institutions. The most important ones affirm that the supernatural reality of the Church must incarnate itself in human structures; that the universal Church is essentially manifested in the local eucharist; that the parish as territory is a part of the bishop's powers; that the parish in the strictly canonical sense is a human institution, but that beyond and before it, the supernatural reality of the Church and the diocese is alive in it. The supernatural reality is indeed present and active in the parish but it is not the parish and must be clearly distinguished from it.

Finally the question of the parish community must once more be discussed. Do the theological statements about the parish allow us to speak of 'parish community'? One thing is certain: the supernatural reality which we find in the parish *ipso facto* includes as such also supernatural community. Christian faith and Christian life are unthinkable without community. But this supernatural community cannot of itself be characterized as parish community. For in this purely supernatural community the believing Christian in China is as near to me as my Catholic neighbour upstairs. Nevertheless, since this supernatural reality of the Church must flow into natural structures and as the Church is not only an invisible, mystical, but also a visible and incarnate community, there are

[1] Cf. Wagner, 'Kult', 218; Dupont, 29.

[2] Cf. 1 Cor. 1: 12 f.; 3: 21 f.; Pius XII's encyclical of 21 April 1957, *Fidei Donum*; Dupont, 18, 24, 41.

differences in the community links. But do these differences, themselves rooted in the human structure, lead to the creation of parish community? By themselves they lead only to communities whose boundaries are fixed by the prevailing human and sociological structures. In as far as the parish boundaries coincide with these natural boundaries, one could speak of parish community, if the human community is also filled and penetrated by the supernatural reality of the Church. Here again the connexion with sociology becomes clear.

On the other hand the actualization of the Church in the eucharist leads to the foundation of a community from the supernatural angle. The question whether this is a way to the parish community will be discussed in the next chapter. Suffice it to say here that so far as the eucharistic community is concerned, no distinction can be made at the parish Mass between parishioners and non-parishioners; and also that many parishioners remain away from worship in the parish church but nevertheless belong to the parish.

The theological examination leads on the one hand to the local community, which is not the same as the parish as such, and on the other to the community of the universal Church and to the community that forms round the bishop. True, this community is also to be found in the parish, but not primarily and it does not coincide with the parish community. Thus the theological approach leads no more to a specific parish community than canon law.

The canonical concept of the parish has a basis in theology. Canon law admits a 'parish' within the parish, that is a number of parishioners who feel themselves as a close community, as a 'family'. But the canonical concept of the parish demands also that this community should not isolate itself but become a missionary nucleus responsible for all the parishioners.[1]

Canon law and theology guard against any sectarianism, any unchristian clannishness or in-breeding in the parish. They see the parish as open, active, dynamic and missionary. Thus it bears the marks of the Catholic Church which should be alive in it.[2]

[1] '. . . in order to keep alive the parish priest's (but also the practising laymen's) conscious responsibility for "the others", I should recommend speaking more of the parish as established by the *C.I.C.* and less of the parish community and family.' Von Nell-Breuning, 'Pfarrei als Zentrum', 462.

[2] Cf. Grasso, 311 f.

CHAPTER FIVE

The Parish as Community from the Liturgical Point of View

THE question of the parish community demands careful consideration of the liturgy; for the liturgy is celebrated essentially in community and its place is the bishop's and the parish church. In the last chapter, the liturgy was discussed principally in connexion with the ministry. This chapter deals with the liturgy itself and with its relation to the people.

Once more the term 'parish' is used here in the inclusive sense, embracing both people and ministry, the worshipping community including all members of the parish, not only a limited circle. As it is impossible to consider all liturgical forms of worship the following discussion is restricted to the Mass as the essence of the liturgy.[1]

I—THE SPHERE OF THE LITURGY

In the liturgy the world of supernatural reality touches perhaps most clearly the world of visible signs. Hence it must first be ascertained which plane of the ecclesial community will be reached by liturgical statements, the purely supernatural, the human or the point at which the two meet.

In the encyclical *Mediator Dei* Pius XII said: 'The sacred liturgy, then, is the public worship which our redeemer, the head of the Church, offers to the heavenly Father and which the community of Christ's faithful pays to its founder, and through him to the eternal Father: briefly, it is the whole public worship paid by the mystical Body of Jesus Christ, head and members.'[2]

[1] Cf. Vagaggini, 115–31: 'Die Messe als Inbegriff der ganzen Liturgie.'

[2] *Mediator Dei*, 20. (Quotations and paragraph numbering are from the translation by Canon G. D. Smith in *Selected Letters and Addresses of Pius XII*, C.T.S., London, 1949.)

A. Stenzel examines[1] the question of the ecclesiastical *domain* to which the liturgy through its public character belongs. Starting from *Mediator Dei*, his analyses lead him to the following observations: the canonical definition of *cultus publicus* in C. 1256, is not in accordance with the active participation of the faithful demanded by *Mediator Dei*, for in the former it is a question of worship by deputies and not by the people.[2]

The criterion must therefore be sought at a deeper level, in fact on the plane of the mystical Body. Now Christ, the head of the mystical Body, is not only the subject of the liturgy but also of private prayer. Consequently a sphere must be found within the mystical Body in which Christ is only the subject of the liturgy.[3] Stenzel sees this in the visible hierarchical society as distinct from the mystical community of grace and yet interiorly related to it.[4] Here he uses the double concept of the Church worked out by Karl Rahner in analogy to the relationship between *sacramentum validum* (*tantum*) and *sacramentum fructuosum*: 'The Church as the bodily presence of Christ and his grace *together with* his grace,[5] and the Church in that it must be essentially distinguished from this grace and interior union with God and yet even so remains a valid Christian reality.'[6,7]

Stenzel thus summarizes his results: 'The distinctive place of the visible, hierarchical society is that dimension of the Church in which she is "at home" as a *Heilskollektiv*, or collective of salvation, where she acts *as* a community or her members *as* members. This is *publicitas* in an eminent sense and hence the liturgy must be assigned to this sphere. Every action within this sphere has a share in the laws proper to it.'[8] Thus the place of the liturgy, of the *cultus publicus*, is the hierarchical Church constituted by the *potestas ordinis* and *iurisdictionis*.[9] The structural principle of the Church as a worshipping community is not the

[1] Stenzel. [2] Ib., 178 f., 182. [3] Ib., 182. [4] Ib., 190–93.
[5] = *Sacramentum fructuosum.* [6] = *sacramentum validum tantum.*
[7] Cf. Karl Rahner, 'Gliedschaft in der Kirche nach der Lehre der Enzyklika Pius XII *Mystici Corporis Christi*', in *Schriften*, II, 80. This distinction is neglected by Martimort, for example. True, he also starts from the analogy of the Church to the *sacramentum* and the *res sacramenti*, but he blurs the boundaries in that he sees the liturgical assembly realized on both planes, the visible one of the *sacramentum* and the invisible mystical one of the *res sacramenti*. As a liturgical assembly it must remain on the plane of the *sacramentum*. Cf. Martimort, *Assemblée*, 8 f.
[8] Stenzel, 198. [9] Ib., 202.

character of baptism and the universal priesthood implicit in it, but the character of the consecrated hierarchical priesthood. 'Whenever Christ makes ministerial use of one of the members of the visible Church appointed to his service, there in principle is action of the Church. No intervention of collective consent is necessary, since the people of God is entirely "from above" (being and continuing, end and means).'[1]

Accordingly, the statements of the liturgy about community apply directly to this visible, hierarchical plane of the Church, and only indirectly also to the actual mystical community of grace with Christ. In other words, the statements of the liturgy apply in the first place to the visible ecclesiastical society and community which precedes all legislation and to which the liturgy belongs as a world of symbols[2] as the great sacramental of the original sacrament, the Church.[3] In so far as the liturgy is enlarged by positive precepts of the Church,[4] it reaches into the natural visibility of the ecclesial community, without however leaving the essentially liturgical sphere.[5]

Two facts will guide us in the following considerations: first, the subject of the liturgy is, after and with Christ, the *Church*; second the liturgy is always celebrated by the *members* of the Church, especially in the case of the parish Mass. From this dual point of view we shall discuss whether and if so to what extent the parish is a community on a liturgical basis.

II—The Church and the Liturgy

There is only one *liturgos*, Jesus Christ, and only one liturgy, the liturgy of Jesus Christ,[6] as quite clearly follows from the theology of the epistle to the Hebrews. The earthly liturgy of the Church is only a manifestation and epiphany of the heavenly liturgy of Christ. Indeed, Christ himself is the real active *liturgos* in all human liturgy,[7] he is 'the first performer of the Church's liturgy',[8] for Christ is priest for ever, indeed the only real priest in the Church.[9] The liturgy of Christ is the one

[1] Stenzel, 203 f.; cf. de Broglie, 455. [2] Cf. Vagaggini, Chap. II–IV.
[3] Stenzel, 200. [4] Cf. *Mediator Dei*, 53.
[5] Cf. Stenzel, 210–13: 'Die Liturgie kirchlicher Einsetzung.'
[6] Vagaggini, chap. VIII., 'Der eine Liturge und die eine Liturgie'.
[7] Ib., 176. [8] Jungmann, *Feier*, 25.
[9] In the New Testament and in writings up to nearly the end of the second century the words ἱερεύς and ἀρχιερεύς are used only for Christ—

liturgy of the one kingdom of God in its cosmic dimension and oneness, founded in Christ according to the epistle to the Colossians.[1]

From Christ, too, the people, the second subject of the liturgy, has its unity: 'It is the *plebs sancta*, ascended from the baptismal font, it is the new humanity, whose head is the new Adam.'[2] The unity of the liturgy signifies at the same time its universality, which embraces everything belonging to Christ.[3] The liturgy 'is the whole public worship paid by the mystical Body of Jesus Christ, both head and members'.[4]

The liturgy of the Church, of the members of Christ, is particularly important for our discussion. The Church itself celebrates the liturgy and offers the sacrifice of the Mass: this is the sacrifice of the Church, not only that of Christ.[5] This thought was definitely neglected by counter-reformation and post-tridentine theology, but becomes immediately apparent in the liturgy.[6] The central sacrificial prayer of the Mass speaks exclusively of the sacrifice offered by the Church; Christ the first subject of the liturgy remains entirely in the background.[7] 'Indeed we may say: the sacrifice of Christ appears in the liturgy of the holy Mass as it were enveloped in the sacrifice

---

later also for the Christian people: cf. Jungmann, *Feier*, 25 f. On the evolution of the term *sacerdos*, see M.Gy, 'Bemerkungen zu den Bezeichnungen des Priestertums in der christlichen Frühzeit', in Guyot, *Das apostolische Amt*, 92–109, particularly 99–109—*Sacerdos, sacerdotium*.

[1] Cf. Vagaggini, Chap. XI and XII, 'Die Liturgie und das Gesetz der kosmischen Einheit des Reiches Gottes'; E. Peterson, *Das Buch von den Engeln*, 52 ff., 81.

[2] Jungmann, *Feier*, 48.

[3] 'The liturgy is borne, not by individuals but by the totality of the faithful. Now this totality is not made up of those men who happen to be in church; it is not simply the assembled community. It reaches right beyond the space in question and embraces all the faithful of the whole world. It reaches out also beyond the barriers of time in that the community praying on earth knows itself to be one with those who have gone before and are in eternity. But the definition of the all-embracing character does not exhaust the liturgical concept of community. The 'I' of the liturgical action is not just the sum of all believing individuals; it is their totality, but to the extent that unity as such is something apart from the multitude of those constituting it, the *Church*.' Guardini, *Vom Geist der Liturgie*, 22. Cf. also Harnack, *Ausbreitung*, I, 204 f.

[4] *Mediator Dei*, 20.

[5] Cf. Denz., 938, 940; *Mediator Dei*, 91, 102; Jungmann, *Missarum*, I, 3.

[6] Jungmann, *Missarum*, I, 229 f.

[7] Ib., II, 270.

of the Church.'[1] This was a self-evident truth to the Fathers[2] and still very familiar to the great schoolmen.[3]

1. *The Holy People*

What does it mean that the Church offers a sacrifice? First of all the Church is seen as a whole, as a unity, and not as this or that individual community.[4] The *plebs sancta* is in the first place—even though not exclusively—the one holy, catholic and apostolic Church. True in the first prayer after the consecration the term is used to distinguish between clergy and laity, but in the vast majority of cases the word *populus* in the Roman liturgy refers to the Church, the people of God of the new covenant, not to a concrete or individual community.[5] This, by the way, is quite in keeping with the New Testament which, following the Old, refers to the Church as the people of the covenant, the people of God.[6]

In the same way the *familiae tuae* of the *Hanc Igitur* refers primarily to the whole Church and only secondarily to the congregation present. In the remaining liturgical texts, too, the family of God, i.e. the Church, is meant.[7] Augustine calls

[1] Jungmann, *The Eucharistic Prayer*, 15.

[2] 'According to his intention the mysterious daily representation of this event (the sacrifice of Christ on the Cross) should be the sacrifice of the Church, whose relation to him is that of body to Head, and who therefore learns to offer herself through him: *se ipsam per ipsum discit offerre*.' Augustine, *De Civ. Dei*, 10, 20; *P.L.*, XLI, 298.

[3] Cf. Jungmann, *Missarum*, I, 231 f. Duns Scotus and the theologians of the end of the Middle Ages emphasized the activity of the Church somewhat one-sidedly so that the role of Christ was obscured. Ib., I, 232. Cf. also Jungmann, *Messe*, 7–29, 'Das Opfer der Kirche'.

[4] Cf. de Broglie, 453. [5] Backes, 114. [6] Ib., 112 ff.

[7] '. . . whereas *familiae tuae* refers to those present *and* to the Church, as in the prayer which the Gregorian sacramentary assigns to vespers of the feast of SS. Peter and Paul.' Batiffol, *Leçons sur la Messe*, 250.

In the Roman *orationes de tempore* the new people of God designate themselves almost exclusively as *populus, plebs, gens* (and in a diminishing number reminiscences of *corpus*).' Stenzel, 188. In the following places there is mention of the people or the family of God the Father or of Christ: Ember Saturday of Advent; 5th collect; collects of the 1st, 2nd, 5th Sundays after Epiphany, collect of Septuagesima; *oratio super populum* of 1st Thursday and Friday in Lent; collect of 1st Sunday of Lent, *oratio super populum* of Monday, Tuesday and Thursday in Passion Week; 3rd collect of Ember Saturday in September; in the Proper of Saints for 18 January (2nd secret), 19 Jan. (collect), 25 Jan. (secret), Candlemas (collect before the procession), 4 Feb. (collect), 2 April (secret), 18 May (collect), 13 June (secret), 23 June (collect), 28 June (secret), 30 June (secret), 12 July (collect), 25 July

it '*redempta familia Domini Christi*'.[1]

Philologically, *familia* here means 'community of all the servants and spiritual blood relationship of all the children of God their Father'.[2] It is used in this universal sense in the canon of the Mass; Tertullian, too, uses it of the Church.[3] 'After Tertullian the word *familia* for the Christian people of God is not found again until Jerome and Augustine, except in the canon of the Mass.'[4] 'At the altar only the general community is still named: instead of the various donors and recipients the great Christian community consisting of clergy and people in which every special group is included: *Hanc igitur oblationem servitutis nostrae, sed et cunctae familiae tuae.* All offer sacrifice for all.'[5]

Further, the very constitution of the Church from above involves that the universal Church as a unity should always be envisaged first.[6] For the Church is essentially hierarchical. The Church is in action not because a community is gathered here, but because here is 'Church from above', the assembled people constitute a community and are themselves 'Church'. The liturgical and ecclesial character cannot be derived from below, from the social sphere.[7]

Besides, the liturgy is precisely where the individual does not act as an individual, where the individual congregation, too, does not act as such, but where both individual and congregation act as the Church. For this is precisely the condition for the very existence of liturgy. For this it is not enough that a number of Christians should do something in common; they must do it as Church. This is only possible in union with the hierarchy, the Church from above.

(collect and secret), 29 July (collect), 11 Aug. (secret), 9 Sept. (postc.), 15 Sept. (collect), 16 Sept. (secret), 27 Sept. (postc.), 9 Oct. (collect and secret), 26 Oct. (secret), 23 Nov. (secret). Cf. Backes, 114.

[1] *De Civ. Dei*, I, 35. Cf. Card. Lercaro, *La Santa Messa*, 16 ff.; cf. 32 ff., 42 ff.

[2] Rütten, 45. [3] Tertullian, *De patientia*, C. 2.

[4] Rütten, 45; cf. Schoenen, *Die Gottesfamilie*.

[5] Jungmann, *Missarum*, II, 225; cf. Lercaro, op. cit., 44.

[6] Cf. Stenzel, 182–89; 'Der Kult des Volkes Gottes.'

[7] 'That is to be rejected: a *publicus*-socialis, collectivus from below.' Stenzel, 181. 'Another confirmation would also be that *Mediator Dei* accepts practices that are eminently social and thus in fact public and yet leaves no doubt that no liturgical character can be derived from the social as such.' Ib.

'Hence the life and grace of Christ flowing from the head do not first seize the individual and then gather those favoured in this way into a community; on the contrary, the life of Christ first seizes the community and through and from the community is shared out to the individuals. Thus the Church as community takes precedence over individual Christians'[1], i.e. the whole Christ, head and members, exists before the individual members. In order rightly to understand the liturgy of the Church, one must always start from the whole Christ, from the unity of the liturgy. For in the liturgy the Church acts always as such, the individuals as its servants and members, as Church, family and people of God. 'That is why the divine efficacy of liturgical action far exceeds the power of the individual ministers or worshippers.'[2]

This ontological precedence of the Church as the people of God is closely connected with the hierarchical order. This order constitutes those embodied into Christ by baptism into a community of worship: 'The hierarchical priesthood constitutes a group of individuals into a community, into a Church. In Catholic teaching there is no Church without the hierarchical priesthood. The faithful constitute a community, a Church, only in so far as they are united to this priesthood. In Catholic thought the priest is not the delegate, not even primarily the representative of Christ, the head of the mystical Body. . . . The priest is also the representative of the people only because he is delegated by Christ. This is expressly taught by Pius XII in *Mediator Dei*: ". . . the priest acts in the name of the people precisely and only because he represents the person of our Lord Jesus Christ, considered as Head of all the members and offering himself for them; that the priest, therefore, approaches the altar as Christ's minister, lower than Christ, but higher than the people." '[3]

2. *Community and Church*

Two conclusions may be drawn from these facts. First: because the liturgy is always concerned with the Church as such in its entirety, the size and type of the congregation which celebrates it is unimportant in itself, always provided that the Church is involved through the ordained priesthood. According

[1] Hoffman, 499.
[2] Vagaggini, 188 f.
[3] Vagaggini, 183 f.; *Mediator Dei*, 88.

to tradition[1] and to the encyclical *Mediator Dei*[2] the sacrifice of the Church is offered in the same way in a pontifical Mass with a large number of assisting priests and people as in the private Mass of a priest without even a server.[3] 'Every time the priest re-enacts what the divine redeemer did at the last supper, the sacrifice is really accomplished; and this sacrifice, always and everywhere, necessarily and of its very nature has a public and social character. For he who offers it acts in the name both of Christ and of the faithful, of whom the divine redeemer is the head, and he offers it to God for the holy Catholic Church, and for the living and the dead.'[4]

The liturgical community of the Church, then, is very largely independent of particular sociological forms of community. The liturgical community and the sociological community are governed by essentially different laws.[5] To that extent the sociological community of a parish is completely accidental to the liturgical community of the Church. Or, conversely: the liturgy does not necessarily form a parish into a closed and distinctive community; on the contrary, in the liturgy all parish barriers merge into the one Church where there is neither this parish nor that, 'no more Jew or Gentile, no more slave and freeman, no more male and female', for 'you are all one person in Jesus Christ'.[6]

Above all, the liturgy does not create any closed local com-

[1] Cf. Jungmann, *Missarum*, I, 248–94.

[2] Nos. 98–102.

[3] Nevertheless a priest should not celebrate without a server. *Mediator Dei*, 102. Cf. C. 813.

[4] *Mediator Dei*, 101.

[5] '. . . the liturgical assembly transcends the laws of sociology and, far from coinciding with human societies anterior to it, tends, as it were, to destroy them.' Martimort, 'Assemblée', 19.

[6] Gal. 3: 28; cf. Col. 3: 11. This passage is cited (e.g. Michonneau, *Paroisse*, 44) as an argument for the parish which is in itself an image of the universality and unity of the Church in that it embraces all estates, sexes, ages and classes. But as soon as the parish sees itself as a complete unit—whereas it is only a part—it hurts the principle that it adduces and thus becomes the image of separation: 'I am for Paul, I am for Apollo, I am for Cephas, I am for Christ' (1 Cor. 1: 12). This principle of division, which is diametrically opposed to the spirit of the liturgy, was emphasized by the parish 'ban' in that non-members of a parish were by legal compulsion excluded from divine service, a part thus became absolute. It is incidentally significant that this forcible hold on the liturgy could only be maintained by severe Church punishments. Cf. Dom Beauduin, 'L'esprit paroissial', 80–90.

munity. Naturally the liturgy must be celebrated in a particular place and at a particular time, and the Church is actualized in the local community. But precisely because the Church is actualized, the local community is always absorbed into the all-embracing Church and the liturgical assembly is by its very nature raised above time and place.

One argument against this assertion seems indeed to be precisely the original form of the Mass where the bishop in the midst of the congregation and surrounded by his clergy celebrated the one sacrifice. This ideal form lived on in the consciousness of the western Church for a long time, and still remains in the east.[1] The sayings of St Ignatius of Antioch on the one eucharist with the one bishop at one altar are well known. However, this ideal form could only be realized in very definite conditions which depended not on the liturgy but on the concrete sociological structure of the Church. That is to say, a sociological structure of the Church can be imagined —and has in fact sometimes existed—which can symbolize the reality of the liturgy, i.e. the liturgical-ontological unity of God's people. This, however, is only an accidental coincidence of the liturgical with the limited sociological symbolism.

Sociological and pastoral exigencies soon made it necessary to increase the number of Masses in many places, without thereby prejudicing the liturgical unity of the Church. This happened with the Masses in the titular churches of Rome where another symbol—this time a liturgical one, the *Fermentum*—was used to express the idea of unity.[2] Leo the Great allowed several Masses to be celebrated on feast days precisely that all the faithful might participate in the one sacrifice.[3]

The existing ontological unity could no longer be symbolized

[1] Jungmann, *Missarum*, I, 248 f.

[2] Cf. Jungmann, op. cit., II, 379 ff.; and p. 47 above.

[3] 'Ut autem in omnibus observantia nostra concordet, illud quoque volumus custodiri, ut cum solemnior quaeque festivitas conventum populi numerosioris indixerit et ea fidelium multitudo convenerit, quam recipere basilica simul non possit, sacrificii oblatio indubitanter iteretur, ne his tantum admissis ad hanc devotionem qui primi advenerint, videantur hi qui post modum confluxerint non recepti, cum plenum pietatis atque rationis sit, ut quoties basilicam in qua agitur praesentia novae plebis impleverit, toties sacrificium subsequens offeratur. Necesse est autem quaedam pars populi sua devotione privetur, si unius tantum missae more servato sacrificium offerre, non possint nisi qui prima diei parte convenerint.' Leo the Great, Ep. 9. 2, PL, LIV, 626 f.

liturgically or sociologically in the same way owing to the increase in the number of the faithful and the dioceses, and the extension of the parish system. Nevertheless, unity with the bishop is preserved in every 'parish' Mass and in every 'private' Mass[1] if not on the sociological, at least on the sacramental and liturgical planes. For the sacrificial community is only constituted on the basis of the hierarchical priesthood of the bishop.[2]

The liturgical is essentially prior to the sociological plane. Hence it is false to assume, for example, that by baptism a Christian becomes first a member of a certain parish, and through the parish a member of the diocese and the universal Church.[3] Exactly the opposite is the case: by baptism, which as an *opus operatum* is an act of the Church through which Christ acts, a person is first incorporated in the mystical Body of Christ and thereby also absorbed into the visible structure of the Church. A man does not become a member of the Church by becoming a member of a parish, but because he becomes a member of the Church he is assigned to a parish, according to the present legal system. For the liturgical community is not the manifestation of the local community. It is the assembly of a local congregation, and as a liturgical assembly it is a manifestation of the Church as such and not simply of a local community.

Although the liturgy must always be celebrated in a particular place and time, nevertheless this factor does not enter into its constitution so that it would become an element of the Church as a hierarchical society. Consequently no community

[1] This is in essence also a public Mass, and one should avoid the expression 'private Mass'. Cf. Martimort and Piccard, 25 f.

[2] From early Christian days there has been a presbyter Mass, especially where several churches with their own clergy existed within the territory of a bishop. 'Although this second basic type even then must have been much commoner than, say, the great station Masses, we have hardly any detailed knowledge of it.' Jungmann, *Missarum*, I, 263. 'Mass in a private house or in a domestic oratory, was fairly common till the Council of Trent, which restricted it considerably on account of abuses that had crept in.' Jungmann, *Gottesdienst*, 113.

[3] This view seems to come through even with Martimort. 'For the believer does not form an anonymous part of a vague universal Church: if he attached himself to the *catholica*, that Church which is everywhere on earth, it is by means of a local Church, or at least of a part of a local Church, since the episcopal church was divided into a number of secondary assemblies, parishes or titles.' Martimort, 'Assemblée', 9.

that depends on space and time can be established on the liturgy. In other words, the community of the territorial parish cannot be constituted on the basis of the liturgy.

3. *The Congregation and the Hierarchical Priesthood*

The true structural elements of the liturgy are not on the plane of time and space, they are functionally determined. As characters of baptism (completed by confirmation) and consecration they enter into the constitution of the Church as a hierarchical society. This leads to the second conclusion: the liturgy necessitates a close co-operation between the priesthood of baptism and the priesthood of ordination. Precisely because the Church is the bearer of the liturgy this cannot be restricted to the clergy alone,[1] but demands the active participation of all the faithful: for the liturgy represents the worship of the whole mystical Body, head and members.[2] Nevertheless, the priesthood of baptism is essentially directed to and supplemented by the consecrated priesthood.

Besides Christ, the faithful and not only the priest are subjects of the liturgy in the second place: 'The second partial subject of the liturgy is the faithful in their entirety. The liturgy is the divine service of the Church; the Church is the community of the faithful; hence the community of the faithful is the subject of the liturgy. That really goes without saying.'[3] In *Mediator Dei* this truth is frequently emphasized.[4] Jungmann shows very well how originally the term *ἱερεύς* was used in the first place of Christ and in the second place of the Christian people, but not of the ordained priesthood. This term was applied to the head of the people only at the end of the second century because he exercised special functions among them. 'In the New Testament, however, this step had not yet been taken, but the faithful themselves were called priests.'[5]

The participation of the faithful in the liturgy is thus nothing accidental; indeed it is more essential than in any other great

[1] Cf. Arnold, 'Vorgeschichte und Einfluss der Trienter Messopferdekretes auf die Behandlung des eucharistischen Geheimnisses in der Glaubensverkündigung der Neuzeit', 158–61. 'Verengung des Subjekts der Messfeier.' Cf. Jungmann, *Liturgisches Erbe*, 89 f., 90 ff.

[2] Cf. *Mediator Dei*, 20. [3] Jungmann, *Feier*, 28 f.

[4] *Mediator Dei*, 84 f., 95–99.

[5] Jungmann, op. cit., 30. Cf. also p. 154, note 9.

religion with the exception of Judaism.[1] The plan of the house of God and the whole divine service are designed for the congregation as the principal executor of the liturgy[2] '. . . in the central acts of the liturgy, in the actual *cultus latriae*, the whole congregation always appears as the subject; so much so that in the form of words practically no other partial subject appears. Prominence is nearly always given to the congregation: we pray, we thank, we offer.'[3] Although this truth may have been neglected for a long time, today it is once more coming to life and has already penetrated the consciousness of the faithful to a considerable extent.[4]

But, as has been said, the congregation of the faithful is only constituted by the ordained priesthood.[5] In the central sacrificial action of the consecration only the ordained priest is active. 'The unbloody immolation by which, after the words of consecration have been pronounced, Christ is rendered present on the altar, is performed by the priest alone, and by the priest in so far as he acts in the name of Christ.'[6] 'The priest acts in the name of the people precisely and only because he represents the person of our Lord Jesus Christ, considered as Head of all the members and offering himself for them.'[7] Even though the faithful do not consecrate themselves, they offer their sacrifice through the priest, for the priest represents them at the altar. 'He consecrates the bread and the chalice in order to present the sacrifice of Calvary to God as their sacrifice. As in the whole celebration of the Mass he speaks and acts not simply in his own name but in the name of the Church, so this does not cease at the moment of the consecration because he then receives the commission of Christ; for precisely the Church bids him accept this commission so that as bride she may enter anew into his sacrifice.'[8] The consecration is the work of the Church, because it is the work of the priest.[9]

Hence the eucharist as the sacrifice of the Church presupposes a profound unity between priest and people. The Canon recalls the twofold division of priest and people at

[1] Ib., 33. [2] Ib., 34–38. [3] Ib., 35 f.

[4] Jungmann, *Missarum*, I, 215–324: 'Wesen und Gestaltung der Messe in der kirchlichen Gemeinschaft'.

[5] Vagaggini, 183; cf. Stenzel, 202 f.

[6] *Mediator Dei*, 96. [7] Ib., 88. [8] Jungmann, *Missarum*, I, 243.

[9] de Broglie, 455.

least four times; but it does not choose the word *ordo* for the priest, a term 'that would remind every Roman citizen of the *ordo senatorius* and the *ordo equester*' in contrast to the common *plebs*, but it uses the humble *servitus nostra*, *nos servi tui*. By contrast the people is called *familia* and *plebs sancta*.[1]

Priest and people together form one community, one Church. St John Chrysostom regards the assembled congregation as a unity because all eat of the same sacrifice: 'for all are equally admitted to the same food, not as in the Old Testament where the subordinates eat different food and it was not permitted to the people to partake of the food of the priests. Now things are quite different, for all are offered one body and one chalice.'[2]

Chrysostom sees this unity also expressed in the great prayer of thanksgiving. 'The prayer, too, through which the eucharist is offered to God, is common to both, for he (the priest) does not celebrate the thanksgiving alone, but the whole people celebrates it with him; for the eucharistic prayer does not begin until they join their voices to his raised voice so that it may 'be done worthily and rightly. . . .'[3] 'He (Chrysostom) therefore also warns the presidents against proud isolation: their rule is an *imperium spirituale* in which a man takes the higher place in the name of the others, not in order to receive honours but "because in caring for your salvation he accepts the greater care. For all are dwellers in the Church as in one house; thus all should care as for one body, just as there is one baptism, one table, one font, one creation, one Father." '[4]

St Augustine sees this unity of all in Christ realized even

[1] Rütten comments on the profound difference between the Greek mentality which chooses for the liturgical functions the words *κλῆρος* or *πρεσβύτεροι* and *λαός*, where *λαός* does not imply any contrast of status, and the Latin terms *ordo* and *plebs*. '. . . the first witness of Christian Latin also wrote the following sentence: "*Differentiam inter ordinem et plebem constituit ecclesiae auctoritas*" (Tertullian, *De exhortatione castitatis*, C. 7). So he calls priest and people *ordo* and *plebs*, and at once it is clear how the Roman-Latin Christian thought. *Ordines* in Rome were the two classes of senators and knights; the rest were *plebs*.' Rütten, 44. Cf. Plöchl, I, 60 f.; Häring, *Macht*, 113 f.; M. Gy, 'Bemerkungen zu den Bezeichnungen des Priestertums in der christlichen Frühzeit', in Guyot, *Das apostolische Amt*, 92–109, especially 92–98: I. *Ordo, ordinare, ordinatio*.

[2] Chrysostom, *Hom.* 18 *in* 2 *Cor.* (PG., LXI, 527).

[3] Ibid.

[4] Gülden, 181; previous quotation from Chrysostom also quoted, ib., p. 180 f.

more profoundly in the sacrament of the eucharist: 'For we too have become his own Body and by his mercy, we are what we receive: as the apostle says, "The one bread makes us one body". (1 Cor. 10: 17.)'[1] 'If then you are the Body of Christ, it is your mystery that is laid on the Lord's table. To what you are, you answer Amen and in so answering you seal it.'[2] '*You* are there on the table, you are in the chalice.'[3]

The whole congregation then, consisting of priest and faithful, offers the Church's sacrifice. 'Liturgy means the worship of God in the community by the community and for the community.'[4] This community ought not to be seen in the people alone. Nor should priest and people be played off against each other in the liturgy, as if the role of the priest consisted in representing Christ while the people were a sort of sacramental sign of the presence of the whole Church. It has already been pointed out that the faithful are constituted as a community through the hierarchical priesthood and that they can consequently represent the Church in the liturgy. And by representing Christ, the priest also acts in the place of the people.[5] Through baptism the priest belongs to the people; the baptismal character is not destroyed by the priestly character. The priest is taken from among the people and appointed to serve God on behalf of the people.[6] Thus the community can represent the Church in the liturgy only in unity with the priest—and not as an opposite pole to him—whereas the priest can represent both the congregation and the Church without any other representative of the community.[7]

Thus we arrive again at the same conclusion as before, namely that the liturgical unity of the congregation is not locally circumscribed but consists in the unity of any group of baptized persons with the hierarchical priesthood—that is ultimately with the bishop (or the pope).

[1] Augustine, *Sermo* 227; PL, XXXVIII, 1099 ff.
[2] Ib., 12466 ff.
[3] Ib., *Sermo* 229; quoted by Hofmann, 504.
[4] Häring, 'Gemeinschaftstiftende Kraft', 206.
[5] *Mediator Dei*, 88.
[6] Cf. Heb. 5: 1–3.
[7] Cf. *Mediator Dei*, 102.

III—Liturgy and Congregation

1. *The Sacrifice of the Congregation*

Though the universal and ecclesial aspect of the liturgy is highly important it is nevertheless also a fact that the liturgy is always celebrated by a concrete community in an exactly defined space and at a certain time.[1]

Hence it is a necessary prerequisite for the sacrifice of the Church that the members of this certain, fixed assembly should take part in Christ's sacrifice, and actively offer it with him.[2] This happens especially and essentially through a personal spiritual act. It presupposes communion with the mind of Christ: 'Yours is to be the same mind which Christ Jesus showed' (Phil. 2: 5).[3] The surrender of self must spring from this.[4] The self-immolation of the Church is 'the real end which the eucharistic mystery should serve'.[5] 'In this context the term Church includes not only the whole Church in general and the priest representing her at the altar but just as much the gathering of the faithful which assembles round the priest at each celebration of the Mass.'[6]

In his sermons Leo the Great speaks frequently of the sacrifice of Christian life which the faithful offer in union with Christ. Their whole life, which is absorbed into Christ through baptism, should be a sacrifice. 'Whoever receives the Body and Blood of Christ, the victim of redemption, acknowledges thereby that he wishes to participate in the saving act of the passion of our Lord, in the sacrifice of the cross, in the death of Christ and through his dying to gain a share in his life. Thus he and all his actions will be offered to God.' The sacrifice of the eucharist and the daily sacrifice of the faithful in their Christian life are *one* sacrifice. Leo can speak of the ascetic efforts of Christians in terms of sacrifice only because the faithful themselves have become both sacrifice and priest through their integration and transformation into Christ.[7] This sacrifice of the faithful is an important bond uniting the Church's sacrifice with real people in real life and absorbing them into itself.

[1] Cf. pp. 140 ff. above. For the relationship between individual communities and the Church as a whole, cf. Harnack, *Ausbreitung*, I, 200–20.

[2] Cf. *Mediator Dei*, 84. [3] Ib., 84. [4] Ib., 103.

[5] Jungmann, *Missarum*, I, 241. [6] Ib., 241 f.

[7] Eizenhöfer, 'Das Opfer der Gläubigen in den Sermonen Leos des Grossen', 106; cf. Jungmann, *Missarum*, I, 245.

In the Mass, however, the faithful offer not only the sacrifice of their own lives but also the sacrifice of Christ himself. This they do in two ways, as explained by *Mediator Dei*: 'first because they offer the sacrifice through the priest, and secondly because, in a certain sense, they offer it with him. And because they have this part in the sacrifice, the people's offering also pertains to liturgical worship.'[1]

The participation of the congregation in the sacrifice must of course be expressed in the form of the liturgy, by their joining in the prayers and singing, by their verbal confirmation of what the priest says and does in their name, especially through the presentation of the sacrificial gifts, the kiss of peace and their share in the sacrificial meal.[2]

2. *Community of the Congregation*

'A basic condition for significant forms of communal participation to emerge in the Mass was the existence of a community welded together by a common faith and love.'[3] This was originally achieved by excluding catechumens, public penitents and public sinners from the actual sacrifice. Today the boundary between Church and world is not so clear-cut. The exclusion of members of other parishes from parish services by the medieval parish 'ban' had quite different reasons and physically excluded from a community those who belonged to it spiritually.

It is interesting to note that in the course of history the congregation was on the one hand more and more circumscribed locally (parish 'ban') in order to preserve its unity, and that on the other the unity between clergy and people, based on the principles of the liturgy itself, was diminishing. This is evident from the steady decline of those liturgical forms that indicate the participation of the people, even to the opinion that the people's joining in the responses at a *missa lecta* was a presumption and contrary to C. 818. Something similar might perhaps be said of the so-called 'parish Mass' at which prac-

[1] *Mediator Dei*, 96.

[2] Cf. Jungmann, *Missarum*, I, 294–308: 'Formen der Teilnahme des Volkes'; Nickl, *Der Anteil des Volkes an der Messliturgie im Frankenreiche von Chlodwig bis auf Karl den Grossen*; Gülden; Martimort.

[3] Jungmann, op. cit., I, 295.

tically no one receives holy communion and everyone is purely passive; where, in fact, the effect attained is precisely the contrary of the parish congregation service originally aimed at.

Undoubtedly the fact that the language of the Mass is no longer understood by the people must bear a large share of the responsibility for the separation between clergy and people in the liturgy.[1] The one language throughout the world—at least in the Roman rite—is probably more a symbol of the uniformity of the Church than its unity, for unity presupposes diversity. At the same time it expresses unmistakably the separation between clergy and people.[2] And there again the language does not take the difference between clergy and people into account: uniformity makes unity more difficult.

It may be worth mentioning in this connexion that St John Chrysostom saw a sign of the inner strength and unity of the Church precisely in its multiplicity of languages. With great pleasure he allowed the Goths in Constantinople to celebrate the liturgy in their own language. On this occasion he himself preached a sermon, which he had translated and in which he said: 'I wish there were Greeks present today so that they could hear the words and learn how great is the strength of the Crucified, how strong the power of the cross, how sublime the majesty of the Church, how sure the faith, how shameful error and how ridiculous the demons. For the teachings of the philosophers are refuted by people of their own language, but our teachings have great weight even among foreigners. The views of the philosophers are more easily destroyed than spiders' webs; our belief is more firmly wrought than iron. Where are the teachings of Plato, of Pythagoras or the Athenaeans? Extinguished! Where is the sermon of the fisherman and tentmaker? Not only in Judaea does it shine forth but also in foreign tongues, more brilliant than the sun. So you people have heard it—Scythians, Thracians, Sarmatians, Moors and Indians, and the inhabitants of the ends of the earth meditate upon holy writ which has been translated into their language. . . .'[3]

[1] Cf. Häring, 'Gemeinschaftstiftende Kraft', 208.

[2] Cf. Häring, *Macht*, 114 f.

[3] PG, LXIII, 499 ff.; quoted by Gülden, 183 f. In another passage he says: 'If you pray in the language of foreigners without knowing what you are saying and being unable to translate, then no layman can answer

The concrete liturgical assembly, however, must also live its sacrifice, continuing the liturgy in daily life, especially in brotherly love.[1] Above all this brotherly love, which it demands, makes it clear that the liturgy breaks down all bounds and restrictions. The love, to which the kiss of peace testifies, cannot simply be restricted to this particular assembly, but must include the wide perspectives of the kingdom of God and its tasks.[2]

3. *Sacrificial Assembly and Parish Community*

Thus the actual liturgical assembly has an extremely important role to play and it must now be asked how this affects the parish community. It goes without saying that the liturgy must have a central place in the life of the parish. 'The liturgy is not only indispensable for the cure of souls, it is its centre and summary, for given the requisite disposition on the part of the subject, the liturgical action provides the closest contact between Christ and the people on account of the *opus operatum* and the *opus operantis ecclesiae.* Hence the liturgy may not only be regarded as a means and a way, but as the goal and starting point of non-liturgical activities. The cure of souls fulfills its vocation not *through* the liturgy, but *in* the liturgy.'[3] The liturgy also preserves especially the communal nature of the cure of souls. In this sense it can be said: 'The soul of the parish is the celebration of the liturgy.'[4]

It must once more be asked, if the concrete liturgical assembly actually establishes a parish community. Only in the rarest of cases, of course, will the liturgical assembly and the parish community coincide, if only for the very simple reason that not all members of the parish will be practising (even in Catholic areas). Further, for the larger parishes there is the question of space: where the church is not large enough for

---

Amen.' 35*th Hom. on* 1 *Cor.*, PG, LXI, 300. Cf. 'Zur Diskussion über *Veterum Sapientia*', in *Orient,* 26 (1962), 63–65; I. Baumer, 'Sprache und Kirche', loc. cit., 76–79.

[1] Cf. Martimort, 'Assemblée', 24–29: 'Le renvoi de l'assemblée et le retour du chrétien à la vie quotidienne'; E. von Severus, 'Kult und Aktion'; Floristan, *La Parroquia,* 175–89.

[2] 'That is why the charity expressed in the assembly of the brethren is an eschatological sign, and the dismissal of the people imposes on the Christian a different way of living the true charity of Christ.' Martimort, op. cit., 28.

[3] Vagaggini, 406.

[4] Ib., 414.

the whole community, several liturgical communities will come into being. Naturally these will not always be composed of the same worshippers, but often the Mass at a particular time is attended by and large by the same people.[1] It must further be asked whether the whole liturgy is in practice performed by the clergy with the servers and choir or if, and to what extent, the faithful really actively co-operate in it both inwardly and outwardly.[2]

The main criterion will probably be the life of brotherly love which is the continuation of the liturgy in daily life. The actualization (*Ereigniswerden*) of the Church in the local celebration of the eucharist must be continued and enlarged in love as the fruit of the sacrament of unity. This will be evidence of how far the liturgical community radiates into the daily life of the parish and forms it into a fully ecclesial and not simply a mystical or worshipping community.

This, however, cannot be determined by liturgical criteria alone. We need the assistance of sociology.[3] This is possible because in the life of brotherly love, in the real Christian life nourished by the eucharist, the supernatural community of worship passes over into the natural community. The ecclesial community is accessible to sociological observation at least in its outward manifestations. At this meeting point of the invisible with the visible it is also evident that the question of the parish community cannot be answered by the liturgy alone but needs sociology.

The question whether the concrete liturgical congregation turns the parish into a fully ecclesial community is not quite the same as whether the liturgy is a principle establishing community in a parish, since the parish is more than just a worshipping assembly. But in as far as the parish comprises other strata of ecclesiastical reality, in the full sense of the term,

[1] For example, principally women at early Masses, the men mainly later, children at a children's Mass, etc. Cf. Häring, 'Gemeinschaftstiftende Kraft', 207 ff.: 'Unterschiedliche Zusammensetzung der Gottesdienstbesucher; Suk, 'Das Bild einer Grosstadtpfarre', 117 ff.

[2] Jungmann, *Sacrifice*, 46–63: 'Communal Celebration of the Mass in jeopardy.'

[3] Cf. Fichter, *Social Relations*, 207–9: 'Social implications of the sacraments and the liturgy'; Häring, 'Gemeinschaftstiftende Kraft', 209–12: 'Einfluss der Liturgie auf das Leben'; Häring, *Macht*, 38–42: 'Die integrierende Macht der Kultgemeinschaft.'

namely, in as far as the worshipping community is to permeate and form the natural community and be carried on by this community, other criteria must be found which can determine the effect of the worshipping community in the non-worshipping sphere. These criteria are to be found in sociology.

CHAPTER SIX

The Parish and Sociology

Introduction

THE nature of the parish (in the wider sense) as defined by canon law tacitly presupposes a community already constituted from some other source, and this at two levels.

First it must presuppose the supernatural community of the Church. For this is the most important element in the community of the Church and cannot be established by human law. However, as we have tried to show, this supernatural community has no specific and exclusive relationship with the parish, not even on the plane of public worship. It transcends all barriers and times, and as a local worshipping assembly is not identical with the parish community.

In order to form a truly ecclesial community the supernatural community of worship must be integrated into a human, natural community. This genuinely human, 'natural' community is the second prerequisite of the canonical parish. Apart from the canonical, this natural element limits the supernatural community so that a specific parish community can be established. It is indeed theoretically conceivable that a canonical institution might not presuppose this human community but would in fact establish it, as for example in the case of the religious orders. The first Christian communities were certainly of such a type, although at that time the legal provisions were minimal; they were integrated by the spirit. This could also happen in communities which formed as it were spontaneously, around an existing monastery church or any other church, wherever the parish was the foundation of a village in the course of development. But today's parish no longer constitutes a natural human community. On the contrary, it presupposes to a large extent already existing communities which it tries to fill with the supernatural life of the Church. In the history of the parish there is a clear tendency to accommodate diocesan and parish boundaries to the existing profane structures.

Hence the existence of a true parish community depends essentially upon whether the existing human groups contained in the parish already constitute a community independently of the parish or whether they are integrated into a community by the parish and its organizations or not. To determine this is the task of parish sociology. Where such communities exist, it must examine to which sociological laws they are subject and what influences come into play to the profit of the parish itself.[1]

Thus the parish must mediate between the supernatural community of the Church and the natural community and society of men. It must be so adapted to both that it becomes the place where they meet and unite, so that a genuine religious community in the global sense will result. For we can only speak of a parish community if all members of the parish constitute a community in the full ecclesial sense.

The question that concerns us here is whether the human structures can be put to the service of the supernatural reality in such a way that we can truly speak of a human community that necessarily belongs to a fully ecclesial community.

In our context this question does not apply to this or that concrete parish, nor to the type of urban or rural parish, but to the structure of the (territorial) parish in general. Hence we shall examine in this chapter whether the parish shows the structure of a human community because the parish people shares in its constitution, or because the parish itself is an integrating force or because it is a supernatural community of worship. Hence we must examine the human structure of the parish people in itself and in its relation to the parish ministry.

Until now a thorough structural analysis of the parish has been neglected both by pastoral and parish sociology. It is only possible after the study of many individual parishes, and since pastoral sociology is still in its beginnings, the available material is relatively scanty. In addition, most studies have been made

[1] Cf. Winninger, 'Que dit le Code?'

with some pragmatic end in view; they are designed to serve pastoral work as directly as possible. The scientific character of pastoral sociology suffers from this, for it easily leads to dilettantism.[1]

Before turning to religious parish sociology we propose, with the help of general sociology, to analyse the basic structures of society of interest to the parish. For the parish must build on and derive from them in great part its own incarnational structure. Further, general sociology shows the structures within which the Church has to function. Pastoral sociology will then show how the Church uses them. Hence from the structures, established by general sociology, we would choose those that have a particular affinity with the parish. This is particularly the concern of community sociology, a science which has so far been neglected by parish sociology, though it is relevant to both town and country parishes.

I—Sociology of the Community[2]

1. *Significance and Concept of the Community*

Apart from the family, the community (in a sense to be defined later) probably has the greatest importance for the social life of man.[3]

The community here to be discussed is not an administrative

[1] There is the danger that pastoral sociology will develop into a pragmatism with the right answer for every situation (like casuistry) instead of providing a solid, scientifically adequate foundation for the serious reflexion that must precede all apostolic action. In this connexion it is significant and gratifying that at the sixth meeting of the Conférence Internationale de Sociologie Religieuse in Bologna in 1959, the participants worked in two separate groups, one with the accent on science and the other directly apostolic-pragmatic. Cf. Morel, 'Wissenschaft im Dienste der Kirche'. It is interesting to note that an analogous observation can be made in the parallel field of community sociology. Cf. König, 146–54.

[2] This chapter follows König's ideas. He divides the sociology of the community into three fields, ecological, structural and typological. König, 68.

[3] 'Above all it can be said that all social connexions beyond the narrow family circle a man experiences from childhood through adolescence to adulthood are met in the first place in the community.' König, 9, cf. 26, 45; 136–41—'Die Funktion der Gemeinde im Aufbau der sozial-kulturellen Person'.

unit but a social fact,[1] i.e. a special form within society. This can coincide with the local government unit, but need not do so. As a social fact it is a primary form of society.[2] Today the community may be regarded as an elementary social phenomenon which not only meets particular needs but is actually a 'totality of life' as regards both rural and urban sociology.[3] This concept does not exclude 'that such a community be built up of a whole hierarchy of functions and a profusion of individual groups and other, including cultural, social formations, without thereby imputing isolationism or self-sufficiency to such a community'.[4] The concept of community implies on the one hand a wealth of inner variety and on the other a fundamental openness to all social institutions of a higher order.[5] It has nothing to do with 'isolation, autonomy, autarky or self-sufficiency'.[6]

The community as a living social unit has by no means disappeared from the modern social scene. René König constantly emphasizes that there is no fundamental structural difference between a small community and a large one.[7] He tirelessly opposes the prejudice and idyllic romanticism that see the ideal realized only in a small community. Hence the community 'is still the most important intermediate social formation between the family and large formations like the nation . . .; in it the socialization of man, begun in the smallest space of the family, is carried into a wider sphere where the social world in all its depth and breadth first is opened to him'.[8]

In view of the manifold interplay of social realities within the community, König proposes a complex definition in the form of a provisional description: 'Community is, first, a global society of the type of a local unit, embracing manifold functions, social groups and other social phenomena which postulate innumerable forms of social interaction, interconnexions and

[1] The distinction is necessary in German, for the word also means that local government unit corresponding roughly to the English civil parish or French *commune*. Cf. König, 7, 28, 39, 61.

[2] Ib., 8–11. [3] Ib., 179. [4] Ib., 26.

[5] 'For the advanced industrial societies of today the community can and may only be a part of a greater context.' Ib., 44. The parish would thus meet in the natural sphere conditions analogous to those already given by its supernatural reality.

[6] Ib., 26. [7] Ib., 9, 10 f., 16, 26, 90, 101, 109, 123. [8] Ib., 180.

scales of values; besides it also has, of course, its external organization.'[1] In this sense 'community' is a comprehensive term embracing family, neighbourhood, calling, etc.; in other words a social system, of which its members are quite aware.[2]

This social system is determined particularly by its communications systems, its groups within the community, its social control, internal tensions, power and class stratification, and cultural traditions and customs. Naturally religious tradition and custom are also included. Thus many specifically social factors work together 'which, independent of the many individual demographic, economic and ecological features and also of the administrative organizations, guarantee the survival of the social reality'.[3]

2. *The Most Important Elements of the Community*

The community is a global society on a local basis. Since there are still other social institutions on a local basis, the community must be defined not only in relation to larger regional or national complexes but also in relation to smaller phenomena which do not have the character of a global society. Hence the concept of the community must be neither too narrow nor too broad. It must be a global society, and not just a part of it, yet it must not lose the character of the local community. One of the most important elements making this definition possible is the principle of neighbourhood. This, though the most general, is yet the most important and decisive condition for the community as a global society on a local basis.

[1] König, 28. [2] Ib., 28 f.

[3] Ib., 29 f. König draws special attention to the fact 'that the organizations (political parties) and associations (in the strict sense) within the community are not more important sociologically than the free and spontaneous societies such as clubs, charity committees, study circles, etc., to belong to which can be of the greatest importance to a newcomer, deciding whether he settles down or not; or even informal groups, cliques and coteries which behind the scenes exercise on community business a pressure which cannot be pinned down but which on that account can in certain cases be all the more enduring and effective; individual personalities with prestige, or loose connexions of friendship or common interest and so on. The sociological study of a community is quite especially interested in such centres of gravity which can become of the greatest importance in the community not only in the matter of social prestige but even more for the creation of opinion.' Ib., 40.

On the other hand it is only a partial aspect of the spatial problem in the community, which is the subject of ecology.[1]

(a) *Spatial Relationships in the Community.* Ecology studies the spatial relationship of living beings with inanimate nature as well as with other members of the species. It is 'the science of the conditions of existence and interactions of living beings and their surroundings'.[2] Ecology examines these phenomena, which can also be the subject of geography and sociology, 'exclusively with a view to their spatial disposition or distribution'.[3] Space in this context is conceived as social space, the essential form of which is the neighbourhood.

The special spatial relationships concern above all the arrangement in space of horizontal and vertical relationships,[4] for example the separation of antagonistic groups.[5] The small community may split into two or more ecological sub-units which can occasionally produce remote hamlets. The larger community is more richly diversified: it is made up of a multiplicity of neighbourhoods, the smallest neighbouring formations. The larger spatially separated districts of a community are called natural areas.[6]

The smaller units or the neighbourhood. The concrete or factual neighbourhood must be distinguished from the neighbourhood principle which 'exists quite generally in every "permanent or transitory coincidence of interest due to physical proximity" (Max Weber).'[7] The factual neighbourhoods in which the principle has actually been effective are designated by König as 'integrated neighbourhoods'.[8] The principle applies in the country just as much as in the town, even though its manifestations are not the same.[9]

However, it would also be wrong to regard the small local community as only one single neighbourhood. 'Even the village community, the most important realization of the neighbourhood principle, always divides into several concrete or integrated neighbourhoods based on relatives, friendships,

[1] Ib., 51, 53. [2] Ib., 14 f. [3] Ib., 54. [4] Ib., 55.
[5] Ib., 32, 69, 118. [6] Ib., 55 f. [7] Ib., 46. [8] Ib., 47.
[9] Recent research shows that 'today experts have more and more recognized the existence of neighbourhoods in the town, where incidentally they are clearly characterized by the class distinctions of urban society—exactly as in the country'. Ib., 50.

cliques, class, common cultural interests and such like.'[1] The narrow conditions by no means guarantee that the physical proximity will result in neighbourly integration, for without other factors this proximity may create only very slight ties.[2] For this reason functional distance 'has been distinguished from purely physical proximity or remoteness. A neighbourhood cannot be defined in two dimensions: the various groups interpenetrate and cut across each other in the most complicated manner.'[3]

On the basis of her study of the community, Ruth Glass has subdivided the concept of neighbourhood into weak and strong neighbourhoods. In the weak sense neighbourhood means a locally fixed group which differs from similar groups because of certain characteristics of the area and its inhabitants, or quite simply 'people who live alongside each other'. The interactions and relations in this sort of neighbourhood are of a very general nature. The strong sense, however, presupposes that such a group displays neighbourly behaviour and is thus really socially integrated through its many social contacts.[4]

It follows from this that there are considerably fewer integrated neighbourhoods than had at first been supposed. Purely ecological factors[5] are not enough to cause social integration. It is, moreover, remarkable that just the poorer and poorest quarters—regardless of the number of inhabitants—develop into integrated neighbourhoods, whereas the smaller wealthier quarters show only very small beginnings in this direction.[6]

In a strong neighbourhood it might further be distinguished between merely latent or manifest interactions: in the latter the existing readiness would also come into action.

In connexion with these considerations König would like 'to limit the term neighbourhood to the small and very small units which are actually distinguished by a closer social intercourse'.[7] He believes that any broadening would lead to sentimental illusions or that ecological–statistical characteristics could be mistaken for real social interactions. Finally he points out that real neighbourhoods offer better chances for the

[1] König, 47. [2] Cf. ib., 32. [3] Ib., 48 f. [4] Ib., 62.
[5] Similar living conditions, rents, size of houses, etc.
[6] Ib., 62 f. Cf. Quoist; Michonneau, *Paroisse*, 62. [7] Ib., 63.

creation of 'lively interaction units'. 'This has often led to the attempt to link administrative arrangements of some sort with such integrated neighbourhoods.'[1]

The nature of the neighbourhood is such that its range must be very limited. It might correspond roughly to 'the surroundings seen directly at one glance'.[2]

Apart from the outer there is an inner limitation, because the need for spatial proximity is offset by that for the so-called escape distance (*Fluchtdistanz*), which finds external expression in fences, hedges, etc. It appears that 'as the educational level rises, men react with increasing sensitivity to infringements of the escape distance'.[3] Since physical proximity is both appreciated and resented, König asks 'if there may not be a kind of happy mean between too far and too near within which neighbourhood relations can function smoothly and positively'.[4]

Distance is not a purely spatial factor but is conditioned by other elements such as social antecedents, a sceptical attitude towards too-friendly relationships, etc.[5] There is, further, the desire to choose one's intimates and friends freely according to one's taste 'without being compelled as it were by the ground plan of the settlement to be constantly crossing one's neighbour's path'.[6] Family and relations, too, have to be considered. Finally the influence of the general surrounding society on the neighbourhood must not be forgotten.

The larger units or 'natural areas'. Besides these smaller and very small units of the neighbourhoods the larger, separate partial zones, the so-called natural areas, are important for the larger, particularly the urban communities. The 'natural area', a term not always used in the same sense in sociology, starts beyond the neighbourhood where personal acquaintance predominates, but it differs from the whole district. 'It can mean areas composed of definite population groups (workers, middle class, upper class), or sections often deriving from smaller towns or villages absorbed into a city, or ecologically

[1] Ib. This was also the aim of parish planning.

[2] Ib., 64. An exception is the 'open-country neighbourhood' still found in Canada and the United States in widely separated settlements.

[3] Ib., 65. [4] Ib.

[5] It appears 'that a more or less expressed aversion seems to exist to too personal relationships in too close proximity'. Ib. 56.

[6] Ib., 65.

separated areas such as shopping centres, "theatreland", etc.,[1] in the English-speaking world–frequently known by street and other names such as Whitehall or the White House for the seats of Government, Broadway for theatres, Harley Street for doctors, Savile Row for tailors, etc.

Even if these 'natural areas' be not considered as separate entities as has wrongly been done, the term is questionable, for the statistical homogeneity of certain quarters disappears under microanalysis. 'It follows quite clearly that the characteristics that may be predicated for most natural areas (French *quartiers*) are exclusively statistical concepts which must be clearly distinguished from social complexes.'[2] In order to understand social complexes, the sociological units must be smaller than the 'natural area'. This is rather a logical or statistical construction valid only in certain extreme cases, as for example definite slum areas, or wealthy areas, or again functional areas like the above mentioned shopping centres, etc.[3]

Unfortunately so far the relation of the community to its surroundings has been examined only very one-sidedly, either from a purely ecological viewpoint or as regards the drift from the country to the towns. Migrations between rural communities have been completely ignored, 'and it should be emphasized here that these represent perhaps a relatively new phenomenon, which appeared only after industrial concerns began to move to the country, as has happened strikingly in Switzerland for example'.[4]

Finally König mentions the merely relative value of ecological factors in judging sociological realities. They only affect one aspect. Proximity in space cannot by itself validly explain the sociological structure. 'It is curious to see that each time one tries to tackle the question more closely, the factor of spatial proximity, which at the start seemed to govern everything, becomes less and less definite in its effect.'[5]

(b) *Structural Elements of the Community*. The form which the life of the community takes in space is only *one* side of the community, albeit an important one. In order to grasp 'the totality of life present in a community' one ought to elucidate

[1] König, 56. [2] Ib., 58. [3] Ib., 58–61. [4] Ib., 71; cf. 82 f.
[5] Ib., 66 f.

'not only the interaction of the various living and functional *milieux* but also the constellation characteristic of a particular community'.[1] This should be done 'in the framework of the daily life of the community'. 'Daily' here means 'that the life of the community takes place not only within the institutional, nor in the specifically structural (for example, class) framework, but frequently just outside these in a totality of manifestations'.[2] Informal groups that form spontaneously are of the greatest importance for this study.[3] Among these König gives the first place to leading groups and cliques in the community. People in the 'leading groups have a high though not the highest status in the community. The people who hold the initiative in these are not necessarily those marked out by some office but those who are greatly respected by the community and at the same time outwardly active.'[4] Studies show that 'after membership of a family, nothing places an individual within the community as clearly as belonging to one or more such cliques'.[5] Indeed, these cliques often break vertically through the social class structure. They are not peculiar to small communities, but are found equally in towns and cities.

The failure of such informal leadership can lead to severe crises in a community.[6] On the other hand, many decisive impulses originate in these informal circles. The functioning of the administration is very often 'wrapped up in all sorts of background activity'.[7] All this underlines the significance of informal processes in the life of the community.

As far as authority and power are concerned, the community is always a very important instrument of power which may even include a high degree of informal economic authority. It seems that even with a democratic constitution of the community 'the real exercise of power remains oligarchic and . . . mostly extremely informal so that it is by no means always easy to find out who really has the power'.[8]

The more formal groups. The problem of social stratification (class and caste) is important. According to the American

[1] Ib., 68. [2] Ib., 86. [3] Ib., 87.

[4] Community studies have revealed, for example, that in local elections party members as such do not get the votes; the parties themselves have to get hold of a man held in high esteem and then present him to the electors as their candidate. Ib., 88.

[5] Ib., 89. [6] Ib., 90. [7] Ib., 92. [8] Ib., 96.

sociologist W. Lloyd Warner there is on the one hand the general democratic postulate that all men are equal, while on the other, it has to be admitted, even though not openly, that men are quite different, a few being superior to the many, the rest inferior to all.[1] Certain studies have shown that people are very well informed about the distribution of influence and power in groups; and 'that the cliques of young people follow very closely the classes of the adults, the influence of class prejudice being stronger than that of the parents'.[2] Whereas before puberty all children play together, class is decisive when choosing a marriage partner.

The old class distinctions retain their vitality especially in villages and small communities, whereas new differences appear in cities and industrial areas. Classes are often distinguished by an internal unity and distance from others.[3] 'Social classes are not, however, stable, but highly dynamic units with different structures.'[4] For rarely does class depend on profession, income, social status and such things, but 'rather on a tangle of actual situation and one's own and others' opinion'.[5] Naturally birth, family, occupation, education, school, wealth, and similar factors make a difference. But traditional ideas of value are just as important.

Thus as regards the social classes in a community two factors intermingle: '(1) A stratification based on objective factors and determining the whole style of living as well as the separation of the various strata. . . . (2) A stratification on the basis of subjective factors which determine the rank and prestige of a member of the community apart from his socio-economic status.'[6] At community level all depends on the subjective factors since the members of the community will always see objective factors from a subjective point of view. Here, concepts of value will have a much more decisive influence than prevailing economic facts.[7] 'As soon as ideas of values enter into consideration all comparison becomes extremely difficult; on the other hand the structure of a community only develops with these

[1] König, 100 f.; cf. 104.
[2] Ib., 101. [3] Ib., 101 f. [4] Ib., 103. [5] Ib., 104. [6] Ib.,
[7] Ib., 105; cf. 84. '. . . where the population is extremely mobile no common scale of values can develop. It is accordingly important whether institutions such as schools and churches which contribute much to the building of character are community-minded or not.'

ideas. This is perhaps the greatest dilemma which modern community research has to face.'

The problem of social control, that is of the prevailing norms regarded as 'correct', is very closely linked with the idea of value.[1] At the community level class and value cannot be separated. The most important and decisive share of social control belongs once more to informal elements, such as custom and usage, gossip, rumour and public opinion. Both inwardly and outwardly the scale of values of a community can be so disturbed by social changes that 'no integration is possible, or at least considerable conflicts of loyalty between various systems of values will originate'.[2]

3. *The Central Problem: Integration of the Community*

The *basic* mistake pointed out by König is to presuppose unquestioningly the integration of the community and to consider all other problems in the light of this false assumption. It is also quite wrong to regard even the small community as an integrated whole, specifically on account of its smallness.[3] Integration does not depend on the type but on the structure of the community. It would also be wrong to include in the definition of a community the demand that it must be an integrated whole. For the local community by no means excludes interior tensions and differences. The chances of conflict are often much greater in a small community than in a large one, for in a town it is much easier to preserve the 'escape distance' and avoid clashes or lessen their impact.

As has been said before, the space factor can be excluded from the causes of integration except perhaps in new estates. On the other hand social and spiritual harmony, though always related to surroundings, will be much more potent elements. This relationship to space and surroundings might be called with G. C. Homans the 'outer system', while the interior unity is the 'inner system'. Whether there is integration or not depends on how the inner and outer systems work together.[4]

[1] Ib., 107. [2] Ib., 108. [3] Ib., 109, 111.

[4] Ib., 114. In this connexion it is also clear that community sociology needs and must be completed by social psychology.

Only very rarely will all groups in a community be integrated.[1] The failure of integration may be expressed ecologically (separate settlements, tesselation) as well as in people's attitude to the world.[2]

Hence the possibility of integration has its limits which can be expressed ecologically either as 'tesselation' or as ecological 'segregation' or as columnization.[3] 'Tesselation' means that different groups live separately near each other; although they settle among each other, interact and trade together, there is no real integration into a community. Integration is prevented mostly by class differences. 'If a community . . . can among other things be defined by the presence of common values, this means that there may, in principle, be groups which live as sub-groups in a larger complex without sharing its values.'[4] Further, integration has its limitations in the case of children and young people who will be only half integrated, and in that of old people who are 'dismissed' from the community.[5]

König comes to the conclusion that 'the structure of the community creates fundamental differentiations which may in some circumstances (not all) hinder integration. This means that even in small communities men are not necessarily integrated by neighbourhood or inter-reactions or common values and links. This is particularly noticeable in the case of values—which immediately create strong differences between those who live according to them and those who do not. . . . Thus social discrimination will always appear precisely where common values are present, paradoxical though this may seem.'[6]

Nevertheless, the structure of a global society does not exclude the presence of numerous phenomena which cannot be attained through structural processes. Hence another kind of integration can be achieved alongside social integration.[7] So, for example, integration may be realized in a symbol, when it

[1] König rejects Tenhumberg's concept of 'the unconscious community of the whole village' as untenable. 115.

[2] Ib., 117. [3] Cf. ib., 129.

[4] Ib., 119. Both phenomena are important for the parish.

[5] Ib., 118–20.

[6] Ib., 123. Also an extremely important insight for parish sociology.

[7] 'We should like to express the opinion that an integration can nevertheless be possible even when it cannot or can only seldom be reached in the social sphere on account of its complexity and the diversity of interests concerned.' Ib., 124.

is unattainable on the social plane. Such a symbol might be the notion of *native land*, for as such the community is not only a social form but an element of culture. There may, however, also be other cultural media, symbolisms and collective identifications, which lead to integration.[1]

The local paper has shown itself to be the most important means to community integration, if it 'tries to maintain local unanimity by underlining common values rather than by resolving conflicts'.[2] It has further been found that the growth of large organizations in modern urban culture has by no means resulted either in separation into impersonal individuals or in outsize social organizations. 'On the contrary, between these two extremes a whole series of intermediary social systems and means of communication have arisen spontaneously.'[3] Finally the importance of community leaders in the matter of integration ought not to be overlooked.[4]

Sociology has not yet exhausted the study of the problem of integration. Nevertheless there are already fruitful beginnings. However, precisely in the sociology of the community several fundamental questions remain open, particularly concerning the macrocosm of groups and the dimensions of horizontal and vertical integration. 'Horizontal integration is principally concerned with the co-operation of groups in the spatial order and on the same status level; vertical integration by contrast runs from below upwards. In both directions there may be several degrees; but there can be true integration only if it occurs equally in both directions.'[5] Vertical integration has been called *Versäulung* (columnization) of social life.[6]

4. *Community Typology*

A typology of the community must be based on historical, economic and cultural assumptions. The community is a social

[1] Ib., 124 f. Perhaps the concept of 'parish family' is such a symbol in some cases.

[2] Janowitz, quoted by König, 126.

[3] Ib., 127. The type of parish news-sheet must also be considered and planned with this in mind. [4] Ib., 85. [5] Ib., 128.

[6] The basic forms of the various religious denominations in a Dutch community serve as an example. Ib., 129. Cf. Kruijt, 'Die Erforschung der protestantischen Kirchengemeinde in den Niederlanden', 47.

formation that has developed in history.[1] Its structures are essentially, if not exclusively, connected with the prevailing economic systems, and if communities are to be classified according to these systems, 'the cultural determinants must also be made visible'.[2]

The subject is so complex that three branches of sociological research share the work: agrarian sociology, urban sociology and the sociology of town–country relations.[3]

König mentions several attempts at a typology,[4] all rather one-sided and unsatisfactory: they remain in the air, 'as long as they fail to be founded on many more concrete sociological community studies'. The attempts he cites can 'only serve as a temporary expedient as long as we do not dispose of more ample material'.[5]

For modern typology, the sociology of town–country relations will have to be consulted as well as agrarian and urban sociology. 'Industry has in many cases moved out into the country, so that the problems of industrialization occur in an entirely new *milieu*, and to a great extent even urbanization itself has in some measure become independent of the town, as this development may be paradoxically described. Today the urban style of living is found everywhere including the country, and it seems that in the discussion between town and country much more is involved than two types of settlement or two economic systems.'[6]

Community sociology has been discussed in such detail for several reasons: first, it contains many instructive parallels with parish sociology; secondly, studies of parish sociology still take too little account of secular social institutions and are concerned too exclusively with the purely 'ecclesiastical' viewpoints; thirdly, and this is most important, parish sociology should not only consult general sociology but should certainly itself be included in specific community sociology. It ought not to be satisfied with a sociology of age-groups and professional groups, with the ecological and social situation. In fact community sociology has hardly been considered by parish sociology. This is not to minimize the value of what has been done, but to put it in its proper place as indispensable preparatory

[1] Ib., 69.
[2] Ib., 72 f. [3] Ib., 73. [4] Ib., 76–81. [5] Ib., 81. [6] Ib., 82.

work.[1] Finally, community sociology is introduced here because it can contribute in many ways towards filling the large gaps still remaining in parish sociology.

Furthermore, community sociology is relevant to our problem because it shows that the parish does not simply find a ready-made community on to which it could graft itself. On the other hand it analyses the structures and functions that make integration possible and provide elements for one or more communities within the parish.

Naturally community sociology throws light on only one side. It must be complemented by parish sociology and placed in its context by theology.

II—Sociology of the Parish

If parish sociology is now to decide whether on the basis of its own criteria the parish is a community, this question must definitely be applied to the parish as a canonical institution, i.e. to the canonical notion of parish (parish in the comprehensive sense). For only in this way will the answers given from the different standpoints relate to the same reality. Further, the reality defined by the canonical term must be studied in its sociological nature.

Moreover, it is clear from our discussions on community sociology, that the parish can never simply be presupposed to be a sociological community or an integrated whole; this could only be the result of our investigation.[2]

Finally, following community sociology, we may exclude with a clear conscience the attempt to arrive at the present parish community by way of the family (in the old sense of family household).[3]

The best approach to our enquiry is undoubtedly through a

[1] 'Demography, sociography and statistics should be seen for what they are: a valuable preliminary for sociology and a basis of information upon which the sociologist can work. We must not confuse this preliminary research with the central object of scientific sociology: the types of behaviour, the functions and relations and processes of life in the group.' Fichter 'Paroisse urbaine', 84. 'Having gone through all the literature, both European and American, dealing with religious sociology, I could find no report of such a study.' Ib., 85.

[2] Cf. König, 120.

[3] Cf. Szabo, 'La Paroisse'; Fichter, *Social Relations*, 159.

parish sociology starting from the elements of community sociology. For it is at least to be supposed that the parish will partly coincide with the sociological community; that it frequently at least represents an integrating or disintegrating element in the community, and that its structure will show traits related to that of the community. Thus the parish is neither to be compared sociologically with the family, nor with the regional units extending beyond the local community for these would rather correspond to the dioceses or deaneries.[1]

1. *Parish, Parish Congregation*[2] *and Parish Community*

One difficulty appears at once. Rather as in the case of the secular community, the boundaries of the canonical parish too do not necessarily coincide with what one might call sociologically the 'parish congregation'. This is true not only in the territorial sense but also in the sense of a purely legal, but not actually living membership of the Church in general and of the parish in particular. One way among others in which the territorial discrepancy between the parish and the parish congregation appears might be, for example, the regular attendance at Mass in another parish.[3] The personal discrepancy is shown particularly by the lack of religious practice among those who legally belong to a parish. Because of this

[1] Exceptions are found in the diaspora or in areas where there is a shortage of priests and a parish may include several communities.

[2] The term *Gemeinde* has here been translated by 'congregation', even though it does not correspond quite exactly to the German term. In this context, therefore, 'congregation' means the community of regular attendants at the services of the parish church.

[3] So, for example, in Lille 37 per cent of practising Catholics over twelve years of age went to Mass outside their parish church, in most cases to other parish churches; only 5 per cent of those who had a free choice (boarding school pupils are therefore not included) attended Mass in chapels (i.e. not in some parish church). Cf. Verscheure, *Lille*, 12, 15, Tables 7, 10; Quoist 190 ff. Fribourg, which is divided into six parishes, has eighty-two public or semi-public places of worship. Of parishioners over twelve, roughly 50 per cent attend Mass in their parish church, 30 per cent in other churches in the parish area, and 20 per cent outside the parish area. Cf. *Recherches pastorales: Canton de Fribourg*, 1957, 24. In Geneva, too, a high percentage heard Mass in a parish church not their own. In the church of St John Nepomucene in Vienna on 18 March 1956, out of 1,736 people attending Mass 595 did not belong to the parish. Cf. Suk, 'Das Bild', 116.

discrepancy Fichter is obliged to work out a sociological definition of the term parishioner apart from the economic one, since the former alone permits valid sociological statements.[1]

This possible or actual difference between the parish in the canonical and the parish congregation in the sociological sense leads to the following conclusions: it may be stated *a priori* that where parish and parish congregation do not coincide, the parish is not sociologically a community. At best it may contain one or more communities within its boundaries. Where parish and parish congregation coincide, the parish may, but need not, be a community. It may consist of several integrated groups. From this it further follows—and this is important—that strictly sociological studies (including those of parish sociology) must start from the sociological unit of the parish congregation and not from the canonical concept of the parish. In fact parish sociology is always in danger of taking the canonical parish territory as its starting point, quietly assuming that it is a social unit, which in most cases it simply is not. The result of such 'sociological' studies will accordingly at best be statistical material but not genuine sociology. Authentic sociological statements apply to the parish (in the canonical sense) only if it coincides with the sociological parish congregation both as regards territory and persons.[2] Religious sociology has already become aware of this problem, especially in America where official statistics divide towns and larger communities into 'census tracts' which do not correspond to local government divisions. Similar units are found in Canada and Switzerland. Since they are relatively small, they make it easier to grasp the real basic sociological units.[3]

One of the first—if not the first—tasks of parish sociology will be to work out whether and in how far the parish is a parish congregation. Once this has been clarified, the question of the parish community can be approached. The latter, in the

[1] Cf. Fichter, *Social Relations*, 9–20: 'What is a parishioner?'; Ryckmans, 'Qu'est-ce qu'un catholique pratiquant?'

[2] Naturally the sociological parish congregation always includes many formal organizational elements even when it does not coincide with the institutional parish.

[3] Cf. Santopolo, 63; Houtart, *Planning*, 104; Fichter, *Social Relations*, 152 f.

sociological sense, will be found wherever there are integrated groups within the parish, or where this as a whole represents one single integrated group. Parish community in the fullest sense will exist wherever the integrated groups are also the bearers of the supernatural community of the Church.

2. *The Parish Congregation*

The parish community is defined as a local community by its relationship to the area on the one hand and on the other by the personal relationships and interactions within this area.

(a) *Relation to the Area.* Canon law provides that the territory of each diocese shall be divided into different parts, and calls these parts parishes[1] without, however, specifying how this division is to be made, or for how long. Indirectly, such a division will be made according to the population within an area[2] so that the parish priest may know the souls assigned to him.[3] The fact that the necessary legal bases are present for the further division of a parish or for the amalgamation of several parishes[4] indicates that a division once made is not to be considered as absolutely definitive. The law presupposes that changes will have to be made.

It follows that, considered from a purely canonical point of view, the parish is on the one hand related to a definite territory, but that, on the other, this relation is not absolute in the sense that a new division would be undesirable or unnecessary. Undoubtedly, as regards both territory and people canon law can and will also be influenced by extra-legal considerations.

The parish is not only a canonically defined part of the diocese, it is also part of a geographical area characterized by a definite religious sociology usually independent of the canonical boundaries.

Studies of average religious practice[5] in individual parishes of a large area or a whole country revealed that the intensity of practice varies within larger zones, others showed that the religious activity of individual vocational groups also varies

[1] C. 216, §§1, 3.
[2] C. 216, §1.
[3] C. 467, §1.
[4] Winninger, 'Que dit le Code?'
[5] Sunday Mass, Easter duties, etc.

with the region.[1] The number of vocations to the priesthood or the religious life over a definite period of time showed similar regional differences.[2]

Religious sociography attempts to chart these homogeneous zones on the map[3] and thereby reveals that the individual parish is not self-contained but is embedded in a larger, fairly homogeneous, zone whose characteristics it shares.

Several elements contribute to the formation of such different homgeneous zones. There is, first, the influence of the geographical area. Religious sociology has shown that there are certain relationships between religion and area, so that the geographic and geological structure of an area can exercise a certain influence on religious conduct.[4]

Don Aldo Leoni calls his thesis on the practice of religion in the diocese of Mantua: *The Religious Sociology and Geography of a Diocese.*[5] He also examines the geographical and geological structure of the diocesan territory and believes he can establish an influence on social and religious human conduct.[6] His last chapter is devoted to the religious contrasts between the different regions.[7]

Just as the nature of a region is always marked by human culture, the geographical influence must be seen in close connexion with cultural and historical factors. The religious situation of a district is always affected by economic, cultural and political influences that have developed historically.[8] In

[1] Boulard, *Itinéraires,* 60 ff.

[2] Ib., 120; *Recherches pastorales: Canton de Fribourg,* 17 ff.

[3] The *Carte religieuse de la France rurale* of Canon Boulard and Prof. Le Bras is famous. On its model a European map is to be produced which, however, will come up against fundamental difficulties on account of the great typological differences in the individual countries. Apart from the map of the Canton de Fribourg (*Recherches pastorales: Canton de Fribourg* 1957), one has also appeared for western Switzerland (*Diocèses de Suisse romande. Aspects sociologiques et religieux,* Lausanne, n.d.). Cf. Pilloud, 'Vers une pastorale d'ensemble'; Berz, 'Pastorelle Folgerungen aus der religionssoziologischen Untersuchung der französischsprechenden Schweiz'; For Belgium cf. Collard, *Carte de la pratique dominicale en Belgique par localité.*

[4] Cf. Iribarren, *Introducción,* 39–47: 'Influjos geográficos y físicos en la sociedad religiosa.'

[5] Leoni, *Sociologia*: 'Sociologia e geografia religiosa di una Diocesi.'

[6] Ib., 127 f.

[7] Ib., 189–206.

[8] Boulard, *Itinéraires,* 49; Iribarren, *Introducción,* 49–60; Kruijt, 'Die Erforschung der protestantischen Kirchengemeinde in den Niederlanden', 38.

Germany, for example, the principle of the Reformation, *cuius regio, eius religio*, must still have some effect.[1]

Another point affecting the religious situation of a country is the distribution of priests in the course of its history.[2]

It is obvious that town and country produce different types of people. Rural and urban parishes, too, show differences which from the Council of Trent onwards Church legislation has unfortunately ignored.[3] This problem belongs to the relations between town and country not yet sufficiently studied by religious sociology.[4] On the basis of available studies, but with the necessary safeguards, Chélini puts forward two hypotheses concerning the fulfilling of the Sunday obligation in religiously homogeneous regions. It seems that the religious state of the hinterland has a decisive influence on the practice in the town and not only the other way round.[5] Further, the religious practice in a town whose rural surroundings show a low degree of religious activity is higher than that of its surroundings. When, however, the surroundings enjoy a high percentage, that of the town is lower.[6]

In any case, religious geography, which can only be touched on here, shows that the parish congregation is part of an area which shows more or less the same degree of religious practice.[7]

[1] For example, good or bad pastoral work in a diocese, intense missions in certain areas, the tithe obligation of many monasteries, urbanization and industrialization. Cf. Boulard, op. cit., 35–50

[2] Cf. StdZ (1958–59), 139 f.; 'Le problème des trop petites paroisses', in *M-D*, 57 (1959); Houtart, 'L'évolution', 49. The article 'Priestermangel in der Schweiz' and the following discussion in *Civitas*, 14, 10–16, 233–79, only brings out a limited aspect of the problem which can only be solved as a whole. Moreover, the scientific and sociological foundations are completely lacking. For these two reasons this presentation gives no objective picture and no valid conclusions can be drawn from it.

[3] Cf. p. 89 above; Nuesse and Harte, 100–53.

[4] In profane sociology the town-country relationship is a branch of its own!

[5] Chélini, 67, 94.

[6] Ib., 67 ff. Bilbao, which lies in an area where practice is good but uneven, shows a lower percentage than its surroundings. But wherever industry has spread out into the country, it is lower than in the town. Chélini believes that in the town, where industrialization is of long standing, the clergy have already adapted themselves to new conditions, which cannot be said for the newly industrialized country areas: the sudden falling off is a result of this. Ib., 72 f.

[7] Cf. Laloux, 'Planning'. Chélini attempted to co-ordinate and compare as far as possible the religio-social findings for towns. Chélini.

This knowledge is of great practical significance for pastoral work. It is also important in the present context, because it calls to mind that a parish community can never be treated in religious sociology as an isolated whole.[1] Hence religious sociology arrives at conclusions similar to those of community sociology: but built into larger religio-sociological formations which can be geographically defined. It is an important task for pastoral-sociological planning to adjust the larger ecclesiastical administrative and pastoral units to the sociological areas (*zones humaines*).

It would, however, be wrong to consider the larger zones as absolutely homogeneous. For zones always result from statistical averages. Micro-analysis shows a much more differentiated picture. With the help of community sociology it is possible within the larger units to distinguish smaller groups which bear, indeed, the general marks of the zone but which represent nevertheless closed groups and 'congregations' distinct from one another.

These groups and 'congregations' do not, however, necessarily coincide with the boundaries of the canonical parishes, for parish boundaries came into being at a particular time in history and in particular social and religious conditions.[2] At the time of their origin they may have enclosed a parish congregation. But do they still? In many cases, certainly. One might be tempted to say, 'In the country, yes'. But such a generalization is not tenable. There are country parishes which contain several sociological communities, often with their own places of worship. Besides, according to community sociology there is no direct relationship between the size of the community and integration. The social changes which are spreading increasingly also to the country, 'loosen the bond between Church community and local society'.[3]

Conditions in towns are more complicated. Here very often the boundaries of the canonical parish and those of the sociological territory of the parish congregation overlap, where old parish divisions have obstinately survived demographic and

[1] Cf. Houtart, 'L'aménagement', especially 520 ff.: 'La paroisse urbaine actuelle est autarchique.'

[2] Szabo, 'La paroisse', 23.

[3] Freytag, 'Aufgaben', 1.

sociological developments.[1] It is one of the most important tasks of parish sociology (particularly parish planning) to adapt parish boundaries in towns to the social conditions. One criterion is the number of parishioners, which ideally should be somewhere between five and ten thousand souls.[2] On the other hand, the boundaries should take account of the sociological features of the area, such as large squares, avenues, streets with a great deal of traffic, railway lines, rivers and so forth, because they act as psychological barriers and determine the ecological structure of a town.

Today these elementary notions no longer suffice: real ecological studies should help in understanding the spatial relationships of the community so that the parish can be adapted as well as possible to the existing ecological area. Today exact ecological studies are indispensable. This is also true for larger country parishes including those related to towns. So far, however, investigations seem to have been limited to town parishes.

In conjunction with ecology the study of social groups, especially, will make it possible to determine the sociological boundaries of the parish community.

Religious ecology no longer necessarily regards the parish as the basic sociological unit. As religious sociography and geography have discerned zones within the larger area, ecology, too, has discovered smaller ecological areas within the parish boundaries.

Religious ecology is even more in its very first stages than religious sociology in general and has only recently been brought into the service of pastoral sociology. Until now the practice of religion has been studied too one-sidedly in connexion with the whole town or the whole parish area, but not in terms of the '*quartier*', that is of the 'congregation' and the groups within it.[3] The first relevant studies were made chiefly in America.[4]

[1] Szabo, loc. cit.

[2] Winninger, *Construire des églises*, 19–39: 'Des paroisses ou unités pastorales de cinq mille âmes.'

[3] Santopolo, 63. Cf. Nuesse, 'Empirical Problems for Social Research in the Parish', 222–28.

[4] For Europe cf. Chélini 145–62: 'Le quartier et la paroisse'; Quoist, *La ville et l'homme*.

Religious ecology studies religious behaviour, or rather the practice of religion in relation to the neighbourhood. Thus it has been established that in the seven sectors of greater Lyons Christians belonging to professions do not everywhere practise equally, and consequently that the ecological *milieu* exercises an influence on religious practice.[1]

In one parish the ecological study was carried further and showed that the parish was, as it were, divided into four sub-parishes, each with its own characteristics. Since there are still far too few concrete studies available, no laws can as yet be established, but it seems that some are beginning to stand out.[2]

A study in the Roman suburban parish of Maria Immacolata al Tiburtino produced similar results.[3] If the relevant tables of the sectors of Rouen investigated by M. Quoist are placed one on top of the other,[4] it is easy to see that the boundaries of the three-and-a-half parishes do not coincide with those of the five natural sociological quarters but that a large number of those practising do not come from the parish territory. Even more striking, however, is the very clear divergence between groups of practising Catholics and neighbourhood groups. Only a very small number of those who go to church come from neighbourhood groups, that is to say that they have neighbourly contact neither among themselves nor with non-practising Catholics: they are evidently individualists all along the line. Today the parish congregation is scarcely held together any more by the social relations of a common dwelling place. Going to church is not practised in the neighbourhood 'but obviously resembles attending a function where people of similar interests meet'.[5]

[1] 'These observations seem to invite us to attach great importance to the role played by different ecological areas in the field of practising religion. Religious sociology in towns would see new horizons opening up before it if this question could be studied with the care it deserves.' Daille, 'Pratique', 68.

[2] Cf. Santopolo, 65 f.; Grond, 'Nature et fonction du quartier d'une grande ville'.

[3] Sr Maria-Agneze Censi, 'L'étude écologique d'une paroisse des faubourgs de Rome', 59 ff.

[4] Quoist, 'Planches': Table 20 (Sunday observance at Saint-Maclon), Table 21 (Sunday observance at Saint-Vivien), Table 25 (the *quartiers*) and Table 26 (neighbourhood groupings).

[5] Freytag, 'Aufgaben', 5.

In Brussels an average of 24 per cent of the total population[1] attends Sunday Mass. Divided among the different quarters, however, the result is that in all working-class areas together 6–15 per cent of the total population are practising, whereas in the middle-class districts the figure is over 40 per cent. It also emerged that in parishes where there was no alternative place of worship 20 per cent practised, while in parishes with an alternative place of worship the percentage rose to 36 per cent.[2]

Studies on the distribution of priests within towns are also very informative. In the centre of Brussels there is one priest for every 1,000–2,000 of the faithful in the middle-class districts; in the working-class districts, one priest for 2,000–3,000 of the faithful. Just outside the centre, half the parishes with over 5,000 souls have only one priest; four out of five parishes in which there are over 5,000 souls to one priest are working-class parishes.[3]

A study of two Paris *arrondissements* shows unmistakably that in comparison with bourgeois parishes working-class parishes are worse treated by the Church all along the line.[4] Abbé Houtart clearly acknowledges this, pointing out that working-class quarters in European and South American cities (in contrast to those in North America) have always too few parishes and too few clergy. 'This is a very important hint for the future. These quarters must be very closely watched.'[5]

On the other hand, there does not seem to be any direct relationship between the size of an urban agglomeration and Sunday observance.[6]

As regards frequent changes of residence, Fichter's studies of American parishes produced the following results: the frequent changes have an unfavourable effect on social participation in the life of the parish only when the parish boundaries are crossed but not if the move is within the parish. A move, however, has no appreciable effect on religious practice whether it remains within the parish or not.[7] These results, incidentally, support the hypothesis that social mixing and religious practice

[1] Equivalent to 27 per cent of those obliged to attend.
[2] Houtart, 'L'évolution', 48. [3] Ib., 49. [4] Daniel, 'L'équipement'.
[5] Houtart, 'Planning', 107. [6] Chélini, 93.
[7] Fichter, *Social Relations*, 104.

are two independent factors in the life of the American city Catholic.[1]

Religious–ecological studies of the country still lag far behind those for the town. It is very probable that with the country communities' loss of demographic self-sufficiency, the migration to the town and within the country, ecological conditions also have changed.[2]

The influence of types like closely grouped villages or scattered hamlets on Christian life has not yet been established. On the basis of the available material on the French countryside, Canon Boulard is convinced that neither scattered nor grouped living has any direct connexion with the practice of religion.[3] Nor does the numerical or spatial size of the community seem to have any direct connexion with it.[4] On the other hand it emerges that too great distances do not permit any human community and hence no common religious life.[5]

Another task for ecology would be to study the relationship of the parishioners to the parish church and presbytery; that is, whether the situation of the church in the sociological area is favourable or otherwise; whether in a town, for example, its position helps to attract groups which do not legally belong to the parish; and so on.

Ecology is very important for parish planning which today is becoming more and more necessary and also more scientifically developed.[6]

Even the study of spatial relationships alone has led to the conclusion that the canonical parish does not necessarily correspond with a religious community in the sociological sense. The term 'parish congregation' does not mean that the parish is sociologically a true community.[7]

But however important and instructive ecological studies may

[1] Ib., 106.

[2] Cf. Mendras, 'L'influence des divers courants migratoires sur la vie religieuse des campagnes'.

[3] Boulard, 'Le problème d'un "optimum" de population pour les paroisses rurales', 163 f.

[4] Ib., 176. [5] Ib., 174.

[6] Cf. Houtart, 'Planning'; *Les techniques du planning au service de la pastorale*, and 'L'aménagement religieux des territoires urbains'; Bodzenta, 'Critères de planning paroissial urbain'.

[7] Cf. 'Mystifizierung des Raumes und der Pfarrei als Nachbarschaftsgruppe', in Noppel, *Pfarrei*, 195 ff.

be, they still only touch the fringes of the sociological structure of the parish community. They have to be supplemented by the examination of neighbourhood and group relations.[1]

(b) *Sociological Groups* (*Neighbourhoods*). Although the value of ecological factors must not be underestimated, they do not play the most important part in the integration of a community, but generally take second place to other factors. Human and social relations, and the attitude and activities of groups are much more decisive. Here begins the real sociological investigation, and precisely here religious sociology still fails us.[2] One of its most important representatives is Fr Joseph Fichter, whose studies may in part not even be published.[3]

For the study of groups within the parish much will depend upon whether it is a question of a purely Catholic or a mixed population within which Catholics may be in a majority or in a minority. The difference between town and country is not decisive in this investigation.

Theoretically, the parish may become a 'congregation' (*Gemeinde*) either through its own power of integration[4] or by using already existing groups as vehicles. In actual fact both elements will work together so that they cannot always be distinguished. However, a sociological study of the parish community would have to examine both possibilities, study their interaction and analyse their effects.[5] This would show which functions in the parish are exercised by the purely religious and which by the profane groups, whether they are interrelated, whether the religious groups act in unity as a

[1] Cf. *PuPr*, 83.

[2] 'It has always seemed strange to me that the principal object of scientific sociology—the study of social groups—has been largely neglected by religious sociologists. Most research in this field has put the stress on the demographic, sociographic and statistical aspects. Even here one finds that the term "social structures" is interpreted in the sense of social stratification and that the practice of religion is measured in terms of profession, age, matrimonial status and place of residence.' Fichter, 'La Paroisse', 84. Cf. also this author's *Social Relations*, pp. 195–217, 'Major issues in the sociology of the parish'; Goddijn, 'Die katholische Pfarrsoziologie in Westeuropa', 17; Pin, 'La sociologie du catholicisme depuis la Conférence Internationale (Louvain, 1956)', and his 'Dix ans de sociologie religieuse, 1950–60'.

[3] Cf. Chélini, 35.

[4] Religious and cultural values, ideals, symbolism, functions, organizations.

[5] Cf. Freytag, *Aufgaben*, 2 f.

leaven, whether individual Christians belonging to religious groups have a religious influence on secular groups and so forth. In this context the study of informal groups would be of particular importance.

The very limited material, however, allows only little insight which remains specialized and provisional. The following discussion uses almost exclusively material dealing with religious groups of the urban parish, and principally the formal groups.[1]

The study of sociological groups within the urban parish leads Fichter to the conclusion that probably in most cases there is not an integrated 'congregation' (i.e. a community) but a secondary group: that is, a 'number of persons in mutual communication who fulfil common functions, have a stock of common values, show a certain solidarity and are considered as a group by non-members'.[2] This secondary group usually includes a primary group which bears the signs of a true community, constituting an integrated neighbourhood or an integrated element of the congregation.[3] Actually these one or more primary groups make the secondary groups possible and hold them together. The primary group consists of the so-called *Kernpfarrangehörige* (core or nucleus of parishioners).[4] Since the parish is a secondary group, the individual parishioners have not, sociologically, the same relationship with each other as with the parish.

Fichter divides parishioners into four sociological types, while fully aware of their relativity; '(*a*) "nuclear" or active parishioners, the most loyal of the faithful; (*b*) modal Catholics, normal "practising Catholics" who account for the great majority of the Catholic laity; (*c*) marginal Catholics, who actively practise a minimum of observances; (*d*) lapsed Catholics, who have given up the practice of their religion but not joined any other denomination.'[5] Similar typologies have

[1] Cf. Donovan, 'The social structure of the Parish', in Nuesse and Harte, 86–93.

[2] Cooley and McYver; Fichter, 'La paroisse', 86 and *Social Relations*, 143 f.

[3] Cf. König, 137, 140 f.

[4] Fichter, *Social Relations*, 143.

[5] Ib., 22.

been established for other countries.[1] Fichter's four types constitute the 'sociological-canonical' parish.[2] For our purposes, we need consider only the average Catholics and the 'nuclear' parishioners.[3]

In the category of average Catholics, who constitute the majority of parishioners, Fichter studies their social solidarity, which is similar to the question of the community character of this *milieu*. He wants to examine scientifically whether there is 'a distinctively Catholic bond of unity that can be recognized in operation at the parochial level'.[4] His attempt to regard the parish as a community group leads Fichter to recognize that the parish is at most 'a social aggregate'.[5]

The most likely bond of union the sociological observer might be expected to find would be the Christian love of neighbour. For, on the one hand, human agreement, i.e. unity of faith and philosophical outlook, may only be expected to produce

[1] For example, for Italy (and France) (*a*) the lapsed (*separati*), (*b*) the conformists (*conformisti*), i.e. those who receive the sacraments at least once in their lifetime (*saisonniers*); (*c*) the practising (*observanti*) who attend Mass on Sundays and holy days and do their Easter duties (*messalisants*), (*d*) active laymen (*devoti*) who work in the various associations, receive monthly Communion, attend Vespers, do more than the Commandments require of them. Cf. Bruhin, 27. Students of Protestant Church communities arrive at similar groupings. Cf. Freytag, 'Aufgaben', 10; Kruijt, 'Die Erforschung', 46; Abrecht, 'Die protestantische Religionssoziologie in den USA', 85 f.; Luckmann, 'Vier protestantische Kirchgemeinden', 134 f.; Köster, 'Die Kirchentreuen', 144 ff.; Rendtorff, 'Die Kerngemeinde im Verständnis des Gemeindepfarrers', 153 ff.

[2] Fichter does not start from a purely religious sociological concept of the parish community, but mingles with it the canonical feature of residence (and the other one of race). Fichter, *Social Relations*. An 'average' Catholic who has the centre of his religious life in a parish other than his own and only refers to his own parish for necessary administrative matters would, according to the purely sociological concept of community, belong to the first parish, whereas Fichter has to count him as belonging to his legal parish. Hence he compromises in this matter. Further, lapsed Catholics can hardly be included in the parish congregation from the point of view of religious sociology.

[3] For the parishes studied Fichter gives 5·7 per cent hardcore parishioners as the average (in *Social Relations*, 24) while average Catholics amount to 70 per cent (ib., 34). The percentages are based on baptized persons of ten years and older designated by Fichter as parishioners (ib., 24). In one large Brussels parish only 3 per cent hard-core parishioners were found. Cf. Verdoodt, 'Une paroisse urbaine européenne comme groupe social', 95.

[4] Fichter, *Social Relations*, 42.

[5] Ib., 42.

social forms; they cannot be proved to do so.[1] On the other hand, solidarity through the grace of God cannot be studied by sociology. Social virtue, however, is accessible to sociologists, if not in its essence nor in its supernatural character, at least in its external manifestation.[2] The virtue which is most important in this context is neighbourly love: 'See, how they love one another.'

Two questions are posed in this connexion: do Catholics work together socially because they are Catholics? and can the social relationships among Catholics be distinguished from those among non-Catholics?[3]

On the level of society in general the study has shown 'that for the modal parishioner almost every other factor of social solidarity seems to have more practical effect in the quality of human relations than the religious factor for which we are searching . . . that so-called secular factors constitute common interest areas, promote close co-operation, and effectively unite people in a way that religious factors fail to do'.[4]

One would expect a difference of degree between the love of Catholics for non-Catholics within general society and the love of Catholics for Catholics in the supra-parochial world. But the same factors that separate men in ordinary society do so also among Catholics.[5] Nevertheless, it is a remarkable sociological fact that efforts to remove class and race barriers are to be found at the supra-parochial rather than at parochial level. But on the supra-parochial plane the average parishioners of Catholic urban churches show no social solidarity that might be founded on supernatural charity.[6]

If the parish were a religious community group, all parishioners would have to be united in a strictly defined social group and this solidarity would have to appear in the actual human relationship of Catholics. Fichter's studies have shown that this only applies to the small central core of the parish

[1] 'Just as the greatest physical proximity of two persons may be accompanied by the greatest social distance between them, so also two Catholics side by side in a church pew may be theologically similar but have no observable social relations with each other.' Ib., 44.

[2] Ib., 45. Cf. Birou, 161–64: 'L'objet de la sociologie.'

[3] Fichter, op. cit., 46.

[4] Ib., 47.

[5] Ib., 47. A striking example is race segregation in America.

[6] Ib., 49.

and that the most important examples of social solidarity in small groups are not necessarily or even primarily based on Christian charity. Membership of the same class or profession forges closer bonds between Catholics and non-Catholics than belonging to the same parish and the same religion does for Catholics of different classes. The same is true of the influence of differences in education and race.[1]

The theory that the parish is a unifying bond between the various groups is refuted by the conditions in the towns: 'The normal urban parish is said to unite people of all classes, of different education, and of all ethnic backgrounds in its societies and organizations. The rebuttal to this claim is known by every experienced parish priest. The various organizations do not provide a locus of parochial solidarity except for the handful of dependable nuclear parishioners. Modal parishioners who are well educated, who are professional and business people, simply do not belong to these societies, and those who are from the skilled and semi-skilled occupations often form at best a nominal membership.'[2]

'Our tentative generalization, based on the empirical studies so far made in urban parishes, is that specifically Catholic solidarity, motivated by Christian love and operating on the parochial level, is at best an ideal toward which priests and parishioners are struggling with varying degrees of success.'[3] Fichter's statements relate always to the American urban parish. Hence we must be careful not to generalize and to apply them at once to European conditions and rural parishes. Nevertheless, the analogies which indubitably exist between parish sociology and community sociology allow us to assume a certain general structure, which may indeed leave some details out of account.[4]

The parish groups are the formal framework which gives social coherence to the average Catholics within the parish.[5] Hence their structure will offer information on the social coherence of a large section of the parishioners.

On the basis of a comparative study in twenty-three urban

[1] Fitcher, 49. [2] Ib., 51. [3] Ib., 55.

[4] It should be noted here that the above conclusions are valid only for the *milieu* and the groups of average Catholics, not for the hard-core Catholics who often display a high degree of integration.

[5] Cf. Engel, 'Parish Societies'.

parishes, Fichter assembles some facts about lay parish groups. He asks if the organizational form of the groups has an influence on the way in which they work. The following picture emerges: (1) the number of formal groups in each parish is relatively small;[1] (2) they are mass-organizations with large nominal membership and few membership conditions; (3) the number of active members is small,[2] and frequently several important posts are filled by the same person; (4) they are strictly organized by statutes; (5) they are mostly attached to a model of the traditional categories of age, sex and family status.[3]

These factors contain a tendency to artificiality in the constitution of parish societies and the danger of organizations becoming ends in themselves through over-emphasis of the formal institutional character.[4]

Fichter arrives at two general, provisional conclusions: 'The first is that the attempt to include all lay, voluntary, parochial activity into relatively few formal artificial organizations minimizes both effectiveness (achieving purpose) and efficiency (getting people to contribute effort). The second is that the neglect of informal small groupings (sometimes called "natural groups") constitutes one of the greatest social wastes in the apostolic potential of the parish.'[5] However, priests in parish work cling to these few formal organizations since they see in them the only way to maintain parish unity. 'They feel that a multiplication of societies would cause disunity among the parishioners, dissipate their apostolic energies, and probably make it impossible for the priests to moderate the lay activity.'[6] This means in other words that an effective and fruitful solution could be sought in the cell system.

[1] On the average, 13·2; ib., 157.

[2] Fichter arrives at a total of practising and active members of a parish over fourteen years of age by deleting the names of those who attended less than one third of the meetings or did not participate at all in the previous year. This gave a figure of 3·6 per cent of all parishioners over fourteen years old! Cf. ib., 157, 160. In addition, his researches show 'that effective co-operation cannot be achieved in groups of more than twelve to fifteen persons'. Ib., 160.

[3] Ib., 156 f.

[4] '. . . the traditional and systematic procedures do not meet the socio-religious needs of contemporary urban culture.' Ib., 156.

[5] Ib., 156 f. Cf. the findings of community sociology on the significance of informal groups. See above.

[6] Ib., 158.

Neither a common religion nor an organization is enough to ensure effective co-operation. The religious bond is only one among others.

Small informal groups usually form round an outstanding personality assisted by other factors such as national characteristics, education, sex, age, friendship, relationship, neighbourhood, and so on. They are usually short-lived and are therefore not very highly valued by the clergy.[1]

Fr Fichter[2] has also studied twelve parish groups of a German urban parish and these lead by and large to the same conclusion.[3]

When considering the structure he starts from the question whether the social structures are adapted to the people or whether parishioners are expected to adapt themselves to already existing parish structures. The structure of the parish groups has no profound law but is simply factual; parishioners readily follow this structure, because they have grown with it and know no other.[4]

Three factors are decisive in the organization of parish groups. First there is the artificial agreement according to social categories. Then there is the internal organization according to social duties and activities linked with certain social categories by custom and positive regulation. The subdivision of group activities into various 'task-groups' produces sub-groups which, however, remain attached to the parent group. Finally, the most important factor is the social gifts of individual parishioners.[5] 'The existence of social groups is . . . only possible through people and their ability to create community, people whose ability is decisively responsible for the functioning of the groups.'[6] This includes willingness and ability to co-operate in a common task. 'But it is precisely this kind of social ability that is most often lacking. In other words, it may probably be said that it represents the least considered yet one of the most necessary qualities for human associations.'[7] The technical ability to fulfil a function is far more widespread than active readiness to co-operate with others. For parish groups this means that

[1] Fichter, 163.
[2] Fichter, *Soziologie.*
[3] Ib., 60.
[4] Ib., 63 ff.
[5] Ib., 65–68.
[6] Ib., 68 f.
[7] Ib., 69 f.

social ability has a greater influence on the social structure of groups than social activities.[1]

'Sociologically all parish groups are interest groups and not true communities. As a result the feeling of being responsible for the group is less than where there is a common life. True, small circles of friends may form within various parish groups for whom the latter can become living communities. The nature of parish groups as interest groups also explains why the relations among members are fairly impersonal. It is, of course, true that even personal ideals and duties can arouse the spirit of loyalty and responsibility, but actually personal ties will do so much more effectively. Just these, however, are lacking in most groups.'[2] Moreover, there is the danger that all such groups will develop into leisure groups with a certain ecclesiastical flavour, mainly devoted to entertainment.[3]

The co-ordination of groups within the parish is very important for the formation of a community, for it appears that these groups hold the whole social fabric of the parish together.[4] What the 'core' families are for the life of all the parish groups, the latter are for the life of the whole parish. But the groups can only play their part when they are properly co-ordinated and thus form a unity. Hence the question is this: 'Are all groups so linked to one another that the whole represents a well-ordered structural unit? This question must probably be answered in the negative, unless one understands the term "social unit" in the widest sense.'[5]

The first co-ordinating factor would be the relation of all parish groups to the parish priest, in whose person they are, as it were, united. Another factor would be the co-operation between the parish priest and the curate who share the direction of the various groups between them. But because both are

[1] Ib., 70. It may be worth mentioning in this connexion that 'more than four out of five office-holders in parish groups come from less than fifteen family circles all related to each other in some way'. Ib., 80. Cf. the part played by the family in the whole practice of religion: Pin, *Pratique*, 409.

[2] Ib., 103.

[3] Freytag, 'Aufgaben', 13.

[4] 'Although the totality of parishioners does not by any means coincide with the totality of group membership, it must nevertheless be said that in the groups the community life of the whole parish is crystallized.' Fichter, *Soziologie*, 147.

[5] Ib., 148.

in a certain sense above and outside the groups, they are not very decisive for their unity. This depends essentially on the contact between the leading laymen. Official contacts between male group-leaders are rare, due mostly to outside pressure; informal contacts are more frequent, though less than those among the leaders of the women's groups.[1]

Moreover, young leaders often meet each other in their family circles, where contacts are much closer than on the official plane of group-leaders. These family and social contacts are quite unconnected with the parish groups, but all parish groups have such family ties. These families, incidentally, constitute the core of the parish, as we shall see later.[2]

The priests have a closer relationship with the groups, especially with their leaders, than with the other parishioners. The active parishioners are in closer touch with each other than they are with the rest, or than the rest are with one another. 'The majority of non-members find themselves usually in the role of benevolent onlookers who are, however, frequently indifferent both to the existence of parish groups and to their efficiency or otherwise.'[3] In spite of this, a 'spiritual co-ordination' not definable in numbers will develop in the whole parish through the activities of the groups.[4]

Normally the Catholic layman practises his faith and charity in the neighbourhood within the parish; yet neighbourly relations are not consciously made dependent on the denomination.[5] Nor does it mean that a person is for this reason a devoted member of the parish as a social unit or of one of its subdivisions.[6] We might simply say that the members of the canonical parish are sociologically divided into several concentric circles.[7] The outer circle would contain unbelievers, non-Catholic believers and apostate Catholics, though these could not really be included in the sociological parish community. Next would come the lapsed Catholics, and further inside the circle the fringe Catholics. And finally there would be the average Catholics and the active parishioners, who are the main constituents of the sociological parish community. Within

[1] Fichter, *Soziologie*, 152–54. [2] Ib., 154 f. [3] Ib., 161. [4] Ib.

[5] Wurzbacher, *Das Dorf*, 229.

[6] Fichter, *Social Relations*, 142.

[7] For Protestant Church communities cf. Tenbruck, 'Die Kirchengemeinde in der entchristlichten Gesellschaft', 123 ff.

this there are three further circles: the average parishioners who are 'practising' but not organized; the average and active parishioners organized in groups; and finally the firmly established centre which constitutes 'a recognizable social group'.[1] 'The limited sociological research in the urban parish system in this country reveals that the parish can no longer be conceived realistically as an *ecclesiola in ecclesia*, a sort of total Church in miniature. Nor can one say that only the layman who continuously and exclusively lives as a parishioner is "a truly living member of the visible body of Christ". Even if this were a desideratum for all lay Catholics the fact is that it does not (and probably cannot) exist in our urban and industrialized society.'[2]

On the question whether the parish is a sociological community, non-parochial forms of association must also be taken into account. Fichter proposes a typology of the religiously aligned (non-parish) lay organizations of the American town[3] which touches on this subject.

He shows, for example, that the interest-groups of laymen in towns are more often based on the principle of free, supra-parochial association than on residence in a parish. Indeed, just the most active Catholics are often attracted to these groups, or so one gathers from the complaints of the parish clergy. It seems that the appeal is greater and that they can develop their gifts better on the supra-parochial level.[4] 'The religious activities of these interest groups are both more personal and more universal than those of parish groupings. The spiritual satisfaction an individual obtains is placed in a setting which transcends the local and immediate problems of the parish. As one man remarked: "You get a broader outlook of the Church when you join up with these groups. You begin to see the work of the Church in a diocesan, regional, and world-wide perspective." The parochial horizon is extended, and the all-embracing missionary, or universal, function of the Church comes into focus.'[5]

Besides the parish principle and the interest principle, the class principle must be taken into account. Co-operation based on the same class and status in the religious sphere creates

[1] Fichter, *Social Relations*, 143. [2] Ib., 143 f. [3] Ib., 138.
[4] Ib., 145 f. [5] Ib., 147 f.

functional solidarity. *Rerum Novarum* and *Quadragesimo Anno* have contributed much to the establishment of such groups. They know 'that persons who perform similar functions (not merely economic) are "naturally and spontaneously" likely to associate with one another. Similarity of interest and values develops with similarity of functions (and vice versa), so that social integration becomes relatively high among the participants.'[1] Empirical examination seems to support this view. The cells of specialized Catholic Action are also constituted according to class and status. The Catholic likes to associate with other Catholics especially for social reasons. His practice of religion is itself closely connected with these.[2]

The national parish, is based partly on sociological structures other than those of the territorial parish. Its existence is one more proof that canon law would be willing in principle to adapt the parish organization to sociological conditions and to use these for its own purposes.[3] National parishes have played, and still play even today, an important role in the United States.[4] For national groups of immigrants they were the most powerful institution to guarantee the continuance of their national individuality. Adapting itself to the concrete situation, the parish exercised many other besides the religious functions: being, for example, responsible for schools, leisure activities, material assistance and keeping alive the mother tongue. These non-religious functions probably integrated the parishioners into the parish communities more than the religious ones. In addition, cultural and social minorities always like to associate in order to preserve their identity particularly in the case of immigrants.

Immigrants to America, for example, come principally from the working classes, another element that contributes to integration. According to community sociology the poorer classes form neighbourhood groups more easily than the wealthy. Thanks to the national parishes, the working classes of the United States unlike Europe and South America have

[1] Fichter, 150.

[2] Freytag, 'Aufgaben', 3 ff. Cf. the pioneer study by Pin, *Pratique religieuse et classes sociales*. The Marian Congregations had already profited from this knowledge in the sixteenth century.

[3] Cf. Wurzbacher, *Das Dorf*, 219 f.

[4] Cf. Harte, 'Racial and National Parishes in the United States'.

always been well cared for in matters of religion.[1] The national parish also exercised a certain measure of social control which allowed it to withstand the bad influences of the town.[2]

By adapting themselves to the conditions of the times, the national parishes embraced well-integrated groups and lively ecclesial communities. But just these national parishes also contributed very largely to the slow and smooth absorption of these foreign population groups into American society.[3] As assimilation increased and the stream of immigrants dwindled, national parishes became correspondingly superfluous, that is to say they no longer correspond to the sociological situation, which has changed while the parish organization has remained static. True, it has in many cases adapted itself to the new conditions, in that it functions as a territorial parish and has lost its national character. But there has not yet been any legal adaptation, a fact which leads to innumerable difficulties.[4]

(c) *The Relation between Parish Priest and Laity as a Factor of Integration.* Canon law allows for the desire and the theoretical possibility that the parish priest's responsibility for all his parishioners and the resulting personal contacts will lead to personal, community-building relations.[5] Sociology must show whether this is a real possibility or to what extent it becomes reality.

It is obvious that in giant parishes contact between the parish priest and his people is impossible. On the other hand one easily tends to take it for granted that it exists in a small parish. But even if it exists, it need not be a force of integration, it does not necessarily mould the congregation into a community. As we know from community sociology, fundamentally integration does not depend on the size of the community, disagreements and oppositions may clash much worse in a small community than in a larger one where it is easier to escape from them.

The decreasing esteem of the parish priest in the village, which Wurzbacher encountered in his investigations, is accompanied by a corresponding decrease in his effectiveness as an integrat-

[1] In South America the national parish system is hardly known.

[2] 'The national parishes saved the religious practice of the urban masses of America.' Houtart, 'L'évolution', 58.

[3] Cf. Szabo, *La Paroisse*, 25.

[4] Cf. Houtart, ib., 51 f.

[5] C 476; note that this canon talks of the parish priest, and not the curate.

ing force in the parish. On an average parish priests take only the sixth place within seventeen professions, that is after doctors, councillors, factory owners, chemists, graduate teachers.[1] Both professions are esteemed more highly in Germany than they are in England. There is no real difference between Catholics and Protestants in this scale of values, though on the average, Catholics rate the parish priest a little higher. The authority of the office is less and less transferred to the person so that the parish priest is judged more by his personal qualities. 'Like all representatives of academic professions, he is in much closer personal contact, which unavoidably invites stronger criticism.'[2] Thus, the integrating force of the parish priest depends on his popularity and his personal qualities, as can be seen from the examples quoted.[3] For this reason his influence, whether positive or negative, is correspondingly lasting especially in the close relationships of a village.

Concerning the larger parishes, Paul Winninger points out the problem raised by the curates. Young curates are the most important apostolic element in city parishes; they are often at the start of their apostolic work and, more important, are frequently changed.[4] Contact with the parish priest, who is heavily burdened with administrative matters, becomes difficult. The frequent change of curates makes a thoroughgoing continuity of work almost impossible. This being so, the parish clergy cannot be expected to instil the community spirit on a large scale. Winniger in any case believes that the creation of a Christian community is impossible in these circumstances.[5]

[1] Wurzbacher, *Das Dorf*, 33, 192.

[2] Ib., 37. [3] Ib., 187 ff.

[4] 'To put it briefly, and to exaggerate slightly, we might say: the towns are in the hands of the curates. The religious mentality of the towns, relationships between clergy and faithful, the psychological nature of the social group which is the parish are all strongly marked by this fact.' Winninger, *Les villes aux mains des vicaires*, 97.

[5] 'One thing is certain: there is so rapid a turn-round of curates that it is not possible to have in urban parishes a Christian community, a coherent group, a brotherly spirit of unity.' Ib., 101. On the other hand, Winninger sees very clearly the enormous importance of the apostolate of the parish in the city: 'City parish priest is objectively, that is to say pastorally, a more important position than parish priest in a village. When the time comes that we see the priests of little parishes turn into genuine urban priests—an unthinkable thing at the present moment—then a genuine revolution will have occurred in the ecclesiastical mentality.' Ib., 100.

Fichter, who regards the priest as the key figure of every Catholic parish, has also included the relationship between priest and people in his studies of the parish and its groups.[1] As a key figure the priest exercises a manifold influence which is not restricted to the religious sphere. The co-ordination of the priest's different roles is sociologically important. Every priest is a mediator and father who cares about the salvation of souls. In the urban conditions of today this care of souls has been largely bureaucratized in order that the multiple contacts between priest and parishioners might be manageable at all.[2] Their relationship has been largely depersonalized and so the influence of the priest on the moral and social conduct of Catholics has dwindled.[3]

Fichter mentions nine different roles of the parish priest: his 'congregational', administrative, business, civic, recreational, charitable, educational, socio-spiritual, and liturgical[4] roles.[5] We can only discuss some of these that seem important for our enquiry.

There is first his 'congregational' role, in which the parishioner is related to his parish priest not as an individual but as a member of the congregation. 'From this point of view, the components of the Catholic parish are not primarily its individual parishioners but its sub-groupings. That is to say, the parish priest plays a communal or group role toward his parishioners. He participates in a definite *social* relationship with the parishioner as a member of various groups and not merely in an *individual* relationship with him as an unattached person.'[6] According to the way the priest fulfils this role, he can have an integrating influence on certain groups within the parish. This is true also of the other roles which bring the priest into contact with the faithful, each in its own way. The role of preacher is especially worth noting for it is 'the only regular relationship which exists between the priest and most of the

[1] Fichter, *Social Relations*, 123 f.

[2] Fichter makes an interesting comment in this connexion: 'Paradoxically, while the influences of religion have been dwindling in the family life of parishioners, the number of functions have been multiplying in the official life of the parish priest.' Ib., 126.

[3] Ib., 123–26.

[4] Häring, 'Gemeinschaftstiftende Kraft', 211.

[5] Fichter, op. cit., 128–37.

[6] Ib., 128.

parishioners'.[1] In addition, seen as a social function, the sermon is the most important test of the educational role of the priest.

If, however, one examines to what extent the parish priest is integrated with the parish as a whole, or rather with the groups within it, it must be admitted that he has ties only with a small part of it. To a certain, though not easily verifiable, extent the priest actually hinders integration and by his conduct causes the lukewarm to cease practising.[2]

Moreover, the parish clergy are in a much closer relationship with the members of parish organizations than with non-members. They are tempted to regard the former as first-class, loyal and reliable parishioners and relegate the others to a sort of second-class status. This is not, of course, done deliberately, but is due mostly to thoughtlessness.[3]

The connexions between parish clergy and parish groups are not primarily religious.[4] On the contrary, they are very complex, containing many spiritual and intellectual as well as social motives. The most important factor is the attitude and personality of the priest. If he shows interest in the groups and is moreover a likeable personality, he has an integrating effect on them and their success is more or less assured. Naturally the relation is reciprocal: because the groups work successfully they attract a greater interest on the part of the clergy.

But even in the relations between priests and groups, particularly the informal ones, difficulties may arise that make integration impossible. This applies particularly to those where the laity themselves want to take over work and responsibility. There is a certain type of priest who systematically brings up his parishioners to be passive and willing listeners, and who will not tolerate such groups, but vigorously opposes them.[5]

[1] Fichter, 134; the priest 'who thinks of his parishioners in terms of so many communions or so many confessions' is wrongly orientated. Ib., 128.

[2] 'In more than 40 per cent of our interviews with dormant Catholics there was mention of this factor. "The priest terrified me; we were afraid of him when we were kids." Others offered somewhat tenuous explanations, remarking on the priest's aloofness, his lack of cordiality, his boorishness, his autocratic methods, etc.' Ib., 77. Such statements must of course be taken with discretion, but they are nevertheless an indication.

[3] Ib., 158. Cf. the same author's *Soziologie*, 161.

[4] Fichter, *Soziologie*, 136. Cf. F. Boulard, 'Wie sehen die französischen Christen den Priester?', in Guyot, *Das apostolische Amt*, 289–307.

[5] Fichter, *Social Relations*, 163.

In any case the relation of the parish clergy to the generality of average parishioners and their groups is normally not that of an integrated community.

3. *The Parish Community*

Apart from the probably quite exceptional case where a parish is so integrated that it constitutes one single community, it is a fact that within the secondary group or the whole of the 'congregation', primary groups or integrated neighbourhoods form a community.[1] In socially not too complex parishes this will normally be what we have called the 'core' of the parish. In more complex parishes several such cores are conceivable, particularly where there are several places of worship in one parish; though in such cases there may, sociologically, be two parish congregations.

The so-called core-parishioners are only a very small group. They are the centre of the parish whose whole social fabric rests on them.[2]

Such a parishioner 'tends to be an integrated Christian in the sense that he carries over into other institutional activities the high behavioral ideals implicit in his religious convictions'.[3] He will usually, though not always, belong to a family of the same ideals.[4] His education seems to be rather better than that of the average parishioner. Generally it can be said of conditions in the United States that 'the less-educated nuclears are more active in the parish organizations, while the better-

[1] Ib., 188. Cf. Nuesse, 'Empirical Problems for Social Research in the Parish', 220 ff.

[2] Cf. Chéry, *Communauté paroissiale et liturgie*. On the Protestant side, cf. Böhm, 272–346, Part III: 'Parochialgemeinde und Kerngemeinde in der Diskussion um die Stellung der Kirche in der modernen Gesellschaft'; Freytag, 'Aufgaben', 13.

[3] Fichter, *Social Relations*, 25. 'It cannot be repeated too often that there is no necessary correlation between formal religious observances and community dependability. The fact is that there are in any urban community a number of people who exhibit a high degree of social awareness but at the same time are not active participants in the religious group. The opposite is also a common phenomenon: some people who are very religious either resist or neglect the extension of their religious beliefs and obligations into the wider social life.' Ib., 26.

[4] Ib., 26. For a contrary view cf. Häring, 'Gemeinschaftstiftende Kraft', 211 f.: 'Verhältnis zwischen Kinderfreudigkeit und Gemeinschaftsatmosphäre in der Pfarrei.'

educated ones are more notable for their religious observances'.[1] In America newcomers from rural parishes seem to fit into urban parishes and become part of the core better than those from other urban parishes.[2]

The social connexions of core-parishioners are not directed to social advancement. On the supra-parochial level they always or nearly always have religious contacts with other Catholics and tend in general towards a certain religious exclusiveness. The core-parishioner is a firm believer who feels with the Church and is led by her, perhaps even so far as neglecting to develop his own judgment. In his personal life he displays exemplary Christian behaviour which is nourished on the profounder religious values and the sacraments.[3] 'The religious institution is pivotal for him, and in this regard he tends to "go against" the culture in which he lives.'[4] Moreover, institutionalized religion is his centre to which all his other activities are directed. This religious saturation of his whole life unifies him also psychologically.[5]

Hence it is not surprising that he should associate and form an integrated group with other parishioners only to co-operate with them in parish tasks on the basis of Christian love.[6] Though he chiefly associates with his fellow Catholics and for religious reasons, this does not exclude his showing true Christian charity to all men nor using it as a basis for social reform.[7] On the other hand, the analysis of small groups shows that often active and well-integrated people in the groups are not core parishioners in their religious practice.[8]

A closer look at the parish 'core' will reveal that it is a small group consisting of a circle of families and friends.[9] 'Outspoken parishioners who are not members of the inner circle sometimes talk about the "clique that's in control".'[10] The greater part of the younger members of the parish groups, for example, comes from families either one or both of whose parents are active in the

[1] Fichter, 27. Converts are seldom found in the core. Like the educated, they are more involved in supra-parochial organizations. Ib., 28.
[2] Ib., 28 f. This is not true, however, of immigrants.
[3] Ib., 29, 53. [4] Ib., 29. [5] Ib., 30.
[6] Ib., 49, 59. [7] Ib., 46. [8] Ib., 55.
[9] Ib., 160. Cf. Wurzbacher, *Das Dorf*, 74–111: 'Die Familie als sozialer Eingliederungsfaktor'; cf. 205.
[10] Fichter, op. cit., 160.

groups.[1] In general, active, integrated members of such groups will also be friends apart from their religious activities and will belong to roughly the same age-group.[2]

The inner circle has a certain elasticity. It may split into smaller circles, but will not expand into larger formal groups.[3] Moreover, this circle is the one group within the parish into which the parish priest, too, is really integrated. As a result of this he can most easily work with this group and becomes somewhat distant from other parishioners and groups.[4] The 'core' parishioners regard the parish priest as their 'chief', maintain warm and natural relations with him, regard themselves as his assistants, understand his problems, defend his measures and back him up energetically. They are prepared to undertake even thankless tasks.[5]

4. *Conclusions*

The material, unfortunately very incomplete, shows nevertheless that a community in the sociological sense is possible within the parish and—one may well say—mostly also exists.[6] This community, however, coincides neither with the Catholics belonging to the canonical parish nor with the sociological parish 'congregation', but embraces only a very modest part of either.[7] It cannot even be said that the 'core' embraces all active Catholics, for there are genuine, idealistic Catholics who are not integrated in it because they are active on the supra-parochial level outside the parish. Indeed, the clergy often complain that just the best parishioners do not co-operate. One cannot therefore equate 'best parishioner' with 'best Catholic'.[8] Precisely because the 'inner circle' has, sociologically and spiritually, something of a ghetto mentality,[9] open and

[1] Ib., 157. [2] Ib., 53. [3] Ib., 160.

[4] 'The particular relation between priests and parishioners refers again to one of the central problems of lay parochial structure. It is difficult to see how the personalized relation of the priest can or should be translated into a purely "professional" relationship.' Ib., 160; cf. Freytag, 'Aufgaben', 4 f.

[5] Ib., 30.

[6] Cf. Freytag, op. cit., 1.

[7] Fichter, op. cit., 187 f. Cf. 'Die Mystifizierung der Pfarrfamilie', in Noppel, Pfarrei, 204 ff.

[8] Ib., 28.

[9] Cf. Rendtorff, 'Die Kerngemeinde im Verständnis des Gemeindepfarrers', 156.

active minds who see the problems and exercise their apostolate in a larger context attach themselves to supra-parochial groups.

Fichter thus sums up the result: 'It is probably true, as Werner Schollgen points out, that the Christian ethos is not associational (*gesellschaftlich*) but communal (*gemeinschaftlich*). But this is like saying that the Christian spirit is in essence "cultic" rather than "ecclesiastic". In the urban areas, where the sense of community and of neighbourliness on a territorial basis has largely vanished, the parish has become a secondary, associational type of social structure. Perhaps the social ideal may still be held that the parish should be communal, but our empirical studies clearly demonstrate that it is now largely associational.'[1]

[1] Fichter, op. cit., 143.

PART THREE

Conclusions of Pastoral Theology

Conclusions of Pastoral Theology

I—Summary of the Various Points of View

Genuine ecclesial community in the fullest sense is present where the mystical Body and the hierarchical community of worship are expressed even in the natural structures and informable human society. This can happen in various ways: first when a naturally existing community[1] is raised up and informed by a sacrament or by grace, as for example, in marriage, and the Christian family; then, in the freely chosen common life in the spirit of the imitation of Christ, in the 'state of perfection' according to the evangelical counsels or in a similar way. There community of goods[2] is practised in the early sense. Finally it can happen in any group of people, who build and integrate their common life within the Church in the spirit of Christian faith and brotherly love. Here natural community-building forces and the supernatural bond of unity in Christ will influence each other, or the community-building force of the grace of Christ will integrate naturally heterogeneous groups, as for example in the primitive Christian communities and in the completely integrated groups within a parish or diocese.[3]

As regards the parish of today, our investigations have shown that the concept and reality of the parish are not identical with the concept and reality of full ecclesial community; that is to say that in very definite circumstances and fulfilling certain conditions the modern parish can be a full ecclesial community, but it need not, and very rarely will, be this.

[1] Already inwardly directed to grace.

[2] Orders, Congregations, Oratories, secular institutes.

[3] It seems to us that even Pin asserts only the possibility but not the reality of parish community. Moreover, according to his arguments this would extend not to the canonical parish but only to a group within the parish. His arguments show no necessary community *structure* of the parish. Cf. Pin, 'Urban Parish'.

Since the parish is an institution of positive human canon law, the canonical nature of the parish was chosen as a starting-point.[1] The result of this examination was that the canonical nature of the parish does not imply as such a parish community, but does not exclude it either.

Further, in so far as the parish is filled with the mystical reality of the Church, it is absorbed into the supernatural community of the Church which transcends time and space and constitutes the mystical Body of Christ, the people of God, though this does not of course mean that the parish itself is a member of the mystical Body. On the other hand, individual parishioners are: yet not as parishioners but as baptized Christians. There is a clear-cut distinction between parish and Church, for the parish is a human institution tied to the here-and-now and to the contingencies of human civilizations.

In the liturgy, the absorption into the universal Church is expressed sacramentally by the participation of the worshipping congregation in the sacrifice of the Church and its head, Jesus Christ. In the liturgy heaven and earth meet, the liturgy of heaven is celebrated by those who, still pilgrims, are hastening towards their fatherland.[2] Thus, in the liturgy, too, the limited community is lifted up into the all-embracing unity of the Church.

In most parishes there are baptized persons who have fallen away not only through grave sin,[3] but who have publicly apostatized so that they no longer wish to be known as members of the Church. With these should be counted also those who have fallen away and perhaps a large part of the non-practising. According to canon law they belong indeed to the parish, but they are not even in the congregation let alone integrated into the community.[4]

The supernatural reality and community of the Church is bound up with the essential nature of man and of human community. Yet it is not, as such, connected with man's freely

[1] Parish in the wide sense. The canonical term *paroecia* has nothing to do with the people of the parish and consequently with parish community. Cf. p. 33 above.

[2] Cf., Schnitzler, *Die Messe in der Betrachtung*, I, 97 ff.

[3] Which does not end their membership of the visible Church. Cf. K. Rahner, 'Die Kirche der Sünder', in *StdZ*, 140 (1947), 163–77.

[4] Cf. also Böhm on this question.

created institutions, but only in so far as these are in harmony with the essential nature of man. Wherever the boundaries of the parish cut across the sociological boundaries of naturally integrated groups, it will be difficult to establish a community. For the integrating influence exercised by the grace and brotherly love of a supernatural community on heterogeneous secular relations should not be overestimated. The few studies in pastoral sociology suggest that the integrated core of the parish, which represents a true ecclesial community, embraces those who already largely constitute a community in the natural sphere, which is, however, much smaller than the parish congregation.

The parish is neither a supernatural nor a natural but an artificial formation. Consequently the parish community, too, can be neither purely supernatural nor purely natural, nor simply a combination of the two, but must be marked by the arbitrary, artificial character of the parish. In order that a specific parish community may come into being, the parishioners must be grouped in such a way that they are sufficiently disposed to make their supernatural community of grace fruitful even to their remotest human relationships. In the contemporary parish this disposition exists only in a small circle of parishioners, to which the full ecclesial community is actually limited. For the modern parish is very complex and makes much greater demands on the parish clergy and the active laity than an integrated community.

For the modern parish has an essentially missionary structure. The parish congregation is grouped round the integrated nucleus which holds it together and gives it vitality. But in certain circumstances there is a far wider circle of parishioners outside the congregation for whom the parish clergy, the core and the congregation bear a Christian responsibility and who should be drawn from the periphery back into the heart of the Church.

II—The Importance of the Community within the Parish

If in the foregoing discussions it has constantly been emphasized that the parish is not a community this should not be allowed to detract from its great importance in the cure of souls. On the contrary, the very rejection of a superficial view of the parish as a community should lead to a stronger realization of the importance of a true ecclesial community, particularly within the parish. For genuine and fruitful pastoral work is only possible if one knows what true ecclesial communities are. And a genuine cure of souls will always strive towards full ecclesial communities and to train them for the Church's apostolate.

It was stated in the introduction that the activity of the Church is the subject of pastoral theology. A too narrow concept of the Church has an inhibiting effect on the Church's cure of souls and places the responsibility too one-sidedly with the hierarchical priesthood. The full concept of the Church shows that the priesthood of the baptized also bears a pastoral responsibility, that the cure of souls must be based on the community, on the co-operation between priest and people. It is but the logical consequence of the rediscovery of the concept of the Church in its completeness that in recent times the importance of the laity for the apostolate has been so strongly emphasized and ways to fruitful co-operation have been sought.

Today it is a widely recognized fact that the individual cure of souls is not enough but that it is essentially conditioned by the social structure of the Church, that it must begin in the community and also be directed towards the building up of the community. For the cure of souls is nothing but the care for the salvation of men which has been given us in Christ and consists in communion with the triune God. The goal is participation in God's community of love; the way leads through the community of the Church. The goal is akin to the way that leads there, for it already starts along the way. The kingdom of God is already amongst us. But this kingdom, this community must constantly be built up.[1]

The world-wide kingdom of God is built up in small communities in which the Church and the spirit of the Gospel are alive. The main pastoral object is to call such communities into being, to foster and strengthen them, while they themselves must radiate through their surroundings, and act as a leaven in the dough.

The aim is not so much to reach the masses directly but first of all to form genuine Christian communities—small though they may be—to bear witness in this world. These small com-

[1] Cf. Dupont; Pin, 'Urban Parish'.

munities will then carry and inform the whole so that it may share in the communion of saints. Hence the multiplicity, the wealth of forms and possibilities in the kingdom of God. Too great standardization jeopardizes real human community and leads almost inevitably to mass uniformity.

It is the task of small Christian communities to bring the world to God. This does not rest only or primarily on the sociological law that true communion is only possible among a limited number; it is far more due to the laws rooted in the history of salvation. Fr Congar shows how, in the history of redemption, the salvation to which all men are called always begins with a small unit which represents the whole.[1] The salvation of all men and all nations was to come from Adam, Abraham, and the chosen people with its twelve tribes. Today the salvation to which all are called still comes from Christ the new Adam and from the new people of God.

The same law of representative units and groups applies within the Church. Thus the love between Christ and his Church is represented in the individual marriage. In the liturgy the worshipping congregation acts as the Church by itself or through the priest representing the whole Church. Their unity with the whole Church is actualized in the direct or indirect unity with the bishop. The axiom *sit tibi in tribus ecclesia*, too, is based on the view that the part represents the whole. The whole tree of the kingdom of God is already contained in the grain of mustard seed, and the grain of wheat that is sown in the earth brings forth fruit abundantly.

Every group shares in the twofold character of the Church: in so far as it is the people of God, a community, it represents mankind on the way to Christ; in so far as it is a sacrament, it represents Christ, who gives himself to the world.[2] Every individual, every community, is a Jacob's ladder for the place which God has appointed to it.[3]

[1] Congar, *Wide World*, 8–16: 'A small Church in a large world'; and 17–26, 'Jacob's ladder'.

[2] 'Two mediations are joined in the Church, one going up, or representative, the other coming down, or sacramental; and through them she is the place where Christ gives himself to the world, and the world gives itself to Christ, the place where the two meet.' Ib., 19.

[3] 'Each one of us for his own little world, all of us for the world at large we are Jacob's ladder. The representative going up of mankind to God and the representative coming down of Jesus Christ to the world pass through

Every such representative group is both closed and open. It is closed in as much as it embodies the Church. But just because of this each group (and every individual) must also be open to the totality of the Church so that it may always be filled again by the Church in order to radiate it into the world. For, in as much as a community represents the Church in its sacramental character it must be open to others, to the world, which it is to endow with a soul.

These few indications should suffice to demonstrate that the cure of souls within the parish (but also in the supra-parochial sphere) must create and foster community because we Christians are called to communion with the triune God.

III—The Individual Communities within the Parish

1. *The Family*

The most important community within the parish is the family. It is the original cell of mankind, constantly rendered more fruitful by Christ through his Church so that the children of Mother Church may be as numberless as the sands of the sea. In the family, human community is first raised to communion in and with God. The sacrament of matrimony is the image of the love of Christ for his Church and of the obedience of the Church to Christ. If we are to speak of the 'Church in miniature' at all, besides the bishop's community, this could apply at best, even though in a strongly figurative sense, to the family. St John Chrysostom frequently calls the household community (family in the old sense) the Church in miniature.[1]

In the sacrament of marriage the spouses are not only responsible for one another's salvation, they also have a quite particular ecclesial duty towards their children and the larger family circle. 'To the parents belongs especially the office of

---

us. The whole Church is sacramental and missionary, and so is each Christian in his degree. Each of the members of any group (e.g. a parish) that seeks Christ through the Church stands for the whole group. To what extent do they effectively aid the group in its journey to God? It cannot be known. But they are its first-fruits, a sheaf offered up, and they are intercessors for it: had there been ten righteous men in the city, God would have spared it (Gen. 18: 32).' Ib., 21.

[1] Cf. Chrysostom, *In Gen. serm. IV*, 2; *In Eph. hom. XX*, 6; *in Matt. hom. XXXII*, 7; quoted by Schlüter and Hermkes in 'Die Familie als "Kirche im Kleinen" ', 286.

teaching their children . . . parents have a priestly office in as much as they lead the family worship, the family liturgy. . . . To the parents, and primarily to the father also belongs the royal or pastoral office that is the preservation of a truly Christian life, both serious and beautiful, disciplined and loving.'[1] Through the sacrament, marriage and hence the family become a grace-giving sacrificial community of love and faith.[2] Naturally the family is open to the Church, especially also to the hierarchical Church, for the Church is essentially from above. The fruitfulness of marriage becomes fully fruitful for the Church only through the hierarchical priesthood.

If the family is the most important community within the parish, it ought to be given corresponding pastoral care. But is it not the case that due to overwork, or to over-emphasis on groups and societies, the family is neglected or not taken seriously enough? Is not the parish Mass, sometimes based on associations and groups rather than on the family principle? Is it right that in some parishes the family never participates together in the sacrificial meal? How can the family spirit come alive in a parish if the family plays no part, or only a small part, in the building up of the community?

2. *The Community of Priests*

If the parish is to be formed into a genuine community it must begin with those who are most responsible for it. Community within the parish must be lived by the clergy as far as that is possible in the circumstances. 'The development of parish communities is very closely allied to that of priestly communities. This is the crux of the matter and the reason why this problem is always being raised.'[3] The clergy at least must be imbued with the spirit of genuine ecclesial and evangelical community where the perfect parish community cannot be realized.

The present canon law does not prescribe community life, but praises and recommends it. Where it exists, it should be

[1] Bopp, 141. 'Family liturgy' is liturgy only in a very relative sense. It lacks in particular the public character.

[2] Cf. Schlüter and Hermkes, op. cit., 286–98.

[3] Dupont, 15. Cf. Connan, 'Die diözesanen Priestergemeinschaften in Frankreich in den letzten fünfzig Jahren', 109, 113 f. This subject is treated further in Greinacher.

maintained.[1] St Pius X already pointed out the fruits of community life among priests in the history of the Church and asked whether it would not be possible to find a modern form for it. Pius XI, too, desired that this way of life should become widespread.[2] Pius XII also: 'What the Church has wished before (*C.I.C.* C. 134), we also approve and most strongly recommend, namely that the clergy of a parish or of several neighbouring parishes should introduce the custom of community life. Though this custom may entail certain inconveniences, nobody can doubt that the greatest benefits derive from it. First, the zeal of love and devotion will thereby daily be rekindled in the priests. Further, the Christian people will be shown that they have willingly freed themselves from their own interests and their relations. Finally, it will thereby become apparent with what conscientious care priests guard their chastity.'[3]

But even at the present time the need for more community life is noticeable among the clergy of many countries, a need which grows out of the knowledge that the personal priestly life as well as the work of the apostolate find in a true religious community an invaluable source of nourishment.[4] The value of the witness and of the efficacy of the unity of a clergy standing by their bishop as well as of those united to his delegates cannot be sufficiently emphasized.[5]

The common life of the clergy does not simply mean living under one roof and eating at the same table so as to avoid isolation. What matters is to realize the priestly ideal in prayer and the apostolate within the framework of a common discipline. There should be an interior community, an exchange of experiences, a common approach to the tasks in hand, unity in prayer and harmony in brotherly love.[6] The concrete forms can be many and may vary from living together according to a

[1] C. 134. Cf. Connan, 109 f.

[2] Cf. Doncoeur, 'La vie communautaire dans le clergé', 613.

[3] Exhortation *Menti Nostrae* of 23 September 1950, quoted by Ancel, 43; Cf. *HK*, 5 (1950), 62–68, 130–39. On the realization of this in France, cf. the contributions of Connan, Rétif, Hornuss, Moubarac and Ponsar to Greinacher; for Germany, cf. those of Hemmerle, Hünermann, Reher-Baumeister and Gülden.

[4] Ancel, 45–50.

[5] Dupont, Überlegungen, 33; cf. Greinacher, *Zur Frage der Priestergemeinschaften*; Michonneau, *Paroisse*, 400–39: 'Par l'esprit d'équipe.'

[6] Cf. Ancel, 54–56.

fixed norm to making a formal promise or taking the three vows. The religious spirit informing these communities may also vary; it may be entirely centred on the bishop or inspired by the spirituality of the various Orders and movements within the Church. In any case, however, the form must be based on the apostolate.[1]

External conditions, whether in town or country, will also have a determining influence. Far-seeing pastors consider teamwork by priests (and in conjunction with laymen) as an absolute apostolic necessity for the urban cure of souls.[2] In the towns priests may decide to live a community life in one parish, but there is also the possibility of uniting on a supra-parochial level in order to tackle the problems of urban pastoral work in common.

In the country there are certain difficulties stemming from external conditions. Often a country parish will have only one priest living in his presbytery. If community life is to be established in such a case, the priests of a number of parishes must join forces in a community house which would serve as a base for the pastoral work of a whole area. With the present lack of priests, when in some countries and districts not every parish can count on a resident priest, just such communities would present a solution. But such a measure must not be regarded and handled as a 'technical solution'; it must be instinct with the will to a genuine evangelical common life. Indeed, such communities have worked very effectively in France for many years.[3] The great efforts of Canon Boulard in France and in

[1] Ib., 57–81. Cf. the interesting proposal of T. Schnitzler, 'Priesterliche Gemeinschaft auf der Grundlage des Stiftes und Säkularinstitutes', in Greinacher, 84–96. Siegwart's historical study is also very valuable, especially in relation to the community of secular priests so desirable and so sought after today.

[2] Cf. Motte, 'Le prêtre et la ville'; Congar, 'Paroisse', 56.

[3] 'Mgr Roland-Gosselin quoted the example of one of those parishes which previously scarcely gave its resident parish priest two hundred communions a year and which now gives fifteen hundred to a non-resident missionary. The statistics gathered in January 1935 show similar increases everywhere. From 1926 to 1934 two villages rose from 600 communions and 20 communions under a resident priest to 1,700 and 300 under a missionary priest. Some places multiplied their communions by ten. The most perceptible result is a considerable increase in the sacramental life among the good Christians and a gradual penetration among the others.' Doncoeur, op. cit., 616.

western Switzerland are in the last analysis aimed at convincing the clergy (particularly in the country) of the absolute necessity of co-operation and at gaining them for a common priestly life and apostolate.

This is not the place to discuss the problem of community life for the clergy in detail. We would only draw attention to the paramount importance of this community within the parish since it is fundamental for any genuine parish community. It is in fact difficult to see how genuine Christian community can be achieved in a parish unless the clergy forms it first. 'The effort to restore its value to everything communal in the Church is more than just a formula or a concession to the taste of the times. It aims at the very essence of the clergy.'[1]

3. *The Community of the Parish Nucleus*

Priest communities must not be closed in on themselves, they must be open to the laity. The Church does not consist only of the clergy and will not be built up by it alone, but only in co-operation with the laity.[2] There must be in every parish a small community of both clergy and laity which forms its nucleus (or several nuclei) and represents the great mass of those who belong to it canonically.

The necessity for this community between clergy and laity is shown by the liturgy as well as by sociology. The nucleus, embracing both priests and laity, is extremely important for the parish. It bears the pastoral responsibility for all parishioners in relation to whom it has a missionary role to fulfil. Here a twofold effort must be made: on the one hand the nucleus must be consolidated in itself, on the other it must radiate outwards.

Both consolidation and radiation will be achieved mainly by encouraging the vitality of the smaller integrated groups within the parish nucleus. It is advantageous to work out the problems and the concrete pastoral tasks in the small circle of the group and together to seek a solution; further the groups should be entrusted with the execution of concrete tasks according to their special abilities.

[1] Dupont, 35; cf. the theological basis in Tollu, especially 98; Ponsar, 154.

[2] Ib., Tollu, 99 f.; Ponsar, 160 f.

Finally, the supra-parochial groups should not be underestimated as regards their power of radiation in their own *milieux*. Although perhaps no direct benefit to the parish is obvious, today these groups are very important for the apostolic work of the Church. The parish, after all, is not an end in itself, but is entirely devoted to the building up of the Church, and the supra-parochial groups have no other object. Naturally the supra-parochial groups must also pray and work in the closest collaboration with the clergy. The supra-parochial groups, which as interest-groups are mostly already well integrated, are also called to form a common nucleus together with the clergy. They can profitably be interested and engaged in those tasks which force the clergy themselves to unite and co-operate supra-parochially. In towns particularly, certain problems and tasks are not amenable to solution at parish level but call imperatively for town-wide co-operation. But even in the country co-operation is the order of the day. Where openness and readiness or at least the desire for this co-operation in supra-parochial groups are lacking, it is seriously to be asked whether this is not due to a failure of insight into the urgent pastoral tasks, or to lack of real apostolic zeal for the increase of the Church.

4. *The Community of the Evangelical Counsels*

A further form of community, though not belonging canonically to the parish, is indispensable for the building up of an ecclesial community, namely that which lives according to the spirit of the evangelical counsels bound by vows approved by the Church. A community of this sort must in some way be present in the parish if the latter is to be representative of the whole ecclesial community. The parish, being responsible for the cure of souls, has the task of building up the Church, and should mirror Christ as faithfully as possible in its plenitude and dynamism. The parish congregation must never be content to build up a minimal Christianity of the commandments, but the whole apostolic effort must ultimately aim at a life in accordance with the Gospel and the evangelical counsels in close imitation of Christ. The Christian must not only keep the commandments, but beyond this he is called to perfection.

There are undoubtedly in every parish men and women who

live in the spirit of the gospel, who daily follow Christ faithfully. But for a full ecclesial community it is not enough that individual members realize this ideal; it must be practised by a community, which has received a visible ecclesiastical structure. Such are the orders, congregations, institutes and secular institutes.

They are the representatives of the ideal Christian community which involves community of goods, and even more, the common imitation of Christ, the struggle for perfection, the building up of the kingdom of God. The future and perfection of the Church are most impressively anticipated even now in the form of their vows. They are the representatives of the eschatological side of the Church, in the sense of the end and the highest goal. They are most intensely *παροικία* in this world.

A parish in which the Church's visible representation of this eschatological anticipation is lacking will hardly be able to give life to a full ecclesial community because an essential side of the Church would not be present. The parish community must be given the highest perfection, in the life of the counsels. If this witness of eschatological community is not present in the parish, it is lacking (not as a canonical institution but in so far as the ecclesial community must be there in it) something essential, not simply a welcome addition. It is not absolutely necessary that such a community[1] should reside in the canonical parish territory. What matters is the spiritual presence, the witness, that must work as a leaven in the parish. In a town it is conceivable, for example, that the nursing nuns in a hospital bear this witness for all the town's parishes, that they represent the kingdom that is to come for all parishes. In the country a monastery may bear witness to it for a whole district. But it is always necessary that the spiritual presence of these communities should be truly alive in a parish, that their representatives should not be felt to be foreign bodies, but should be co-ordinated and integrated into the parish congregation and community.

Ideally, there should as far as possible be close co-operation between the parish and the religious communities instead of their regarding each other as a kind of competition. Religious

[1] E.g. teaching or nursing nuns, representatives of a Secular Institute, a monastery, the house of a Congregation, etc.

communities should even be integrated into the parish or else, as more or less independent communities, form a nucleus around which a group may gather, not to be drawn away from the parish but to be made into apostles and witnesses to brotherly community.

Above all, secular and regular clergy must co-operate in a spirit of brotherhood and their common work must be inspired by their burning zeal for the salvation of men and the increase of the kingdom of God now and in eternity.

Each of these communities represents a certain aspect of the Church for a certain group, but only in the ensemble of all the communities does the Church shine forth in her full beauty and become incarnate in a particular place. It would be wrong to make any one of these communities into an absolute and exclusive principle. Each must be encouraged in its own way so that as a result of its individual character it may make its special contribution to the whole. Here again, genuine community is not based on uniformity but on diversity. True pastoral care, in so far as it is the activity of the whole Church, must be the task of all these communities in harmonious co-operation.

These communities, however, should not be regarded as ultimate apostolic units. In their turn they are composed of small nuclei or 'cells' (in the sociological sense) which are probably the decisive factor in the interior build-up of the community and in its outward radiation. From them the life-giving impulses go out, not only to the community of which they are a part but also to the non-practising or non-Christian *milieux* in the midst of which they are placed. Today particularly, in view of the special sociological position of the Church in modern society, the importance of the cell is being more and more recognized.[1]

IV—Conclusion

The actual situation of the Church in the world, and the pastoral problems arising from it, make it increasingly clear that the parish is not the final pastoral unit. On the one hand, the parish—precisely in as far as it is a parish 'congregation'—must relinquish its self-sufficiency in order to be open to large units, among which the diocese with the bishop as responsible

[1] Cf. Spitaler, *Die Zelle in Kirche und Welt.*

for the cure of souls takes the lead. In order to prove itself a useful member of a higher unit—deanery, diocese, etc.—the parish must co-operate with these larger organizations, particularly in the solution of those problems which appear in these larger sociological spheres.[1]

Equally, as parish 'congregation' it must take into account the various groups such as neighbourhoods, integrated interest-groups, family groups and groups of friends—and integrate them into the pastoral planning. The cells, the smallest units, and the truly integrated communities must receive special attention.

It seems that the contemporary parish problem cannot primarily be saved by dividing the many outsize parishes into smaller ones as Paul Winninger proposes.[2] Naturally, parishes that are humanly manageable are an ideal to be pursued, but this by itself would not be enough. Community sociology seems to show that the integration of a congregation does not primarily depend on small numbers or a restricted area. More important than an exaggerated multiplication of parishes—which would probably only make supra-parochial co-operation even more difficult—is the adaptation to already existing integrated groups, or to elements that lend themselves to integration, in order to build small communities on these foundations. This does not actually require a multiplication of parish churches[3] but an increase in places of worship within the larger parishes. For only when the various communities have a suitably situated place of worship can pastoral work be built up from the altar. Simple but pleasing places of worship[4] to be developed especially into spiritual centres of these communities will suffice for this purpose. Here would also be an opportunity for better and more fruitful co-operation between secular and regular clergy. Why should the suitably situated church of a religious order not become the centre of a local or supra-

[1] Here it is presupposed that the boundaries of diocese, deanery, etc., correspond with those of the sociological structures.

[2] Winninger, *Construire des églises.* Dr Swoboda was of the same opinion. Cf. p. 105 above. Fr Motte shows the incompleteness of such a solution in 'Le prêtre et la ville', 161.

[3] Which would normally entail multiplication of the whole administration.

[4] They do not at first have to be very lavishly appointed.

parochial group—naturally in close fraternal co-operation with the parish clergy?

The adaptation to sociological groups, moreover, presupposes a reasonable organization of parishes taking sociological structures into account. Finally, there must be common discussion and planning concerning what is to be done within the parish and what at the supra-parochial level.

If it is true that from the pastoral point of view the parish can no longer be regarded as a closed unit for apostolic work, it would nevertheless be going too fast to conclude from this that the parish is today an obsolete institution. On the contrary, precisely because the canonical parish is open to the supernatural reality of the Church and can be shaped by the changing forms of the world, it is still valid and still has its value as a legal institution. The legal form is in itself adaptable enough to embrace a parish 'congregation' and a parish community and yet to remain responsible for all those who are not yet touched by them. The legal term is by and large flexible enough to be adapted to modern sociological conditions.[1] The lack of adaptability lies less in the legal institution as such than among those responsible for applying the law in accordance with changing conditions.

Perfect ecclesial community in the parish demands not only community between priest and people, which is built upon family community, the parish 'nucleus' and the community life of the clergy, but also the presence of the eschatological Church which, as the legally recognized life according to the evangelical counsels, does not indeed belong to the parish but should nevertheless constitute a summit of ecclesial community within the parish.

This community is not indeed canonically but of the very nature of the Church entrusted with the care of the brothers and sisters of the parish congregation and of the whole parish. Moreover, it has a Christian and missionary responsibility that cannot be restricted by any parish boundaries.

[1] This is not to say that no legal constitution better suited to the needs of the modern cure of souls is possible. Cf. Noser, 34.

BIBLIOGRAPHY

Abrecht, P. R., 'Die protestantische Religionssoziologie in den U.S.A.', in Goldschmidt (q.v.), pp. 75–89.

Amato, E., and Houtart, F., 'La démographie paroissiale de Buenos Aires', in *PuPr*, pp. 70–73.

Amberger, J., *Pastoraltheologie*, 3 vols., 3rd ed., Regensburg, 1866.

Ancel, A., 'Die apostolische Begründung des Gemeinschaftslebens beim Weltklerus', in Greinacher (q.v.), pp. 43–83.

Arnold, F. X., 'Das Prinzip des Gottmenschlichen und seine Bedeutung für die Seelsorge', in *ThQSchr*, 123, 1942, pp. 145–76.

'Das gottmenschliche Prinzip der Seelsorge in pastoralgeschichtlicher Entfaltung', in *ThQSchr*, 124, 1943, pp. 99–133; and 125, 1944, pp. 57–80.

Grundsätzliches = 'Grundsätzliches und Geschichtliches zur Theologie der Seelsorge'; vol. 2 of *Untersuchungen zur Theologie der Seelsorge*, Freiburg, 1949.

'Der geschichtliche Weg theozentrischer Pastoralwissenschaft', in *ThQSchr*, 129, 1949, pp. 206–30, 440–71.

'Vorgeschichte und Einfluss des Trienter Messopferdekretes auf die Behandlung des eucharistischen Geheimnisses in der Glaubensverkündigung der Neuzeit', in Arnold and Fischer (q.v.), pp. 114–61.

'Pfarrei' = 'Zur Theologie der Pfarrei', in *Die Pfarre*, pp. 18–36. This article also appeared in the author's *Glaubensverkündigung und Glaubensgemeinschaft. Beiträge zur Theologie der Verkündigung, der Pfarrei und des Laientums*, pp. 74–105, Düsseldorf, 1955.

'Kirche und Laientum', address given at the solemn handing over of the Rectorship at the start of the summer semester, 7 May 1954, in *Reden bei der feierlichen Übergabe*, pp. 23–45, Tübingen, 1954.

'Pastoraltheologie' = 'Was ist Pastoraltheologie?', talk in the radio series *Was ist Theologie?* given on Südwestfunk, Baden-Baden on 8 April 1959, reprinted in *Anima*, 14, 1959, pp. 194–98.

Arnold, F. X., and Fischer, B., *Die Messe in der Glaubensverkündigung. Kerygmatische Fragen*, Freiburg, 2nd ed., 1953.

Backes, 'Die Kirche ist das Volk Gottes im Neuen Bunde', in *TrthZ*, 69, 1960, pp. 111–17.

Bardy, G., 'Sur l'origine des paroisses', in *MO*, 21, pp. 42–59, and *MO*, 22, pp. 42–66.

Batiffol, *Leçons sur la messe*, Paris, 1919.

Baumer, I., 'Sprache und Kirche', in *Orient*, 26, 1962, pp. 76–79.

Beauduin, Dom L., 'L'esprit paroissiale dans la tradition', in *QLit*, 2, 1911–12, pp. 16–26, 80–90, 305–11. The same article later appeared in Vol. 4 of *Cours et Conférences des Semaines liturgiques*, Louvain, 1926, pp. 11–44.

Berz, A., 'Der Standort der Katechetik innerhalb der Theologie', in *FZPhTh*, 6, 1959, pp. 36–43.

'Pastorelle Folgerungen aus der religionssoziologischen Untersuchung der französischsprechenden Schweiz', in *SchwKZ*, 129, 1961, pp. 353–55.

Birou, A., *Sociologie et religion*, with a preface by M. D. Chenu, Collection de Sociologie Religieuse, 5, Paris, 1959.

Bodzenta, E., 'Critères de planning paroissial urbain', in *PuPr*, pp. 143–50.

'Versuch einer sozial-religiösen Typologie der katholischen Pfarren', in Goldschmidt (q.v.), pp. 179–95.

Böhm, F., *Parochie und Gemeinde im 19. und 20. Jahrhundert*, Marburg/Lahn, 1958.

Bonhoeffer, D., *Sanctorum Communio. Dogmatische Untersuchung zur Soziologie der Kirche*, Theologische Bücherei, 3, Munich, 1954.

Bopp, L., *Zwischen Pastoraltheologie und Seelsorgswissenschaft. Eine Einführung in die pastoraltheologischen Grundsätze und seelsorgswissenschaftlichen Grundfragen*, Munich, 1937.

Botte, B., 'Der Kollegialcharakter des Priester- und Bischofsamtes', in Guyot (q.v.), pp. 68–91.

Boulard, F., *Itinéraires* = *Premiers itinéraires en sociologie religieuse*, with a preface by Prof. Le Bras. Collection de Sociologie Religieuse, 1, Paris, 1954.

'Wie sehen die französischen Christen den Priester?', in Guyot (q.v.), pp. 289–307.

'Le problème d'un "optimum" de population pour les paroisses rurales', in *PuPr*, pp. 160–82.

de Broglie, G., 'Du rôle de l'église dans le sacrifice eucharistique', in *NRT*, 70, 1948, pp. 449–60.

Bruders, H., *Verfassung* = *Die Verfassung der Kirche von den ersten Jahrzehnten der apostolischen Wirksamkeit an bis zum Jahre 175 n.*

Chr., pts 1 and 2; this is Vol. 4 of *Forschungen zur christlichen Literatur- und Dogmengeschichte*, Mainz, 1904.

Brugger, W., *Philosophisches Wörterbuch, Ergänzungsband zu Mensch, Welt, Gott. Ein Aufbau der Philosophie in Einzeldarstellungen*, Berchmanskolleg, Pullach, Freiburg, 6th ed., 1957.

Bruhin, J., *Zu den Methoden einer Soziologie der Pfarrei*, typescript, Pullach, 1959.

Brunner, A., 'Glaube und Gemeinschaft', in *StdZ*, 163, 1958–59, pp. 439–51.

Censi, Sr Maria-Agneze, 'L'étude écologique d'une paroisse des faubourgs de Rome', in *PuPr*, pp. 59–62.

Chélini, J., *La ville et l'Eglise, Premier bilan des enquêtes de sociologie religieuse urbaine*, Rencontres, 52, Paris, 1958.

Chenu, M.-D., 'Die Erneuerung der Seelsorge-Wissenschaft', in *Anima*, 1, 1946, pp. 308–11.

'Position théologique de la sociologie religeuse', in *Paroisse et Mission*, 5, 1958, pp. 5–9.

Chéry, H. C., *Communauté paroissiale et liturgie: Notre-Dame-Saint-Alban*, Rencontres, 25, Paris, 1947.

Chiesa, *Parrochia e parrocchiani*, Alba, 1936.

Collard, E., *Carte de la pratique dominicale en Belgique par localité*, Mons, 1952.

Colson, J., *Evêque* = *L'évêque dans les communautés primitives. Tradition paulinienne et Tradition joannique de l'Episcopat des origines à S. Irénée*, Unam Sanctam, 21, Paris, 1951.

Fonctions = *Les fonctions ecclésiales aux deux premiers siècles*, Textes et Etudes théologiques, Tournai, 1956.

'Evangélisation' = 'Evangélisation et collégiate apostolique', in *NRT*, 82, 1960, pp. 349–72.

Congar, Y., 'Paroisse' = 'Mission de la paroisse', in *Structures sociales et pastorale paroissiale. Congrès national de Lille, 1948*, Paris, 1949, pp. 48–65.

Vaste monde ma paroisse. Vérité et Dimensions du Salut, Bibliothèque de l'homme d'action, Paris, 1959. English translation by Donald Attwater, *The Wide World My Parish. Salvation and Its Problems*, London, 1961.

de Coninck, L., 'Les orientations actuelles de la théologie pastorale', in *NRT*, 76, 1954, pp. 134–41.

Connan, F., 'Die diözesanen Priestergemeinschaften in Frankreich in den letzten fünfzig Jahren', in Greinacher (q.v.), pp. 109–17.

Conrad, H., *Rechtsgeschichte* = *Deutsche Rechtsgeschichte. Ein Lehrbuch. 1. Frühzeit und Mittelalter*, Karlsruhe, 1954.

Daille, R., *Pratique* = 'Pratique dominicale et zones écologiques', in *PuPr*, 67–69.

Daniel, Y., 'L'équipement' = 'L'équipement paroissial de deux arrondissements parisiens: les XVIe et XXe arrondissements, de 1861 à 1956', in *PuPr*, pp. 28–43.

Daniel, Y., and le Mouel, *Paroisses* = *Paroisses d'hier . . . paroisses de demain*, Paris, 1957.

Dansette, A., *Histoire religieuse de la France contemporaine*; Vol. 1, 'De la Révolution à la Troisième République'; Vol. 2, 'Sous la Troisième République', 'L'Histoire', Paris, 1948, 1951. English translation with abridgements approved by the author by John Dingle, *Religious History of Modern France*, Edinburgh, 1961.

Delchard, A., 'Constitution Apostolique "Exul Familia" du 1er août, 1952, sur les soins d'ordre spirituel à apporter aux émigrants', in *NRT*, 75, 1953, pp. 309–11.

Deman, 'Grundsätze einer Seelsorgewissenschaft', in *Anima*, 1, 1946, pp. 12–16.

Denis, J., 'La constitution "Exul Familia" et les paroisses territoriales', in *M-D*, 36, 1953, pp. 75–85, 37; 1954, pp. 150 ff.

Denis, N., and Boulet, R., 'Titres urbains et communauté dans la Rome chrétienne', in *M-D*, 36, 1953, pp. 14–32.

Doncoeur, P., 'La vie communautaire dans le clergé', in *Etudes*, 224, 1935, pp. 608–18.

Donovan, J. D., 'The Social Structure of the Parish', in Nuesse-Harte (q.v.), pp. 75–99.

du Cange, C. D., *Glossarium mediae et infimae latinitatis, conditum a Carolo Du Fresne, domini Du Cange, auctum a monachis ordinis S. Benedicti, cum supplementis integris D.P. Carpenterii, Adelungii, aliorum, suisque digessit G.A.L. Henschel. Editio nova aucta pluribus verbis aliorum scriptorum a Leopold Favre*, ten volumes, Niort, 1883–87.

Duchesne, L., *Fastes épiscopaux de l'ancienne Gaule*, 3 vols., Paris, 1894–95.

Histoire = *Histoire ancienne de l'Eglise*, Vol. 1, 3rd ed., Paris, 1907, Vols. 2 and 3, Paris, 1907, 1910. English translation from the 4th ed. *Early History of the Christian Church*, 3 vols., London, 1909–24.

Origines = *Origines du culte chrétien. Etudes sur la liturgie latine avant Charlemagne*, 4th ed., Paris, 1909. English translation by M. L. McLure, *Christian Worship: its origin and evolution*, 5th ed. of 1919 re-issued, London, 1931.

Dupont, P., 'Überlegungen über die Theologie und Spiritualität der Ortskirche', in Greinacher (q.v.), pp. 15–42.

Eizenhöfer, L., 'Das Opfer der Gläubigen in den Sermonen Leos des Grossen', in Arnold and Fischer (q.v.), pp. 79–107.

Engel, F. S., 'Parish Societies', in Nuesse-Harte (q.v.), pp. 178–205.

Ermecke, G., 'Die Sozialtheologie als christliche Gesellschaftslehre und ihre Beziehungen zu verwandten Wissenschaften', in *ThuGl*, 48, 1958, pp. 1–18.

Feine, H. E., *Kirchliche Rechstgeschichte auf der Grundlage des Kirchenrechtes von U. Sturz*, Vol. 1, 'Die katholische Kirche', 2nd ed., Weimar, 1954.

Feiner, Trütsch and Böckle, *Fragen der Theologie heute*, Einsiedeln-Zürich-Köln, 1937.

Fichter, J. H., *Soziologie* = *Soziologie der Pfarrgruppen. Untersuchungen zur Struktur und Dynamik der Gruppen einer deutschen Pfarrei*, Schriften des Instituts für christliche Sozialwissenschaften der westfälischen Wilhelmsuniversität, Münster, 1957.

Social Relations = *Social Relations in the Urban Parish*, University of Chicago Press, 1954.

'Paroisse urbaine' = 'La paroisse urbaine comme groupe social', in *PuPr*, pp. 84–94.

Fischer, A., *Seelsorge* = *Seelsorge zwischen gestern und morgen*, Freiburg, 1961.

Fischer, B., and Fiala, V., *Colligere Fragmenta. Festschrift Alban Dold zum 70. Geburtstag 7.7.1952*, Beuron, 1952.

Floristan, C., *La parroquia, comunidad eucarística. Ensayo de una teología pastoral de la parroquia*, Christus Pastor, Madrid, 1961.

Fraine, J. de, *Adam et son lignage. Etudes sur la notion de 'personnalité corporative' dans la Bible*, Museum Lessianum, Section Biblique No. 2, Bruges, 1959.

Freytag, J., 'Aufgaben' = 'Aufgaben und Methoden der empirischen Erforschung von Kirchengemeinden', in Goldschmidt (q.v.), pp. 1–15.

Füglister, R., 'Die Pastoraltheologie als Universitätsdisziplin. Eine historisch-theologische Studie', *Th.Théol.*, Fribourg, 1951, Basel, 1951.

Funk, F. X., *Patres apostolici*, 2nd ed., Tübingen, 1901.

Geck, A., 'Sozialtheologie', in *Die Kirche in der Welt*, 2, 1949, pp. 471–80.

'Christliche Sozialprinzipien. Zum Aufbau einer Sozialtheologie', in *ThQSchr*, 130, 1950, pp. 28–53.

'Die Sozialtheologie als Aufgabe', in *TrthZ*, 59, 1950, pp. 161–71.

Giftschütz, *Leitfaden für die in den k.u.k. Erblanden vorgeschriebenen Vorlesungen über die Pastoraltheologie*, Vienna, 1787.

Goddijn, W., 'Die katholische Pfarrsoziologie in Westeuropa', in Goldschmidt (q.v.), pp. 16–35.

Goison, M., 'Mission irremplaçable du sacerdoce pour l'animation spirituelle de toutes les réalités humaines du monde moderne', in *Structures sociales et pastorale paroissiale, Congrès national de Lille, 1948*, Paris, 1949.

Goldschmidt, D., Greiner, F., and Schelsky, H., *Soziologie der Kirchengemeinde*, Soziologische Gegenwartsfragen, New Series, Stuttgart, 1960.

Gollwitz, Dominikus, *Anleitung zur Pastoraltheologie*, 4th imp., Regensburg and Landshut, 1836.

Golombeck, Oskar, 'Weltflüchtlingsjahr und die Apostolische Konstitution "Exul Familia" ', in *StdZ*, 165, 1959–60, pp. 199–210.

Graf, A., *Kritische Darstellung des gegenwärtigen Zustandes der praktischen Theologie*, Vienna and Tübingen, 1841.

Grasso, D., 'Osservazioni sulla teologia della parrocchia', in *Greg*, 1959, pp. 297–314.

Greinacher, N., *Priestergemeinschaften*, Mainz, 1960.

Soziologie = *Soziologie der Pfarrei. Wege zur Untersuchung*, Preface by G. Le Bras, Dienst am Heil, Freiburg, 1955.

'Zur Frage der Priestergemeinschaften', in *Orient*, 23, 1959, pp. 13–16.

Griffe, E., 'Premières Paroisses' = 'Les premières "paroisses" de la Gaule', in *Bulletin de littérature ecclésiastique*, 1949, pp. 229–39.

'Paroisses Rurales' = 'Les paroisses rurales de la Gaule', in *M-D*, 36, 1953, pp. 33–62.

Grimm, J. and W., *Deutsches Wörterbuch*, 16 vols., Leipzig, 1854–1942.

Grond, L., 'Nature et fonction du quartier d'une grande ville. Quelques résultats d'une enquête sociologique sur la situation sociale et religieuse d'Amsterdam', in *LV*, 6, 1951, pp. 245–54.

Groner, F., 'Statistik der katholischen Kirchengemeinden in Deutschland', in Goldschmidt (q.v.), pp. 196–208.

Guardini, R., *Vom Geist der Liturgie*, Ecclesia Orans 1, Freiburg, 1934. English translation by Ada Lane, *The Spirit of the Liturgy*, London, 1930.

Gülden, J., 'Liturgische Erneuerung und die Beteiligung des Volkes am Gottesdienst in der Väterpredigt', in *StdZ*, 137, 1940, pp. 178–86.

'Vom Geist und Leben des Oratoriums vom Hl. Philipp Neri', in Greinacher (q.v.), pp. 213–39.

Guyot, *Das apostolische Amt*, Mainz, 1961.

Gy, M., 'Bemerkungen zu den Bezeichnungen des Priestertums in der christlichen Frühzeit', in Guyot (q.v.), pp. 92–109.

Hagen, A., *Pfarrei und Pfarrer nach dem C.I.C.*, Rottenburg am Neckar, 1935.

Häring, B., *Macht* = *Macht und Ohnmacht der Religion. Religionssoziologie als Anruf*, Salzburg, 1956.

'Gemeinschaftstiftende Kraft' = 'Die gemeinschaftstiftende Kraft der Liturgie. Liturgiesoziologische Beobachtungen und Probleme', in *LJB*, 7, 1957, pp. 205–14.

Harnack, A., *Ausbreitung* = *Die Mission und Ausbreitung des Christentums in den ersten drei Jahrhunderten*, 2 vols., 4th ed., Leipzig, 1924. English translation by James Moffat, *The Mission and Expansion of Christianity in the First Three Centuries*, Th. Tr. Lib., 1894.

Harte, T. J., 'Racial and National Parishes in the United States', in Nuesse-Harte (q.v.), 154–77.

Hauck, A., *Realenzyklopädie für protestantische Theologie und Kirche*, orig. by J. J. Herzog, 3rd enlarged and improved edition by Hauck, 24 vols., Leipzig, 1896–1913.

Hefele, C. J., *Conciliengeschichte. Nach den Quellen bearbeitet von Carl Josef Hefele*, 2nd ed. by Alois Knöpfler, 9 vols., Freiburg, 1873–90. English translation in 5 vols., *A History of the Christian Councils, from the original documents*, Edinburgh, 1871–96.

Hefele, C. J., and Leclercq, *Histoire des Conciles d'après les documents originaux*. Par Charles Joseph Hefele. Nouvelle traduction française faite sur la deuxième édition allemande, corrigée, augmentée de notes critiques et bibliographiques par un religieux bénédictin de l'abbaye de Farnborough (Henri Leclercq), Paris, 1907 ff.

Hemmerle, K., 'Die Bewegung der Focolarini und die Priester', in Greinacher (q.v.), pp. 175–82.

Henrici, P., 'Bibel-Philosophie und Bibel-Theologie', in *Orient*, 23, 1959, pp. 214–17.

Hergenröther, J., *Handbuch der allgemeinen Kirchengeschichte. Neu bearbeitet von Dr J. P. Kirsch*, 4 vols., 5th ed., Freiburg, 1911–17.

Hertling, L., *Communio und Primat*. Miscellanea Historiae Pontificiae 8, Rome, 1943. Reprinted in *Una Sancta*, 17, 1962, pp. 91–125.

Hofmann, F., 'Glaubensgrundlagen der liturgischen Erneuerung', in Feiner (q.v.), pp. 485–517.

Homeyer, J., 'Die Erneuerung des Pfarrgedankens. Eine bibliographische Übersicht', in Rahner, H., *Die Pfarre* (q.v.), pp. 125–58.

Hornuss, M., 'Die Priestergemeinschaft in der "Mission de France" ', in Greinacher (q.v.), pp. 127–31.

Houtart, F., 'L'aménagement' = 'L'aménagement religieux des territoires urbains', in *La Revue Nouvelle*, 28, 1958, pp. 517–27.

'L'évolution' = 'L'évolution démographique et écologiques des paroisses de Bruxelles et de Chicago', in *PuPr*, pp. 44–58.

'Planning' = 'Le planning des paroisses urbaines', in *PuPr*, pp. 104–20.

Les techniques du planning au service de la pastorale, Brussels (no date).

Huber, H., *Geist und Buchstabe der Sonntagsruhe. Eine historisch-theologische Untersuchung über das Verbot der knechtlichen Arbeit von der Urkirche bis auf Thomas von Aquin*, Studia theologiae moralis et pastoralis edita a professoribus Academiae Alfonsianae in Urbe, Vol. IV, Salzburg, 1958.

Hünermann, P., 'Unio sacerdotalis Jesus-Caritas', in Greinacher (q.v.), pp. 183–92.

Imbart de la Tour, *Les origines religieuses de la France. Les paroisses rurales du IVe au XIe siècle*, Paris, 1900.

Iribarren, J., *Introducción a la Sociología Religiosa*, Madrid, 1955.

Jone, H., *Gesetzbuch des kanonischen Rechtes. Erklärung der Kanones*, 3 vols., Paderborn, 1939–40.

Jozefcyk, A., *A modern parish as modelled on the life of the Cenacle*, Diss. Angel. Rom, Fribourg, 1951.

Jungmann, J. A., *Feier* = *Die liturgische Feier. Grundsätzliches und Geschichtliches über Formgesetze der Liturgie*, Regensburg, 1939.

Missarum = *Missarum Sollemnia. Eine genetische Erklärung der römischen Messe*, 2 vols., 2nd ed., Vienna, 1949. English translation in one volume, *The Mass of the Roman Rite*, revised edition, London, 1959.

The Eucharistic Prayer = *Das eucharistische Hochgebet*, Würzburg, 1954. English translation, *The Eucharistic Prayer*, London, 1956.

Sacrifice = *Vom Sinn der Messe als Opfer der Gemeinschaft*, Christ heute, 3rd series, No. 8, Einsiedeln, 1954. English translation, *The Sacrifice of the Church*, London, 1956.

Gottesdienst = *Der Gottesdienst der Kirche. Auf dem Hintergrund seiner Geschichte kurz erläutert*, Innsbruck, Vienna, Munich, 1955. English translation by Clifford Howell, *Public Worship*, London, 1957.

'Liturgie zwischen Tradition und Pastoral', in *SchwKZ*, 127, 1959, pp. 49–51, 68–70, 80–82.

Liturgisches Erbe = *Liturgisches Erbe und pastorale Gegenwart.*

Studien und Vorträge, Innsbruck, Vienna, Munich, 1960. English translation by Ronald Walls, *Pastoral Liturgy*, London, 1962.

'Fermentum' = 'Fermentum. Ein Symbol kirchlicher Einheit und sein Nachleben im Mittelalter', pp. 379–89 of foregoing (English, pp. 287 ff.). Previously printed in Fischer-Fiala (q.v.), pp. 185–90.

Kittel, G., *Theologisches Wörterbuch zum Neuen Testament*, 6 vols. issued so far, Stuttgart, 1933 ff.

Klostermann, F., *Das christliche Apostolat*, Innsbruck, Vienna, Munich, 1962.

König, R., *Grundformen der Gesellschaft: Die Gemeinde*, Rowohlts deutsche Enzyklopädie No. 79, Hamburg, 1958.

Köster, R., 'Die Kirchentreuen. Bericht über eine Untersuchung in einer evangelisch-lutherischen Gemeinde Norddeutschlands', in Goldschmidt (q.v.), pp. 144–53.

Köstler, R., *Wörterbuch zum Codex Iuris Canonici*, Munich, 1927.

Krieg, C., *Seelenführung* = *Die Wissenschaft der speziellen Seelenführung*, Vol. I of *Wissenschaft der Seelenleitung. Eine Pastoraltheologie in vier Büchern*, 3 vols., Freiburg, 1919, 1907, 1915.

Kruijt, J., 'Die Erforschung der protestantischen Kirchengemeinden in den Niederlanden', in Goldschmidt (q.v.), pp. 35–49.

Kurtscheid, B., *Historia Iuris Canonici. Historia Institutorum*, Vol. I, 'Ab Ecclesiae fundatione usque ad Gratianum', Rome, 1941.

Labriolle, P. de, 'Paroecia', in *Recherches de Science Religieuse*, 18, 1928, pp. 60–72.

Laloux, J., 'Planning' = 'Planning et remembrement des paroisses rurales', in *PuPr*, pp. 184–220.

Le Bras, G., *Introduction* = *Introduction à l'histoire de la pratique religieuse en France*, 2 vols., Bibliothèque des Hautes-Etudes religieuses, Paris, 1942, 1945.

Leclercq, H., 'Paroisses rurales', in *DACL*, XIII, 1938, pp. 2198–235.

Leoni, A., *Sociologia* = *Sociologia e geografia religiosa di una diocesi. Saggio sulla pratica religiosa nella diocesi di Mantova*, No. 1 of Studia Socialia edita ab Instituto Scientiarum Socialium Pontificiae Universitatis Gregorianae, Rome, 1952.

Lercaro, G., *La santa Messa, assemblea del popolo di Dio*, Bologna, 1955.

Lesêtre, H., *La paroisse*, Paris, 1906.

Lübeck, K., *Reicheinteilung und kirchliche Hierarchie des Orients. Ein Beitrag zur Rechts- und Verfassungsgeschichte der Kirche*, Vol. 5, Pt. 4 of *Kirchengeschichtliche Studien*, Münster, 1901.

Luca, de, *Praelectiones Iuris Canonici*, 5 vols., Rome, 1897 ff.

Luckmann, T., 'Vier protestantische Kirchengemeinden. Bericht über eine vergleichende Untersuchung', in Goldschmidt (q.v.), pp. 132–44.

Martimort, A.-G., 'Assemblée' = 'L'Assemblée liturgique, mystère du Christ', in *M-D*, 40, 1954, pp. 5–29.

Martimort, A.-G., and Picard, F., *Liturgie et Musique.* Translation with commentary of the Instruction, *De Musica sacra et sacra Liturgia*, of the S. Cong. of Rites dated 3 September 1958, Lex orandi 28, Paris, 1959.

Mendras, H., 'L'influence des divers courants migratoires sur la vie religieuse des campagnes', in *PuPr*, pp. 154–59.

Michonneau, G., *Paroisse = Paroisse, communauté missionnaire. Conclusions de cinq ans d'expérience.* Introd. by H. C. Chéry, Rencontres Nos. 21 and 22, 2nd ed. Paris, 1946.

Mickells, A. A., *The Constitutive Elements in Parishes*, Washington, 1960.

Monachino, V., *La cura pastorale a Milano, Cartagine e Roma nel secolo quarto*, Rome, 1947.

Montini, G.-B., 'La paroisse dans l'Eglise. Lettre du 14 août 1953 à la semaine sociale du Canada', in *M-D*, 36, 1953, pp. 9–13.

Monzel, N., 'Parish Research in other Countries. Germany', in Nuesse-Harte (q.v.), pp. 333–40.

Morel, J., 'Wissenschaft im Dienste der Kirche', in *GrEnt*, 15, 1959–60, pp. 210–14.

Mörsdorf, K., *Die Rechtssprache des Codex Iuris Canonici. Eine kritische Untersuchung*, Görres Gesellschaft, Veröffentlichungen der Sektion für Rechts- und Staatswissenschaft, No. 74, Paderborn, 1937.

Motte, J.-F., *Mission générale* = with Dourmap M., *Mission générale, oeuvre d'Eglise. Techniques d'élaboration d'un plan urbain et régional de Pastorale Missionnaire.* Preface by Mgr Garonne, Abp. of Toulouse. Questions pastorales, Paris, 1957.

'Le prêtre et la ville', in *Cahiers de vie franciscaine*, 23, 1959, pp. 146–81.

Moubarac, Y., 'Die Priestergemeinschaft von Sankt Séverin in Paris', in Greinacher (q.v.), pp. 142–54.

Müller, K., *Beiträge = Beiträge zur Geschichte der Verfassung der alten Kirche.* Proceedings of the Preussische Akademie der Wissenschaften (Phil.-hist. Klasse), Year 1922, No. 3, Berlin, 1922.

Kirchengeschichte = Kirchengeschichte, Vol. I/1 edited by von Campenhausen, 3rd ed., Tübingen, 1941.

Nanni, L., 'L'evoluzione storica della parrocchia', in *La scuola cattolica*, 81, 1953, pp. 475–544.

Nell-Breuning, O. von, 'Pfarrgemeinde' = 'Pfarrgemeinde, Pfarrfamilie, Pfarrprinzip', in *TrthZ*, 56, 1947, pp. 257–62.

'Grenzen' = 'Grenzen des Pfarrgemeindegedankens. Eine juristisch-soziologische Studie', in *Anima*, 3, 1948, pp. 105–13.

'Pfarrei als Zentrum' = 'Pfarrei als Zentrum der Seelsorge', in *SchwKZ*, 116, 1948, pp. 461 ff.

Neuner, J., and Roos, H., *Der Glaube der Kirche in den Urkunden der Lehrverkündigung*, 4th improved edition edited by K. Rahner, Regensburg, 1954.

Nickl, G., *Der Anteil des Volkes an der Messliturgie im Frankenreich von Chlodwig bis auf Karl den Grossen*, Forschungen zur Geschichte des innerlichen Lebens, No. 2, Innsbruck, 1930.

Noppel, C., *Aedificatio* = *Aedificatio corporis Christi. Aufriss der Pastoral*, Freiburg, 1937.

Pfarrei = *Die neue Pfarrei. Eine Grundlegung*, Freiburg, 1939.

Noser, H. B., *Pfarrei und Kirchgemeinde. Studie zu ihrem rechtlichen Begriff und grundsätzlichen Verhältnis*, Vol. 13 of the Freiburger Veröffentlichungen aus dem Gebiet von Kirche und Staat, Fribourg, 1957.

Nuesse, C. J., 'Empirical Problems for Social Research in the Parish', in Nuesse-Harte (q.v.), pp. 209–33.

Nuesse, C. J., and Harte, T. J., *The Sociology of the Parish. An Introductory Symposium*, Milwaukee, 1951.

Pascher, J., 'Die Hierarchie in sakramentaler Symbolik', in *Episcopus*, pp. 278–95.

Peichl, H., *Der Tag des Herrn. Die Heiligung des Sonntags im Wandel der Zeit*, Vol. 3 of Studien der Wiener Katholischen Akademie, Vienna, 1958.

Peterson, E., *Das Buch von den Engeln. Stellung und Bedeutung der heiligen Engeln im Kultus*, Leipzig, 1935.

Pilloud, L., 'Vers une pastorale d'ensemble', in *La Semaine Catholique de la Suisse romande*, 89, 1960, pp. 17–20.

Pin, E., *Pratique* = *Pratique religieuse et classes sociales dans une paroisse urbaine. Saint Pothin à Lyon*, Paris, 1956.

'La sociologie du catholicisme depuis la conférence internationale (Louvain 1956),' in *Social Compass*, 7, 1960, pp. 75–86.

'Dix ans de sociologie religieuse, 1950–1960', in *Revue de l'Action Populaire*, 145, 1961, pp. 217–29.

'Urban Parish' = 'Can the Urban Parish be a Community?', in *Social Compass*, 8, 1961, pp. 503–34. Reprint from *Greg*, 61, 1960, pp. 393–423.

Pinsk, J., 'Die religiöse Wirklichkeit von Kirche, Diözese und Pfarrei', in *Der kath. Gedanke*, 6, 1933, pp. 337–44. A free French translation, 'La liturgie et la réalité spirituelle de l'Eglise, du diocèse et de la paroisse', appeared in *QLit*, 18, 1933, pp. 192–205.

Pius XII, *Mediator Dei*, 20 November 1947. English trans. by Canon G. D. Smith in *Selected Letters and Addresses of Pius XII*, London, 1949.

Plöchl, W. M., *Geschichte des Kirchenrechtes*, 3 vols., Vienna, Munich, 1953–59.

Ponsar, A., 'Überlick und Schlussfolgerungen', in Greinacher (q.v.), pp. 155–72.

Pruner, J., *Pastoraltheologie* = *Lehrbuch der Pastoraltheologie*, 2 vols., 2nd ed., Paderborn, 1904 ff.

Quoist, M., *La ville et l'homme. Rouen. Etude sociologique d'un secteur prolétarien*, Paris, 1952.

Rahner, H., *Die Pfarre. Von der Theologie zur Praxis*, Freiburg, 1956.

Rahner, K., 'Die Kirche der Sünder', in *StdZ*, 140, 1947, pp. 163–77.

'Die Gliedschaft in der Kirche nach der Lehre der Enzyklika Pius' XII "Mystici Corporis Christi" ', in *Schriften* (q.v.), II, pp. 7–94.

'Pfarrprinzip' = 'Friedliche Erwägungen über das Pfarrprinzip', in *Schriften* (q.v.), II, pp. 299–337.

'Betrieb und Pfarrei', in *Sendung und Gnade* (q.v.).

'Pfarre' = 'Zur Theologie der Pfarre', in Rahner, H., *Die Pfarre* (q.v.), pp. 27–39.

Schriften = *Schriften zur Theologie*, 5 vols., Einsiedeln, Zürich, Cologne, 1954–62. English translation of Vol. I by Cornelius Ernst, *Theological Investigations*, I, London, 1963.

Sendung und Gnade. Beiträge zur Pastoraltheologie, Innsbruck, Vienna, Munich, 1959. English translation, Vol. I, *Mission and Grace*, London, 1963.

Rahner, K., and Ratzinger, J., *Episkopat und Primat*, Quaestiones disputatae 11, Freiburg, 1961. English translation, *The Episcopate and the Primacy*, Edinburgh, 1962.

Reher-Baumeister, P., 'Die Paulus-Gemeinschaft im Bistum Münster', in Greinacher (q.v.), pp. 193–212.

Rendtorff, T., 'Die Kerngemeinde im Verständnis des Gemeindepfarrers', in Goldschmidt (q.v.), pp. 153–62.

Renninger, J.-B., *Pastoraltheologie*, ed. by Fr A. Göpfert, Freiburg, 1893.

Rétif, L., 'Soubassements sociologiques d'une paroisse', in *MO*, 61, 1951, pp. 69–83.

'Die "Fils de la Charité" ', in Greinacher (q.v.), pp. 118–26.

'Die gemeinsame Arbeit der Priester in den Gemeinschaften der "Boucle" ', in Greinacher (q.v.), pp. 132–41.

Rossi, G. de, 'Ciò che possono dire i dati statistici di una parrocchia', in *Vita e Pensiero*, No. 1, 1915.

Roth, H., 'Pfarrei' = 'Pfarrei und Pfarrprinzip', in *Die Kirche in der Welt*, I, pp. 13–16.

Rousseau, O., 'Priestertum und Mönchtum', in Guyot (q.v.), pp. 158–71.

Rütten, F., 'Philologisches zum Canon Missae', in *StdZ*, 133, 1937–38, pp. 43–50.

Ryckmans, A., 'Qu'est-ce qu'un catholique pratiquant?', in *NRT*, 76, 1954, pp. 965–72.

Sailer, J.-M., *Vorlesungen* = *Vorlesungen aus der Pastoraltheologie*, 3 vols., 3rd ed., Munich, 1812.

Santopolo, Fr A., 'L'importance des zones écologiques à l'intérieur de la paroisse urbaine', in *PuPr*, pp. 63–66.

Schenkl, M., *Institutiones Theologiae Pastoralis*, Augustae Vind., 1803.

Schlier, H., and Warnach, V., 'Die Kirche im Epheserbrief. Aufsätze von Heinrich Schlier und P. Viktor Warnach, Beiträge zur Kontroverstheologie', ed. by Robert Grosche, supplement to *Catholica*, No. 1, Münster, 1949.

Schlüter and Hermkes, M., 'Die Familie als "Kirche im kleinen" ', in *StdZ*, 133, 1938, pp. 286–98.

Schmale, F. J., 'Kanonie, Seelsorge, Eigenkirche', in *Historisches Jahrbuch*, 78, 1959, pp. 38–63.

Schmid, H. F., *Die rechtlichen Grundlagen der Pfarrorganisation auf westslavischem Boden und ihre Entwicklung während des Mittelalters*, Weimar, 1938.

Schmidt, K. L., 'Das Gegenüber von Kirche und Staat in der Gemeinde des N.T.', in *Theologische Blätter*, 16, 1937, pp. Exkurs II, 'Die Kirche als Beisassenschaft'.

Article on *πάροικος*, *παροικία*, *παροικέω*, in Kittel (q.v.), 5, 1954, pp. 840–52.

Schmitt, J., 'Das jüdische Priestertum und die kirchliche Hierarchie in den Urgemeinden Palästinas', in Guyot (q.v.), pp. 52–67.

Schnitzler, T., *Die Messe in der Betrachtung*, 2 vols., 5th ed. Freiburg, 1957–58. English translation by Rudolph Kraus, *The Mass in Meditation*, St Louis, Mo., and London, 1959.

'Priesterliche Gemeinschaft auf der Grundlage des Stiftes und Säkularinstitutes', in Greinacher (q.v.), pp. 84–96.

Schnürer, G., *MA* = *Kirche und Kultur im Mittelalter*, 3 vols., Paderborn, Vol. I, 3rd ed., 1936, Vol. II, 2nd ed., 1929, Vol. III, 1930.

18.Jh = *Katholische Kirche und Kultur im 18. Jahrhundert*, Paderborn, 1941.

Schönen, A., 'Die Gottesfamilie', in *Die Familie, Gotteswerk und Menschenbemühen*, Liturgie und Mönchtum, Laacher Hefte, No. 23, 1958, pp. 7–12.

Schrott, A., *Seelsorge* = *Seelsorge im Wandel der Zeiten. Formen und Organisation seit der Begründung des Pfarrinstitutes bis zur Gegenwart. Ein Beitrag zur Pastoralgeschichte*, Graz, Vienna, 1949.

'Pfarre' = 'Pfarre und Pfarrseelsorge im Wandel der Zeiten', in *Die Pfarre*, pp. 9–17.

Schubert, F., *Pastoraltheologie*, 3 vols., 3rd ed., Graz, Leipzig, 1934 ff.

Schüch, I., *Pastoraltheologie* = *Handbuch der Pastoraltheologie*, new edition by V. Grimmich, Innsbruck, 1896. (The first printing was MS. in 1865–66.)

Schurr, M., 'Die übernatürliche Wirklichkeit der Pfarrei', in *Benediktiner Monatschrift*, 19, 1937, pp. 81–106.

Schwer, W., *Der soziale Gedanke in der katholischen Seelsorge. Ein Beitrag zur Geschichte der Seelsorge und der sozialen Ideen im 19. Jahrhundert*, Cologne, 1921.

Semmelroth, O., *Die Kirche als Ursakrament*, Frankfurt a. M., 1953.

Das geistliche Amt. Theologische Sinndeutung, Frankfurt a. M., 1958.

Severus, E. von, 'Kult und Aktion', in *Liturgische Haltung und soziale Wirklichkeit*, Liturgie und Mönchtum, Laacher Hefte, No. 19, 1956, pp. 86–97.

Siegwart, J., *Die Chorherren- und Chorfrauengemeinschaften in der deutschsprachigen Schweiz vom 6. Jahrhundert bis 1160. Mit einem Überlick über die Kanonikerreform des 10. und 11. Jahrhunderts*, Studia Friburgensia, Neue Folge, Fribourg, 1962.

Siemer, L., 'Pfarrfamilie und Ecclesiola', in *Die Neue Ordnung*, 3, 1949, pp. 37–51.

Spiazzi, R., 'Spunti per una theologia della parrocchia', in *La Scuola Cattolica*, 80, 1952, pp. 26–42.

Spitaler, A., *Die Zelle in Kirche und Welt*, Graz, 1960.

Stauffer, E., 'Die Urkirche', in *Historia Mundi, Ein Handbuch der Weltgeschichte*, 10 vols., founded by F. Kern, Vol. IV, 1956, pp. 298–310.

Stenzel, A., 'Cultus Publicus', in *ZkTh*, 75, 1953, pp. 174–214.

Stolz, E., '*Παροικία*, parochia und parochus', in *ThQSchr*, 89, 1907, pp. 424–48.

'Parochus' = 'Zur Geschichte des Terminus parochus', in *ThQSchr*, 95, 1913, pp. 193–203.

Stutz, U., 'Pfarre, Pfarrer (parochia, parochus)', in *Realenzyklopädie für protestantische Theologie und Kirche*, XV, pp. 239–52.

'Karls des Grossen divisio von Bistum und Grafschaft Chur. Ein Beitrag zur Geschichte der Reichs- und Kirchenverfassung der fränkischen Zeit im allgemeinen und zur Geschichte Churrhätiens im besonderen', in *Historische Aufsätze Karl Zeumer zum 60. Geburtstag als Festgabe dargebracht*, Weimar, 1909.

'Parochus' = 'Parochus', in *Savigny*, 32 (1911), pp. 313–18; 33 (1912), p. 344; 34 (1913), pp. 495–97; 35 (1914), pp. 497 ff.; 37 (1916), pp. 405–12; 40 (1919), pp. 314 ff.; 43 (1922), pp. 415 ff.; 47 (1927), p. 332; 55 (1935), pp. 342 ff.; 56 (1936), pp. 485–88.

Suk, W., 'Das Bild einer Grosstadtpfarre', in Goldschmidt (q.v.), pp. 109–22.

Swoboda, H., *Grosstadtseelsorge. Eine pastoraltheologische Studie*, 2nd ed., Regensburg, 1911.

Szabo, D., 'La paroisse dans la structure écologique de la ville', in *PuPr*, pp. 17–27.

Tenbruck, F. H., 'Die Kirchengemeinde in der entchristlichten Gesellschaft. Ergebnisse und Deutung der "Reutlinger Studie" ', in Goldschmidt (q.v.), pp. 122–32.

Tollu, F., 'Priestertum und Priestergemeinschaft', in Greinacher (q.v.), pp. 97–105.

Trütsch, J., 'Gestaltlose Kirche', in *Civitas*, 17, 1961–62, pp. 189–91.

Vagaggini, C., *Theologie der Liturgie*, translated from the Italian and edited by A. Berz, Einsiedeln, Zürich, Cologne, 1959.

van der Meer, *Augustinus der Seelsorger. Leben und Wirken eines Kirchenvaters*, 2nd ed., Cologne, 1953.

Verdoodt, A., 'Une paroisse urbaine européenne comme groupe social', in *PuPr*, pp. 95 ff.

Verscheure, J., *Lille. La pratique dominicale. Aspects sociologiques*, Lille, 1956.

Wagner, J., 'Kult' = 'Kult und Aktion im Aufbau der Pfarrgemeinde', in *LJB*, 7, 1957, pp. 215–25.

Winninger, P., *Construire des églises. Les dimensions des paroisses et les contradictions de l'apostolat dans les villes*, Rencontres, 49, Paris, 1957.

'Les villes aux mains des vicaires', in *PuPr*, pp. 97–101.

'Que dit le Code? Aspects canoniques du remembrement et de la fusion des paroisses', in *M-D*, 57, 1959, pp. 31–47.

Wintersig, A., 'Pfarrei und Mysterium', in *Jahrbuch für Liturgiewissenschaft*, 5, 1925, pp. 136–43.

Wurzbacher, G., *Das Dorf* = with Pflaum, R., *Das Dorf im Span-*

nungsfeld industrieller Entwicklung. Untersuchung an den 45 Dörfern und Weilern einer westdeutschen ländlichen Gemeinde, Stuttgart, 1954.

Zorell, S., 'Die Entwicklung des Parochialsystems bis zum Ende der Karolingerzeit', in *Archiv für katholisches*, Kirchenrecht, 82, 1902, H.1, pp. 74–98; H.3, pp. 258–89.

ANONYMOUS AND SYMPOSIA

'Was ist ein Bischof? Beiträge zur Kontroverse über den Episkopat', in *HK*, 12, 1958, pp. 188–94.

Diocèses de Suisse romande. Aspects sociologiques et religieux, Publications de l'Action Catholique Romande, Lausanne (no date).

Episcopus. Studien über das Bischofsamt, presented to H. E. Michael Cardinal von Faulhaber, Archbishop of München-Freising, on his eightieth birthday by the theological faculty of the University of Munich, Regensburg, 1949.

Die Kirche in der Welt. Wegweiser für die katholische Arbeit am Menschen der Gegenwart, a loose-leaf lexicon edited by P. Steffes and A. Eickhoff, three numbers issued, Münster, 1947 ff.

Paroisses urbaines—paroisses rurales. 5e Conférence Internationale de Sociologie Religieuse, Paris, Tournai, 1958.

Die Pfarre—Die Pfarre. Gestalt und Sendung. Wiener Seelsorgertagung vom 7–9. Jänner, 1953, Vienna, 1953.

'Priestermangel in der Schweiz?', in *Civitas*, 14, 1958–59, pp. 10–16, 233–79.

Recherches Pastorales. Canton de Fribourg 1957. Centre d'Etudes Pastorales, Grand-Séminaire, Fribourg (no date).

Structures sociales et pastorale paroissiale. Congrès National de Lille 1948, Union des Oeuvres, Paris, 1949.

'Zur Diskussion über "Veterum Sapientia" ', in *Orient*, 26, 1962, pp. 63–65.

SELECT BIBLIOGRAPHY OF WORKS ON THE PARISH WHICH HAVE APPEARED IN ENGLISH

Beck, H., *The Pastoral Care of Souls in South-East France during the Sixth Century*, Rome, 1950.

Carr, J. M., *Working together in the larger parish*, Atlanta, 1960.

Chike, T., 'An experiment in marriage counselling by the New Jersey churches', *Pastoral Psychology*, February 1961, pp. 29–34.

Crichton, J., 'The parish', *Liturgy*, 29, 1960, pp. 1–4, 28–32, 53–60.

Dobriner, W., *The Suburban Community*, New York, 1958.

Fichter, J. H., 'The parish and social integration', *Social Compass*, 7, 1960, pp. 39–47.

Parochial School: a sociological study, Indiana, 1958.

'Social experiences of religious functionaries.' *Compte-rendu, Social Compass*, 5, June, 1960.

Fitzgerald, W. F., *The Parish Census and the Liber Status Animarum:* a historical synopsis and a commentary, Washington, 1954.

Foster, J., *Requiem for a Parish*, London, 1962.

Garasche, E. S., *Modern Parish Problems*, New York, 1929.

Gremillion, J., *The Parish as a Natural Community* (M.A. dissertation), New Orleans, 1958.

Hamer, J., *The Church is a Communion*, trans., Geoffrey Chapman, 1965.

Marx, P., *A Parish that Really Lives*, New York, 1957.

Mundy, T. M., *The Union of Parishes*, 1944.

Navagh, J. J., *The Apostolic Parish*, New York, 1950.

O'Connor, D., *Parochial Relations and Co-operation of the Religious and the Secular Clergy: a historical synopsis and a commentary*, Washington, 1958.

Parres, C. L., 'Secular priest joining secular institute', *Homiletic and Pastoral Review*, 83, 1959.

La Piana, G., 'The Roman Church at the end of the second century', *The Harvard Theological Review*, 18, 1925, pp. 201–77.

Roy, M., *The Parish and Democracy in French Canada*, Toronto, 1950.

Schreuder, O., 'Religious attitudes, group consciousness, liturgy and education', *Social Compass*, 10, 1963, pp. 29–52.

'The parish priest as a subject of criticism', *Social Compass*, 8, 1961, 111–26.

Schuyler, J. B., 'The parish studied as a social system', *The American Catholic Sociological Review*, 17, 1956, pp. 320–37.

Segler, F. M., 'A new understanding of pastoral care', *South-Western Journal of Theology*, 1960, pp. 53–60.

'The pastor and church administration', *South-Western Journal of Theology*, 1959, pp. 26–34.

Shippey, F. A., 'The variety of city churches', *Review of Religious Research*, Vol. 2, No. 1, 1960, pp. 8–19.

Thomas, J. L., 'Family and parish: marriage as an index of parish vitality', *Social Order*, 1, 1951, 291–96.

Tonna, B., 'The allocation of time among clerical activities. A study in a Brussels parish', *Social Compass*, 10, 1963, 93–106.

Vidich, A. J., and Bensman, J., *Small town in Mass Society: class, power and religion in a rural community*, Princetown, 1958.

Ward, C. K., *Priests and People: a study in the sociology of religion*, Liverpool, 1961.

'Priest and people: a study of parish visitation in an English city', *Sociologia religiosa*, 7, 1961, pp. 79–83.

Ward, L. R., *The Living Parish*, Paris, 1959.

Zimmer, B. G., and Hawley, A. H., 'Suburbanization and church participation', *Social Forces*, 5, 1959.

'Parish and catechesis', *Lumen Vitae*, Vol. 14, No. 4, 1959, pp. 606–782.

'The urban parish', *Social Compass*, 8, 1961.

LIST OF ABBREVIATIONS

Anima	*Anima*, a quarterly on practical pastoral work issued by the Seelsorgeinstitut of the University of Fribourg, 1945 onwards.
DACL	*Dictionnaire d'archéologie chrétienne et de liturgie*, 15 double vols. published by F. Cabrol, H. Leclercq and H. Marrou, Paris, 1907–53.
DDC	*Dictionnaire du Droit Canonique avec un sommaire de l'histoire et l'état actuel de la discipline*, published under the direction of R. Naz, Paris, 1935 onwards.
Denz.	H. Denzinger, *Enchiridion Symbolorum . . .*, 31st ed.
DTC	*Dictionnaire de théologie catholique* begun under the direction of A. Vacant and E. Mangenot and continued under that of E. Amann. 3rd ed., Paris, 1923 onwards.
Etudes	*Etudes*. A review founded in 1856 by the Jesuit fathers in Paris.
FZPhTh	*Freiburger Zeitschrift für Philosophie und Theologie*, Fribourg.
Greg.	*Gregorianum*, a quarterly for theological and philosophical studies issued by the Gregorian University, Rome, since 1920.
GrEnt	*Der Grosse Entschluss*, a monthly for active Christianity, Vienna, since 1945.
HK	*Herder-Korrespondenz*, Freiburg, 1946 onwards.
JbLW	*Jahrbuch für Liturgie-Wissenschaft*, published by Odo Casel. OSB, Münster 1921–41.
LJB	*Liturgisches Jahrbuch*, a quarterly dealing with questions concerning divine worship, published by the Liturgisches Institut, Münster.
LThK	*Lexicon für Theologie und Kirche*, revised edition, 10 vols., published by Michael Buchberger, Freiburg, 1930–8.
LThK²	Ditto—a completely revised edition of Buchberger by Josef Höfer and Karl Rahner, up to date 6 vols., Freiburg, 1957 onwards.
LV	*Lumen Vitae*, an international review on religious training, Brussels.
M-D	*Maison-Dieu, revue de pastorale liturgique*, quarterly of the Centre de Pastorale Liturgique, Paris.
MO	*Masses ouvrières*, Paris monthly.
NRT	*Nouvelle revue théologique*, published under the direction of Mm Jean—Joseph Loiseaux and Jean—Baptiste Felix, Tournai, 1869 onwards.
Orient	*Orientierung*. Catholic leaflets for philosophical information, Zürich.
PG	*Patrologia Graeca* (Migne).
PL	*Patrologia Latina* (Migne).
PuPr	*Paroisses urbaines—paroisses rurales*. 5th International Conference on Religious Sociology, Tournai, 1958.

QLit	*Les questions liturgiques et paroissiales*, quarterly. Abbaye de Mont Cécar, Louvain.
Savigny	*Zeitschrift der Savigny-Stiftung für Rechtsgeschichte, kanonistische Abteilung*, Weimar from 1911
SchwKZ	*Schweizerische Kirchenzeitung*, information on questions of theology, care of souls and Church policy, Lucerne from 1831.
Social Compass	*Social Compass*, international review of socio-religious studies, Brussels—The Hague—Fribourg.
StdZ	*Stimmen der Zeit*. Monthly for the spiritual life in the present time, Freiburg.
STh	*Summa Theologica* of Thomas Aquinas.
ThBl	*Theologische Blätter*.
Th Dig	*Theologischer Digest. Theologie und Leben*. Bergen–Enkheim, from 1958.
ThQSchr	*Theologische Quartalschrift*, Tübingen, from 1819.
ThuGl	*Theologie und Glaube*, periodical for the Catholic clergy, Paderborn.
TrthZ	*Triere Theologische Zeitschrift, Pastor Bonus*, Trier, 1892 onwards.
ZkTh	*Zeitschrift für katholische Theologie*, Innsbruck–Leipzig, from 1877.

INDEX

C

P